Taking the Mick

Taking the Mickey

Mickey Arthur
with Neil Manthorp

Jonathan Ball Publishers
Johannesburg & Cape Town

Published in trade paperback in 2010 by
JONATHAN BALL PUBLISHERS (PTY) LTD
PO Box 33977
Jeppestown
2043

ISBN 978-1-86842-383-5

Cover design by MR Design, Cape Town
Set in 11/15 pt Garth Graphic
Printed and bound by CTP Book Printers, Cape

Contents

Graeme Smith

Let me start by saying that I had no idea what was in this book when I sat down to write the foreword. At least, I had not read it. Obviously I had an idea of what it might contain. Mickey fought hard for what he believed in, harder than most people I have known, and there were some clashes with his bosses as a result. I guess they will be recorded in the book. He wouldn't be 'Honest Mickey' if they weren't.

I know Mickey would want me to say, for the record, that my words here should not be construed as an endorsement of everything he said and did.

He fought for the players, and he fought for me. He did everything he could to allow the players to concentrate on performance; he spared us the 'politics' of the boardroom and protected us as best he could. He tried to create an environment in which we could focus all of our energy on scoring runs and taking wickets for the team.

The result was that we enjoyed the greatest year in South African cricket history in 2008 and rose to the number-one ranking in both Test and one-day cricket. We won Test series in England and Australia during that period, achievements I will cherish to the grave. And I don't believe they would have been possible without Mickey. I gave him my man-of-the-match medal after we won the Test series against England with the victory at Edgbaston. I played probably my best innings in that game, so it felt appropriate that I could thank him with a special souvenir. That's how much he meant to me – to all of us.

I first met Mick in Kimberley when I played for a UCB XI against Griquas, right at the start of my career. I was eighteen, and I scored some runs. Mick was in a strange place in his career – at least, he was to a kid like me! I didn't know if he was the senior pro, the coach or the manager! He sat me down with a beer straight after the match and offered me a contract!

He was one of the most decent, polite and honest people I'd met in cricket – and he still is twelve years later. He is a gentleman with a need, and a desire, for people around him to behave with the same sense of respect and decency that he has.

That's not to say he didn't have a mean streak. Mickey would never have been the successful coach he was without it. One of the greatest assets of our relationship was that we could talk to each other without any fear. Right from the beginning, we knew we could speak our minds; there was no holding back because of worries about hurt feelings. That was so refreshing. He made allowances for my age and the 'passion of youth' and knew that we could talk again after a few hours, or a good night's sleep, if we disagreed or had an argument.

I'm not sure what will happen in the future, but the five years I shared with Mickey were the best years of my career. He deserves so much credit for the team's performance and results – more than I can describe in such a short space. At first, as with many great planners and tacticians, his value and worth was appreciated more after the event than during it. But that period didn't last long. By the time 2008 started, we all knew what his vision was and shared in it.

He didn't just accept or tolerate a different opinion from me; he *demanded* it. He insisted that it was the captain's team, not the coach's. He refused to take the credit for success, but was always prepared to face the media and explain the bad days.

When his time was finally up, it was horrible for both of us. We were in constant contact. The media speculation about a 'falling-out' between us was hurtful in the extreme. It was nonsense. But I had already experienced it with speculation that I was responsible for 'Jet' Jennings being ousted as coach. This was worse, though, because we had been together for five years and had shared so much. The idea that I might have 'shafted' Mickey was appalling and upsetting to both of us.

I walked around taking 'daggers' from the public for a couple of days while Mick was lying low in East London. But we both knew the truth, and that was a source of comfort for him and me.

One of the many beliefs we shared was that you should never, ever take anything for granted in this game. You never know what is around the next corner. But if I am fortunate enough to lead the team on another tour of Australia, or even just to go as a player, then I will look forward to the start of it in Perth more than ever before. Mickey's loyalties will be to Western Australia, of course, and by extension to Australia, but he will never be able to stop me inviting myself over for a braai and picking his brains about our opposition!

I am especially happy for Yvette and the girls that they will now be able to see so much more of their husband and Dad. They deserve to be together after the years of dedication to the Proteas. I know a bit about the loneliness that comes with the job – I've experienced it for long enough myself. It is fair to say that, during our five years working together, I admired Mickey as much for his determination to be a good husband and father as for anything else.

Graeme Smith
SEPTEMBER 2010

Chapter 1

Early years

Cricket was always in my blood. From the earliest days, my dad was my biggest influence. Rain or shine, I used to get up early and have throw-downs before school. He would throw to me any time of day or night until his shoulder seized up; then my Mum, brother Richard or sister Diane would take over, although I used to have to pay them most of my pocket money! Dad used to run a team that played in the Natal Country Districts set-up; as I progressed and started high school I would take my kit along to every game, hoping that somebody wouldn't turn up and I could get a game as a last-minute replacement. At that stage, my dream was to play alongside my dad in the Country Districts.

It was interesting that Tony Irish (head of the South African Cricketers Association, SACA) ended up playing for my dad's team. Years later, Tony would play a pivotal role in many key decisions that I had to make as national coach. And he wasn't the only person from my formative years whose path I would cross again later in life. Fortunately, I have never been one to burn my bridges, but it's a lesson that many people wish they had learned earlier: make as few enemies as possible through life – you never know when you might need a friend.

I used to go and watch every game Natal played. Barry Richards was a hero of mine, as were Mike Procter and Vince van der Bijl. They were the greatest players I'd ever seen, but I'm not sure I realised how great they were. Because I grew up watching them, I guess I didn't have many players to compare them with. Van der Bijl and Procter on a green mamba were a lethal combination. Not many teams stood a chance. Then Barry would go out and make it look like a pavement. I used to go every day after school and sit on the grass banks, just lapping it up.

The irony that I would work with these men one day is never lost on me. Barry was a fixture in the commentary box and a good man to chat to after a day's play. Proccie became convenor of selectors during the second half of my term as national coach, and 'Big Vince' was always a pillar of strength. He was always there for me – for anybody, actually. He was a fantastic listener – you don't appreciate people who listen well until you don't have anyone. When Vince took over the High Performance Centre at the University of Pretoria we spent a lot of time together, and I thrived on the calm, quiet authority that he brought to every meeting. Not that he didn't get passionate – far from it – but he was always in control of his emotions.

As a young player, I was totally dedicated to cricket, and trained and practised daily. Throughout my teenage years, I had very strict pre-match routines, and would never go out the night before a match. I made the Westville Boys High first team in Standard 8, and I went through the ranks playing for the Kingsmead Mynahs in Standard 8 and for Natal Schools for two years in Standard 9 and matric. I played with the Ford brothers and Craig Grinyer, and against guys like Shukri Conrad and Gary Kirsten. Later in my career, I would often cross swords with Gary, both at playing and coaching level with Western Province and then of course with India.

All I wanted to do when I was growing up was to become a professional cricketer. Cricket was my life. I remember being asked in a matric careers interview what my occupation was going to be, and I didn't have the slightest hesitation in writing 'professional cricketer'. You have to remember that there were very few people making a living from cricket in those days, at least in South Africa, so I knew I was inviting trouble. But it was the truth and I didn't want to hide from it. I was young and ambitious and I wanted to live my dream.

Cricket was as much a part of my education as school. I used to collect *Wisden* and *Cricketer* magazines and study them all, page by page and paragraph by paragraph. I even used to read every line of the advertisements – I didn't want to miss a thing. Reading about the game in England and, to a lesser extent in the rest of the world, was a constant reminder of South Africa's isolation in the apartheid era. But, without ever knowing how or why, I believed I would be part of cricket in the rest of the world at some point. Or maybe it was just a desperate hope.

After matric, I was more determined than ever to push on with my cricket, and it seemed the obvious choice to accept the offer of a post-matric year at Hilton College. But instead I turned it down in favour of an army call-up to Kimberley. Not that my preference was for the army over cricket! I'd been to Kimberley and had a good look around, and was convinced that I could make a start to my first-class career at Griqualand West and start making a name for myself. And get my army training done at the same time.

Fortunately, my gut feeling was correct, and I broke into the Griquas side early in my army career. I came under the tutelage of Fred Swarbrook, who took me under his wing and became the first major influence on my career after my father. Fred was a classic, old-fashioned disciplinarian and a strict timekeeper, who would react with fury if you were late – especially for a second or third time! But he taught me the value of good discipline and, just as importantly, how to instil it in players by helping them to appreciate it, too.

Once again, I met and worked with a host of people whose paths I would cross again years down the line. Arthur Turner was the CEO of Griquas at the time, before moving to Free State and signing me up as a player to join him in Bloemfontein. I stayed with Reunert Bauser in Kimberley, who would ultimately move to the Eastern Cape and sign me for the Warriors.

I'm not sure how long I would have lasted if I had ever seen any active military service. My army training was mostly spent playing cricket, although I did the basics (well, some of them). I made my debut for Griquas against Kim Hughes' touring Australian team in Kimberley and made a few runs (52, in fact). I went on to represent Griquas for four years; the first two were my army years (1986-87), and after that I signed my first professional contract for another two years (1989-90). My contract was worth R800 per month and included my board and lodging – but no transport. Gordon Parsons and Andy Moles were the two overseas pros in the side, and both went on to have long and successful coaching careers, which must have had something to do with all the evenings we spent talking about the game over a cold beer or two.

Every winter I would go over to England to play for Coventry and North Warwickshire in the Birmingham and District League, and whenever I wasn't playing during the summer I was coaching with Fred in the townships. I absolutely loved the experience, and my passion for coaching was kindled at that time. We spent a lot of time in Galeshewe, outside Kimberley, which still has a very special place in my heart. As a 'privileged' white South African, I hadn't had much experience of township life, and had even less contact with underprivileged cricketers. But, as so many people have discovered, the sense of determination and appreciation for the small things that you experience in the townships can be incredibly uplifting.

I met my wife to be, Yvette, during this period. It happened at the Halfway House Hotel, which was the happening place in town. We met, chatted briefly and arranged to meet there again the following night. And that was it. We never looked back. She has been both the pillar and the foundation of my career, and also managed, somehow, to keep our family together and our three girls on track during the thousands of days I've been away from home. She has been amazing for me, and I'm proud to say I love her as much today as I ever did. And I'm even more re-lieved to say that she still appears to love me.

The move to Free State from Griquas in 1990 was an amazing experience. Although Free State was later to become a routinely successful team in the late 1990s and 2000s, it was still very much a 'junior' province in cricketing terms in the early and mid-1990s, having only recently been given 'A' status and hav-ing yet to win a trophy.

Arthur Turner was well on the way to building a formidable squad. By the time he signed me, Free State already had the likes of Hansie Cronje, Allan Donald, Rudi Steyn, Corrie van Zyl, Omar Henry, Louis Wilkinson, Bradley Player and Philip Radley, all of whom except Philip went on to earn national or South African 'A' colours. It really was a fantastic squad. In the year I arrived, West Indies cricketer Franklyn Stephenson be-came our overseas professional. He can be credited with a lot of the progress and success that Allan and many others achieved in their cricket careers at that time.

After the first year with Free State, perhaps the most significant signing for the province was Eddie Barlow as head coach. He would become my coaching mentor, and was undoubtedly the man to whom I owed the most in later years. I have learned a lit-tle bit from almost everyone I played with or worked under, but he was definitely the man on whom I styled my coaching career.

I marvelled at the ability 'Bunter' had to get the best out of his players, and was often amazed at what he could do in terms of managing players. Although ruthless and unforgiving in so many ways, yet he could take you under his wing and into his confidence in so many other ways. As a coach, you can never be afraid of telling the truth, but if you have to knock a player down then you also need to know how to help him pick himself up again. When I became director of playing affairs at Griquas, I would sign Eddie to come and coach for a period of time, a few days or even weeks, and I constantly bounced ideas off him. He always believed he was right, but that never stopped him listening to a different point of view and giving you the confidence to go with your own idea, even if it differed from his. One of my few regrets (and I don't have many) is that Eddie didn't live longer – not for my sake but for South African cricket.

In five extremely happy years at Free State, we won everything there was to win. Even more happily, Yvette and I started our family with the births of Brooke and Kristin. Ashton was a Kimberley baby, and completed our beautiful family. In some ways, though, I felt I had unfinished business at Griquas. I had reached the pinnacle of my cricket, and played 110 first-class games averaging 34 or 35 (33.45 to be exact). There were also 150 or so one-day games. It was the 'hardest' cricket I would ever play, and I mean 'hard' as in ruthless as well as physical. This was in the days before the expansion to eleven provinces, so every game was a strength-versus-strength encounter, with teams like Western Province, Transvaal, Northerns, Eastern Province and Natal almost always at full strength. The intensity of domestic cricket back then was still pretty eye-watering, even though the Currie Cup in the 1970s and 1980s was no doubt even more brutal. It was a period in which my cricket philosophy was formed, and in which I tried to mould my thinking and 'scenario planning'.

I was back with Griquas for another nine seasons, and it felt right. I returned to play and captain the side initially, but then became the *de facto* 'cricket manager' while I was still playing. We had the likes of Kepler Wessels, Pat Symcox and Ottis Gibson as senior players, and I enjoyed, dare I say it, the most successful period in Griquas' history towards the end of my playing career. We won the Standard Bank Cup (1998-99), with me winning the man of the match in the final (83 off 106). Then Fred Swarbrook moved on, and Eddie Barlow took charge before Fred came back again. But the Griquas' board felt it was time for a change. When the position of head coach came up in 1999, I threw my hat into the ring. It took a lot of courage for them to appoint me, but I believed I was ready. It was an exciting time.

At just 31, I was a very young coach, but I wanted to make coaching my career and saw a huge opportunity to go for it. I felt as strongly about coaching as I had done about playing when I was a teenager. I felt it was almost my vocation. I will forever be in the debt of board members Ahmed Jinnah, AB Williams and Brian Kidson for giving me that chance. Experience is a priceless commodity in the world of sport, and to all intents and purposes I had none. But I had the 'feel' of the club; I was determined, I was prepared to work hard and I was prepared to learn. They felt I was the right man for the job, but it was still a risk.

There was an extraordinary mix of players in the Griquas' squad – probably the most diverse range of cricketers in any first-class squad in the world. On the one extreme we had some senior, well-travelled pros who had been playing for over a decade, and on the other we had some youngsters who were literally learning the game – and I mean the laws of the game! I threw myself into the job with total commitment. I had learned important lessons from Fred and Eddie, but also from Johan Volsteedt, who, as headmaster of Grey College in Bloemfontein and a master coach, knew a lot about managing people. I tried to use all their strengths to mould my own coaching strategies and philosophy.

There was a lot of technical work to be done with the young players – we signed a lot of young players – and so my technical knowledge improved all the time. Not so much cricket technique, but the technique of coaching. Having cricket knowledge is one thing, but it doesn't make you a coach. Being able to impart that knowledge successfully is the most valuable skill for a coach. And all the time I was learning how to manage people and run a successful team. I studied other successful teams and tried to identify what they did, and kept doing so in order to remain successful. I read extensively and tried to absorb as much as possible. I studied coaching. It was my degree.

During my time with Griquas, I also coached at the National Academy and I was appointed to take charge of the South African 'A' team, both under the leadership of Vince Barnes, who would become a close friend during my time with South Africa and still is one of my best friends in cricket. It was ironic that I coached under him at the Academy and South Africa 'A', and he would later coach under me for the Proteas, but we remain true friends. It was a source of anxiety to both of us that he was perceived by some people as being a 'tactical' appointment in both jobs – that he was there because he was coloured. Not true. He is exceptionally talented, and has a brilliant way with players. It was never, ever an issue between us, although we shared the frustration, and sometimes anger, caused by uninformed speculation.

When Cricket South Africa (CSA) eventually made the move in 2004 to cut the first-class system from eleven provinces to six franchises, following the Australian model, I was fortunate enough to have done enough as a coach to survive the 'cut'. Because of my record with Griquas, and the reports of what I'd done at the Academy and with South Africa 'A', I kept a job.

I was then 'head-hunted' by Reunert Bauser to coach the

Warriors franchise, and was to be based in East London. It was a difficult time for many people, having to amalgamate resources and administration. Free State and Griquas probably struggled most, but Border and Eastern Province weren't far behind.

I had a great year with the Warriors and enjoyed every moment; it was my total focus. But at national level Eric Simons lost his job as national coach and the position was advertised. Ray Jennings was given an interim position in October 2004. I recall sitting in the office of Greg Hayes, cricket operations manager at the Warriors, and asking: 'So do I go for this job, or don't I?'

I wanted to show that I was keen, and I needed to illustrate that my passion and ambition was coaching, so I had to throw my hat in the ring. I wanted the powers that be at CSA to be aware that I was keen and ambitious. But, realistically, I didn't think – at that stage of my career – that I had a chance.

I submitted my application and CV and waited. A couple of weeks later, I received a letter from Gerald Majola to say that I had made the short list and that I was required to go to Johannesburg for a series of psychometric tests and an interview. I was the last one to be interviewed and the last to do psychometric testing, which was extensive, to say the least. They really grilled us, with a host of problem-solving scenarios and tasks to complete under time pressure. It was a tough process, lasting close to six hours, but no doubt the examiners learned a thing or two about the characters of the applicants. We all learned something about ourselves.

Three days after returning home, I was back in Jo'burg on the eve of our semifinal in the Standard Bank Pro20. This was my interview, and I had put together a business plan for the panel. As preparation, I had spent several hours with Barend van Graan, who was on the Warriors board as well as on the board of rights management company SAIL and the Blue Bulls Rugby Union (with whom he later became the CEO). I bounced a lot of ideas off him regarding my philosophy, and I took all that information away and developed a business strategy that I believed would be sustainable and successful.

Naturally, my plan was based around taking South Africa to number one in all forms of the game. I presented the 'vision' in a booklet, which I presented to everyone before the interview. The panel comprised Gerald Majola, Andrew Hudson, Norman Arendse, Ray Mali and Mike Procter. Errol Stewart was supposed to be there, but was absent. I was humble, and kept reminding myself that I was an 'outsider'. Nevertheless, I couldn't help feeling that the interview had gone really well. Whatever happened, I knew I'd prepared as well as possible, and made my views clear. I had an answer for everything, even if that answer was: 'I don't know, but this is how I would find out.'

When I returned to Port Elizabeth, my future wasn't even on my mind. It was out of my hands, but I was satisfied that whatever the result I'd given my best shot. So, with a happy heart, I threw myself into preparing for the semifinal against the Free State Eagles. My opposite number, Corrie van Zyl, had been my roommate for five years while I was playing for Free State. The ironies never cease. Later, as national coach, I employed him to take over at the High Performance Centre, and then he took over from me as national coach when I was sacked. The lesson, once again, is 'don't burn your bridges'!

I'll never forget the morning of that game. I was lying in my hotel room in Port Elizabeth – it was a 6.00 pm start, so I was having a sleep-in. My mobile phone woke me up at 7.04 am. It was Gerald. My only thought was: 'Why would he be calling me this early?' My heart never skipped a beat. What he was about to say never occurred to me.

He told me I had the job. It was all very hush-hush at the time because South Africa were about to embark on a tour of the West Indies with Ray Jennings in charge as interim coach, and he had also put his name forward for the job. It was only as I started talking that I felt my heart beating faster. Gerald didn't get straight to the point, so I began hearing the words 'thanks for applying, but ...' I started consoling myself with the fact that I was on the radar and would, hopefully, get another chance further down the line.

Then he said: 'Are you sitting down?' I said 'Yes, er, no, actually I'm lying down.' He then said: 'Congratulations, we would like you to be the coach of South Africa. Can I meet you for breakfast?' I then raced off to his hotel, the Garden Court King's Beach, met Gerald for breakfast and we thrashed everything out. It was a fantastic day. I couldn't have been more proud, but I couldn't tell anybody. Well, almost nobody. I called Yvette immediately, and she called her folks while I called mine. Apart from the kids, for just over a month they were the only people who would know. Much as I love my family, in retrospect it still seems amazing that nobody let the cat out of the bag.

When I eventually returned to Jo'burg for the official announcement on (19 May 2005), I was blown away by the size of the press conference and the subsequent demands of the media. I thought I was prepared, but I was still taken by surprise. There must have been thirty or forty people at the announcement, and it felt like eighty. I'd never seen so many television and media cameras, never seen so many flashes. The difference between life as a franchise coach and life as national coach could hardly have been more graphically illustrated. I'm not sure how, or what, I would have felt if I had realised that it would remain that way for the next five years!

Fortunately I had five months to prepare before my first assignment with the national team. I did interviews with news stations from around the world. One of the first was with Daniel Davini from 6PR radio in Perth. When my time was finally up with the Proteas, and I was appointed head coach of Western Australia, who was my media manager? Dan Davini. It is amazing how things work out.

My first job with the national squad was to have one-on-one meetings with all the major role-players and the cricketers themselves. I was full of ambition and determination, but there was a problem getting my new colleagues to share my vision and belief, considering that we were ranked sixth in the world in Tests and fifth in one-dayers.

I soon became aware that a lot of people, and media, were starting to speculate about how South Africa had taken on a young, inexperienced coach who couldn't possibly deliver on his plans and promises. I may have been rattled initially, but it didn't last long. Within weeks, my resolve was firmer than ever. With the support of my family, I was going to make this job work. I had three practical goals: to become number one in Tests and one-day internationals (ODIs), and to win an International Cricket Council (ICC) event. There was a lot of scepticism about our ability to achieve the Test and ODI rankings. But we did it. The failure to win an ICC event remains my only regret in five years as national coach.

Chapter 2

The South African job

October to November 2005

The first assignment – New Zealand's tour to South Africa in October-November – was the beginning of a tempest from which there was little respite. The New Zealand series was quickly followed by a five-match ODI series to India in late November. Still to come was the 'marquee' tour of Australia, in which we were, as usual, desperate to do well. The history was part of our daily thinking, albeit subconscious. South Africa had never won there.

For three months, however, I had the opportunity to simply look at the squad, searching for the players we wanted, seeing if those who were in place were actually the real deal and having extensive meetings with captain Graeme Smith to decide on which way, and what 'brand' of cricket, we were going to play. I was absolutely clear about what I wanted to achieve, and the qualities that I sought in the administrators, support staff and players. I had no doubts or questions.

My vision was to take South Africa to number one in the world in Tests and ODIs – T20 cricket did not figure in the beginning although it very quickly became a huge factor. It's not true to say that I was obsessed with winning – I was obsessed with helping the team to become the best it possibly could be. I just happened to believe that they would win everything and beat everybody if they played to their potential.

In order to realise my vision, I wanted to have the most professional support staff, and I wanted to identify, expose and develop the most talented franchise players and turn them into good international cricketers. I wanted to cultivate an ultra-professional environment, an environment that would allow players to develop fully with the aid of medical science and the very best in sports psychology. We all agreed that we wanted to play a style that would encourage the public to support the Proteas, a style which involved playing positively at all times, with the emphasis on being prepared to take risks in order to win. We wanted to eradicate the fear of failure from the team game plan.

Finally but very, very importantly, we wanted to operate unconditionally in an environment of transformation. It was a key component of the business plan: we needed to work in a space in which everybody knew where we stood on selection and there were no doubts or suspicions. We were committed to transformation, but also dedicated to excellence. It was an extremely difficult thing to do. As much as we wanted to get rid of the 'grey' areas, some people would always question – if not others, then themselves. But I was very strong on the subject because I believed in both transformation and excellence. Operated correctly, with sensitivity and common sense, I didn't believe that they were mutually exclusive or even that one had to compromise the other.

I have lived my life, and built my career, on the principle of forming strong and sincere relationships with key people. Even if it isn't possible to share another man's principles or philosophies, it is important that you know where you stand. If your relationship is, at worst, based on mutual antipathy, then I want that to be made clear. Mostly, though, I am the kind of person, and coach, to find some area of positive, shared ground. On that basis, when I became national coach I knew it would be critical to have a strong and trusting relationship with the captain and the convenor of selectors.

Successful coaching can be applied with a stick, but such an approach will only ever be short-term. You will never have sustained, long-term success with a bullying approach. My coaching philosophy is based on personal pride and communication with players, media and board members of relevant stakeholders. I always believe that, by standing still, you will move backwards. In professional sport, now more than ever, you need to be striving to improve all the time – not just physically, but in the fields of emotional intelligence, strategy, tactical planning and logistics. I felt South African cricket, as a result of the years of isolation, had done too much 'following' since the return to international cricket. I wanted us to be innovative and to be leaders in every aspect.

Discipline was also going to be an essential ingredient of our future success. The South African team hadn't always been held in the highest esteem around the world, for a variety of reasons, but chiefly because of the conflict it seemed to attract, and that was something we wanted to change. We wanted to be leaders on and off the field. In no way was this a climb-down or a 'softer' approach to the game – quite the opposite. Aggression was still a cornerstone of our game, but, to use a tennis analogy, we wanted to have more of the Bjorn Borg 'Iceman' approach than John 'The Brat' McEnroe.

I was very keen to find out what made cricketers like Jacques Kallis tick – and then to bottle it and hand out regular doses to the other players! Everybody is different, but I was keen to try and develop a system whereby the players could understand why they were strong in certain areas and weak in others, and then to share their strengths with each other and learn from their weaknesses.

My principle for successful cricket is based on a very simple 'adult learning' cycle: preparation, assessment, execution, analysis, strategising. And then the whole process starts again. It is the simplest way to ensure that you are always looking for ways to improve rather than running the risk of resting on your laurels – not that I have anything against a good celebration if things are going well!

Fortunately, I am blessed with a very small ego, which can be an asset for the coach of a major sports team. With the Proteas, it was never going to be about me – provided things went well. If things went badly, of course, then I would have to take the blame. I knew that was how it worked, and I was under no illusions. Although the job was the fulfilment of a dream for me, I had no visions of raising my arms in triumph and taking credit for anything. That was the players' privilege.

It sounds simple, but I believed that by creating an environment in which the 'marquee' players – Kallis, Graeme Smith, Shaun Pollock, Mark Boucher, etc – could raise their games by 10 percent, then the other players would find an extra 20 percent. Once again, I had no doubt that we would become champions if that happened.

The starting point was to identify our 'cornerstone' players, and then the areas where we felt we needed to improve, either in terms of personnel or performance. We certainly needed an improved system for bridging the gap between what was required for success at franchise level and what was required at international level. We certainly weren't alone in having that problem; even the Australians struggled to make the transition and they had the strongest domestic cricket in the world at the time.

One of my plans was the implementation of a consultancy programme, using people with highly developed, specialist skills to work with the team on an intensive but short-term basis. Jonty Rhodes and Duncan Fletcher were top of the shopping list, and fortunately both were available. No coach can do everything, no matter how good he is, but even if he is able to do everything the players still need variety and a second, even a third, opinion. I hope that future Proteas' coaches do something similar; I'm convinced that it is the way forward. Rather than travelling with a vast, full-time coaching squad, as England do, I think short and sharp 'refresher' courses are more effective. Too many coaches on a permanent basis can become cumbersome and lead to confusion. But feedback from different experts, in different conditions, helps a player to find his own answers and grow as a cricketer.

I always saw the job as far more than just coaching the players. It was about 'managing' the coaching process, which included the whole coaching staff and the structure that was put in place. I wanted the players to be confident that they were being given as much information as they could possibly get, that their roles were clearly defined at every stage and that they always knew exactly what was expected of them.

Communication, as I always said, was crucial. Once the captain and coach had decided on the game plan, there was no point in the convenor of selectors giving us a team based on his vision of what was required. There is an old saying in sport that the best XI or XV players doesn't necessarily equate to the best team. But that information needs to be shared openly and freely with the players and the selectors in order to get a consensus. The key was honest and open communication with everyone – the captain, players, coaching staff, cricket operations manager, CEO and the board, supporters, media, sponsors and franchise coaches. I must admit I was chuffed when the Australian media nicknamed me 'Honest Mickey' on our first tour there (even though we lost).

I knew I needed to lead by example and set the standards

in all aspects of life. The job comes with a certain amount of respect, but that doesn't last long unless you earn it. And you earn respect by providing the players and the administration with something new, some insight and some knowledge that they didn't have before. You also have to practise and be up to date with all the latest trends and news and be able to offer some advice and guidance about what is relevant or important – and what isn't. Often, a senior player will know what is best for him, but sometimes that player needs to realise that his routines and habits are not quite as good as he thinks they are – like having a 'good night out' two days before a Test match in the belief that he will sleep well the night before.

I wanted to develop a 'brand', a style of play that was successful, sustainable and exciting. The theory was great, but we needed the facilities and coaching aids to make it happen, things like the latest video analysis equipment and wickets that simulated conditions around the world. Preparing a dry and dusty pitch in South Africa to simulate conditions on the Indian subcontinent isn't easy.

As far as playing technique was concerned, my input was far less than at franchise level. No surprise there. The majority of the national squad were exceptional cricketers, among the best in the world, and their skills were good enough to help them reach the top and, in many cases, stay there. At the same time, however, my challenge was to observe their techniques like never before – to watch and study and learn at a level I had never attained in my career. If Jacques Kallis was suddenly to hit a bad patch and not know how to get out of it, I needed to be able to offer something practical. Only hundreds of hours of observation, and communication, would make that possible.

Our technical preparation, fielding and fitness would give us the competitive edge. Fitness and fielding are controllable because you can measure them. Coaches enjoy things we can 'measure' – it makes our lives that much easier! So many of the other crucial elements can only be measured subjectively, but fitness tests, catches and hitting the stumps are all a matter of numbers, and it is no wonder that coaches fall back on them.

Our goals were to win 60 percent of our Test matches and 65 percent of our ODIs. I had calculated, as far as possible and taking into account other likely results, that a success rate like that would take us to the number one ranking in both forms. So that was my time frame. Three years.

Attention then turned to the support staff. I had Vincent Barnes as my assistant coach and right-hand man from the start, and he proved to be brilliant. Sadly, he never enjoyed the recognition he deserved, particularly for his work with the bowlers. He was more than just adequate; he was often inspirational. But I also cherished the fact that he trusted me and I trusted him. I always allowed him to grow in his area of expertise, and I know he appreciated that.

After Duncan and Jonty, I employed Jeremy Snape as our sports psychologist. Mohamed Moosajee, too, was a very successful appointment as team manager. Goolam Rajah was superb in what he did, although often under-appreciated by players and administrators alike, but he was a 'preparation and logistics' man and that was what he needed to be allowed to do. Doc Moosajee had the time and temperament to deal with player issues, and the strength of personality to make difficult decisions.

Video analysis has become a critical factor in the modern game, and both Gustav Obermeyer and Hendrikus Koertzen were outstanding. I had very little to do with the change in staff, but I know it involved money. Gustav was entitled to a share of prize money, but because he was working for an outsourced company, they claimed the money. It was an internal affair, and all I was concerned with was that we had an adequate replacement, which Drikus certainly was.

Our physiotherapist, Shane Jabaar, was sound and very

knowledgeable, and everybody respected him. He had been in the job for a long time, and there wasn't much he hadn't seen. Perhaps he'd seen everything a little too often, actually, because there were times when his enthusiasm for the job seemed to have waned, and he could be a real grump at times. He was brilliant with his hands, though, and I never had the slightest doubt that the players were getting the best treatment, but personality is also a critical ingredient in a cricket team, especially on long tours when you are living in each other's pockets for months at a time.

Sometimes I felt like we were working against each other. As coach, I was desperate to have my best players on the field for every game – but Shane kept telling me they were injured and needed rest! Perhaps we were both at fault – there are always two sides to every story. We had our first serious falling-out in England in 2008 and eventually parted ways six months later, after gradually increasing disharmony during the tour of Australia. Brandon Jackson took over and became an extremely popular addition to the squad. But I guess everyone has a shelf life.

As for fitness trainers, I was very lucky to work with Adrian le Roux, who was one of the very best, and Grant Compton, who was much better than average. For the last couple of tours, the excellent Robbie Walter took over, and I hope he goes a long way with the team. Adrian was outstanding at his job, but was perhaps a little too intransigent and inflexible in a team environment. Perhaps this is a trait of all good physiotherapists and biokineticists. Sadly, we had a major disagreement at the 2007 ICC World Cup and our relationship never really recovered. More on that later.

Riaan Muller was a fantastic masseur, a position often regarded as fairly 'lowly' but one which can be more important than any other among the entire backroom staff when it comes to keeping a star player on the field. I never heard him complain once, even when an injury required hourly attention through the night and there was a queue of aching bodies competing for his time.

We had a couple of security men, but the main man was the incomparable Faisal Nagel. It is clearly essential for the very best in the security business to have a gold tooth – to enhance their reputation as 'enforcers' – but Faisal was unquestionably the real thing. Half of his job, I suppose, was simply to make us 'feel' safe and secure and he most certainly did that. His vigilance was amazing; he was always scanning rooms for alternative entry and exit points, always keeping one eye somewhere else – even when he was talking to you. He was inadvertently caught in the Taj Mahal Hotel during the Mumbai terror attacks of November 2008, and helped dozens of guests to escape through the hotel kitchen.

Michael Owen-Smith was our media man, and illustrated to everybody the value of having a guy with extensive experience in that position. We started with Gordon Templeton – who was a bit of a disaster, to be frank – and then Moabi Litheko, who was a lovely guy but who couldn't handle the pressure of the job.

Finally, Doc Moosajee was able to double up as the team doctor as well as team manager without any difficulty. His background in the pharmaceutical industry made him especially useful in the Indian subcontinent, where he had an uncanny knack of knowing exactly why somebody was feeling a bit sick, or 'bowely', and he always seemed to have the pills or potion to limit the damage.

* * *

In the three months before our first tour, Graeme and I often sat together discussing what we wanted in our players, who we thought were underrated, who had the potential to step up and make an impression, and even who we thought were overrated.

I was pretty adamant that every single player in the squad had to be outstanding in two of the three disciplines. You could make an exception if somebody bowled like Allan Donald or batted like Don Bradman but was useless in the other discipline and couldn't field, but I didn't believe there was anybody in South Africa competing for a place in the squad with credentials like that. And besides, we both believed that it was the responsibility of cricketers with a special or rare talent to add another string to their bow through sheer, bloody-minded hard work – much like Glenn McGrath learned to bat. A good example among the Proteas was Paul Harris, who was blessed with modest batting ability and was seen by some as a liability in the field when he first started. But within a couple of years he was our regular night watchman, played some fairly heroic innings and was fielding in the gully.

Ideally, I wanted players with a certain amount of flair and the potential to be genuine match winners, but you can't have a team full of stars. They had to be strong of character, and they had to be genuine fighters with a sound work ethic in terms of both skills and fitness. There would be no room in the Proteas' squad for players who were soft and content to sit in a comfort zone. They would have to want to push themselves and explore the limits of their capabilities. Even if they hadn't shown these qualities at franchise level, I wanted to believe that we could identify the potential to do so and then give them a chance to prove us right or wrong.

Identification of these players would require intimate work between the captain, coach and convenor of selectors, as well as the other national selectors and the domestic coaches. As for the incumbent squad members, all I wanted to stress was that it was privilege for them to be there, not a right. Having said that, once the squad was together I wanted them to feel 'elite'; it was important that they knew they were the best in the country and had a duty to live up to expectations and not let people down.

The cricket style that I wanted to implement was based on pushing limits and not simply accepting what was and wasn't possible. History plays far too big a role in cricket; the game has moved on far more than we realise, but we are still beholden to convention. I wanted the team to be brave, and subsequently coined the phrase 'brave cricket', for which I took a lot of flak – an unnecessary amount, in my opinion!

I thought it would take three years to implement 'brave cricket' on a sustainable level and give the nation a team that would be exciting and attractive to watch on a consistent basis. That didn't mean they would win everything, but if they lost then they would lose with a roar.

My first assignment was, without wishing to be too disrespectful, a red-nose-and-giant-wig affair. I'm sure the Afro-Asia Cup (held in August 2005) was well intentioned, but it wasn't what I needed to kick-start my international career. It was hard to do justice to the 'team' when I wanted to concentrate on the South African players. Still, I was able to learn a couple of useful lessons, and also made the right impression myself. I can't even remember what the result of the series was. Or how many games there were, for that matter ...

One of the men whom I most respect in cricket is RMB chairman Paul Harris, who was an independent director on the board of Cricket South Africa. Brilliant men like Paul make such a difference to a board of directors who, sometimes, are a little too close to their subject matter to be able to step back and make an objective decision. The ICC, for one, could do with a couple of independent directors on its board to look after the health of the global game rather than just the interests of the individual member nations.

Paul had introduced me to Francois Hugo, who is an industrial psychologist by training but, as with many people in that field, wasn't limited by titles or qualifications. I felt we needed to add Francois to the team, particularly at the beginning of my appointment. There had been issues within the South African side before I came in, and I wanted them out in the open, to be acknowledged and addressed. There was a deep lack of trust in the selection system and, consequently, doubt and suspicion among teammates. Black players were wary of being selected for the wrong reasons, and some white players felt they would be regarded as disposable no matter what they did on the field. This all needed to be brought into the open and discussed without fear of reprisal.

It was vital for everyone to start with a clean slate. I didn't want players to be hampered or constrained by old 'baggage'. So we went away for a two-day camp in the Pilanesberg, and Francois facilitated the process of talking through old problems that were still nagging away at certain people. The dynamic of the team was important if we were to achieve everything I hoped we would. It was a great few days from that perspective.

There were some fascinating moments. Jacques Kallis spoke about the perception that people have of him as a perpetually calm, unruffled personality; he explained that he suffered from nerves like everyone else, but had learned what worked best for him when it came to dealing with tension. Makhaya Ntini gave a heartfelt account of what it felt like, for him and other black players, to be perceived as being in the team because of the colour of their skin rather than merit. Nobody could believe that he still felt like that – he was already a South African legend – but clearly he did from time to time. He was more concerned that future players be spared the kind of emotional battering that he had endured at the start of his international career.

* * *

The first 'real' series was against New Zealand – five ODIs at home (21 October – 6 November). We won the first three games, and all of them were pretty close, which can do wonders for team spirit. You learn more about the character of your team-mates, and yourself, in tight contests. Massive, one-sided victories are great but they often don't teach you much. The fourth match, in Durban, was washed out but we completed a 4–0 series win at Centurion on 6 November. It was a good start.

South Africa in India (14–28 November 2005)

The second tour was to India in mid to late November for another five one-dayers. India was an eye-opener, a complete contrast and contradiction in so many ways. I said to myself several times during that tour that I loved India with all my heart – and hated it with a passion. When we were at the cricket ground it was wonderful – the vibe, the colour, the noise, everything within the stands. Away from the cricket grounds, I really didn't enjoy it much at all that first time. Fortunately my view changed in later years; the major cities are very different to the second- and third-rate venues, where facilities, particularly off the field, are a bit of a lottery. I didn't moan – that's not my style. I was never concerned about myself – it didn't matter if I got sick or couldn't sleep. But I became stressed when the players battled to prepare properly, because that jeopardised their performances and therefore the fortunes of the team.

It was, nonetheless, a fabulous series, which we drew 2–2. In the first game, in Hyderabad, we had India 35–5 before a Yuvraj Singh century helped them to 249, but we chased it down with seven balls to spare, which set the tour up beautifully. We were hammered in Bangalore, to leave the series level as we went to Kolkata for the fourth game on 25 November (the third, in Chennai, having been abandoned). My first experience of Eden Gardens was when the enormity of the change in my life hit me: 80 000 people in a cauldron of frenetic, heaving activity. It was a long, long way from the De Beers Diamond Oval and Buffalo Park. The magnitude of the job hit me hard, but in a very pleas-

ant way. I was daunted, but not intimidated. I knew I could
cope, but more than that, I believed I would thrive.

We bowled India out for 188 and Graeme played an extraordinary innings – 134 from just 124 balls. Ten-wicket victories
don't come along very often in ODI cricket, and this was a very
special one.

My appointment as national coach created a huge amount
of interest around the world. A significant amount of speculation concentrated on the possibility that I was a 'soft' and in-
expensive appointment. There were some interesting questions
asked about whether I would simply be there to run around for
Graeme and the players, and would bow down to orders from
the administrators and the board. The end of my career at national level proved that I was nobody's yes man, and that my
principles were strong, but they were just as strong at the beginning as they were at the end.

Chapter 3

Taking on Australia

December 2005 to March 2006

It was the ultimate prize. More than winning a World Cup, or anything else, the chance to win a Test series in Australia was a dream opportunity, and I mean that literally. I had dreamed about it several times in the months before we actually boarded the plane for Perth.

The fact is, we weren't facing just any Australian team; it was a great team. They weren't even on their way to becoming great; they had already done it. Langer, Hayden, Ponting, Warne, McGrath, Gilchrist ... if an ODI at Eden Gardens had been eye-opening, this was going to be eye-watering.

Tour of Australia (9 December 2005 – 7 February 2006)
Our preparations went well, as far as I was concerned. In retrospect, there are always one or two things that you might have done differently, but at least we were decisive and had a plan. We flew out early to practise and acclimatise for ten days. Graeme and I had spoken at great length about the need to be

strong in our attitude and approach, and to make it clear we weren't scared of, or intimidated by, Australia. Perhaps that was wrong, or perhaps we overdid it, but we were conscious of the fact that the last South African team to visit Australian shores had been so humble that they were perceived as weak.

Graeme took a lot on his own shoulders in terms of what he said in the media. He even took on Shane Warne, which the tabloids loved but which probably wasn't the best move, given that Warne was paid a fortune to write a column for the biggest tabloid in Australia, and could have a crack at Graeme whenever he wanted. To be fair, Graeme was only responding to what Shane had said, and actually did so with sharp wit and humour. Just before the Boxing Day Test, Warne said that we were the worst team to have left South African shores. The following day, in clear reference to Warne's latest sex scandal, Graeme told the tabloids that Warne was probably just feeling very frustrated about the fact that he would never captain his country. It was, of course, absolutely true, and it hurt Warne very deeply. From then on, Warne stuck the knife in at every opportunity. The media distractions probably didn't help our cause, but I take consolation from the fact that they happened because we didn't want to be bullied, and there's nothing wrong with that.

I will never forget a session we had with Francois Hugo in the team room in the hotel in Perth a few days after arriving. Everybody said all the right things and spoke about not being intimidated, having no fear and having the confidence and self-belief to play to our potential and do ourselves justice. It all sounded so good at the time, but ultimately it was all just bravado.

The Perth Test (16–20 December) had a number of tense and exciting passages of play, during which we earned a small first innings lead but ended up having to bat out the entire fifth day to save it. Jacques Rudolph, despite a double century against Bangladesh, had never really done himself justice or established himself in the Test team, and the same could be said for Justin Kemp. However, both showed fabulous character on that final day, and were an unlikely but very popular pair of heroes.

Makhaya Ntini bowled beautifully to limit Australia to 258, but we messed up by not extending the lead beyond 38 in our first innings. On a good pitch, showing no signs of deterioration, it was inconsequential. Australia went huge in their second innings, and at one stage I thought we were in serious trouble until it became apparent that Ricky Ponting was going to allow Brad Hodge the chance to get to a double century. Instead of batting the best part of five sessions to save the game, it was only four. Our target was 491, but far more relevant was the time Ponting had unnecessarily wasted. It was a bad omen for the home side, and I believe it probably cost them the Test.

I know history is littered with examples of touring teams coming 'second' when it comes to umpiring decisions in Australia, and I certainly felt that way during the Test. Umpires are not biased – at least, since the advent of neutral umpires they haven't been – but that does not stop them from being significantly intimidated, and consequently influenced, by strong and wilful characters, of which there were many in that Australian team. But it's not just the team that influences players. The size and volume of the crowd, and the enormity of the occasion, also play their part. Steve Bucknor and Billy Doctrove were in charge in Perth. I enjoy the company of both men, but I also think they were among the most easily influenced of the umpires on the international circuit.

* * *

The Boxing Day Test in Melbourne is one of the great sporting events in the world, never mind the cricket calendar. Our families had joined us for Christmas, the atmosphere and mood of the camp was great and, because we'd taken more from the

draw in Perth than Ponting and his team, we were full of confidence. The Melbourne Cricket Ground (MCG) is one of the
world's greatest sports theatres. We'd had a few days' practice
there before Boxing Day, but there can be no doubt about the
impact on first-timers when they walk out and see 80 000 people
in the stands. I experienced my second MCG Boxing Day Test
three years later; far from being a lesser experience, it was even
better. The result helped, of course!

What really surprised me about Australia, even though I had
done my research and tried to prepare for it, was the hostility of
the spectators whenever we practised. There were many friendly
people (and plenty of South Africans in Perth, of course), but
there were also always people who came to barrack and abuse
us – every day, without fail. It was the unashamed and unsubtle
hostility that I wasn't expecting. A chirp here and there is no
problem, but this was deliberately unpleasant. And there were
always plenty of kids around the nets, too, which made it harder
to stomach. After the first day of the MCG Test, Graeme went
to have some throw-downs in the nets, which are in full view of
the spectators as they file past. He is a tough character, and puts
up with just about anything, but he was forced to come back to
the changing room almost immediately for the sake of the innocent and/or sensitive among the passers-by. He had quickly
become a strong magnet for even stronger language.

The worst thing about the Test was that we did so much of
the hard work and played ourselves into a great position before making basic mistakes – mostly dropping catches – and
letting Australia off the hook. They batted first after winning the
toss, and at 154–1 things were looking bleak. To make matters
worse, we had dropped Ponting on nought, and he had added
152 with Hayden for the second wicket. But Shaun Pollock,
Makhaya Ntini and André Nel then launched an amazing fight-
back, which saw eight wickets fall for 100, and they had their
backs to the wall at 248–9 with McGrath walking to the wicket.

I could hardly believe how well we had hit back and, although it was a drop-in pitch and not easy to bat on, I was sure that, with determination and application, we could earn a decent first innings lead.

Mike Hussey edged a Pollock delivery straight to Kallis at second slip, and that was that. No safer pair of hands in the game. I felt a sigh of relief as the ball flew straight into Jacques's hands. And then a wave of disbelief and shock as it bounced straight out again. The result couldn't have been worse, as Hussey brilliantly manipulated the strike and coaxed a century stand out of McGrath, of all people.

You say the right things after something like that, and you talk about 'putting it behind us and moving forward', but in retrospect I'm not sure we ever recovered mentally from that partnership. Apart from half a dozen dropped catches, we also had a series of umpiring decisions go against us, notably an LBW decision against Ponting, which was absolutely plumb on about 10 or 11. Of course, it wouldn't have mattered if we hadn't dropped him.

We were chasing 366 in the fourth innings, which was worth about 500 on a decent wicket; it was never going to happen, and it was only thanks to an innings of 67 from Polly at number eight that we managed to get to 181. So we were 'thrashed', and the media let us know all about it, both at home but certainly in Melbourne. But Graeme and I knew how close we had been to upsetting them. We knew that they knew there wasn't as much between the sides as the result suggested. Although Ponting, Hayden and Hussey had scored fine centuries, it was our mistakes which had given them all the chances. Strange as it may sound, we were able to take comfort from the fact that our destiny was in our hands. If we had created nothing, it would have been different, but we had created many, many chances. We just hadn't taken them.

Graeme and I compared notes on the performances of the

players, and tried to analyse why we had faltered when we were so close to a winning position. In line with the 'style' of cricket and brand of character we were looking for, the process of evaluation started.

As amazing as the Boxing Day Test match experience is, the New Year Test in Sydney ranks very firmly alongside it. The only difference is the difference in capacity of the stadiums – 100 000 at the MCG and 45 000 at the SCG. But in Sydney you get to stay close to the famous harbour and watch the greatest fireworks display in the world on the iconic Harbour Bridge on New Year's Eve.

The ground was packed for the first three days, and we played some very, very good cricket. We included Johan Botha in the XI at the last minute, on a pitch which was notoriously spin-friendly towards the end of the match, and then won the toss and batted first, which was perfect. At domestic level, I had played a role in helping Botha reinvent himself as a spinner, having never threatened as a seamer, and his ability to bowl a 'doosra' made him especially exciting – although it was undoubtedly a gamble, too. He'd been bowling off-spin for only a couple of years, and here he was being given a Test match!

It was an overcast morning and the ball was nipping around a bit. At 86–3 the innings could have gone either way, but Kallis and Ashwell Prince applied themselves – as only those two can – and batted magnificently during a stand of 219, which helped us declare with a first innings score of 451–9. We bowled extremely well, too, and despite yet another brilliant Ricky Ponting century we earned a lead of 92, which should, and could, have been enough to make a match-changing difference. We batted well again in the second innings, and were well on target to put the game beyond Australia's reach and also give ourselves enough time and overs to win it.

But the fourth day was almost completely washed out, with only 20.3 overs bowled, and we were left kicking our heels in frustration. Cricketers are actually surprisingly level-headed when it comes to coping with bad weather; we have to do it on a fairly regular basis, so you learn to switch off and not waste any emotional energy over it. It's our families and supporters who seem to suffer a lot more than us.

But it left Graeme and me in an interesting position. Would we live up to our new mantra and be brave enough to risk losing the game in order to give ourselves the chance of winning it and levelling the series? Whichever way you did the sums, and however well we batted for the rest of our second innings, we would always be giving Australia a genuine chance of victory if we wanted to have enough time to win the match. For over a hundred years, conventional cricketing wisdom and logic had dictated that you never declare until the match is 'safe', that is, you always take a draw if you can't win and never, ever give the opposition a chance. Were we really going to challenge that – in a Test match?

Yes, we were. Graeme was adamant that we should do everything we could to try and square the series. His view was simple: a one-nil series defeat was no different to a two-nil defeat, and it didn't matter if a bold declaration backfired.

There was nothing wrong with our calculations – in theory – but two unexpected factors conspired against us. The cold and wet weather meant the pitch hadn't deteriorated nearly as much as usual, and there was nothing for the seamers or spinners. It was like a pitch on the third morning rather than the fifth day; everything was flying straight off the middle of the bat. The second spanner in the works was a heel injury to André Nel, which prevented him from bowling. He'd got better and better through the series, and was our best bowler in the first innings. To lose him for the second innings was a serious blow.

Having said all that, Ponting was, yet again, brilliant. He sensed the chance to bury us early, and attacked from the start. He simply never allowed it to get close or tense. Makhaya was missing, too, having picked up an injury before the game, and any hopes that 'Botes' was going to make a dream debut were dashed almost immediately when Hayden and Ponting tore into him straight away and belted him for 77 in 12 overs.

To make matters even worse, match referee Chris Broad reported Botha after the match for a suspect bowling action. It was horrible. He had worked so hard on making himself 'different', on giving himself the best possible chance of playing international cricket. The issue of 'chucking' (throwing the ball instead of bowling) has been demystified a little in the last decade, but it still retains a good deal of stigma.

So that was that. The Test series was lost two-nil, and Shane Warne could say that he was right about us being the worst team to leave South Africa. But we weren't, not by a very long way. We were bitterly disappointed, but after a few days to recover we could point to how close we had got to disturbing Australia's aura of invincibility. Now we needed to look at ourselves, and our own games, in order to learn how to get the job done. We had a young, talented and very strong captain, and our relationship was growing well. Graeme and I both believed we had most of the players we needed to make the team a success.

The disappointment continued into the triangular series afterwards, when we failed to reach the final. We needed to beat Sri Lanka in Hobart on 7 February to make the final, but we capitulated meekly. When the heat was on, we couldn't take it. We did win a couple of games, and played some decent cricket at times, but there was an important ingredient missing. I wasn't certain what it was, but I was bloody well going to find it.

Towards the end of the triangular series, a day before the ODI against Sri Lanka, Gerald Majola made an impromptu visit to Perth. It was an excellent piece of management, and one which had exactly the desired effect. He was understandably concerned that Graeme and I might have become a bit despondent about the way results were going and about the inevitable battering that we were taking in the media. He took us both out for dinner the evening he arrived, and assured us that he – and everyone else who mattered – could see that we weren't as far off the pace as the results suggested. He said that perseverance and hard work were required, and that they would ultimately pay off.

Gerald was consistently supportive throughout my time as national coach. He supported me even when it may have been difficult or awkward to do so. Ultimately, he couldn't save me – perhaps by then he'd had enough of the fights between me and the board – but through all the trials and tribulations before the final week he took the view that, as chief executive, he had appointed me, and as chief executive he was going to support me. It meant a hell of a lot to me.

Australia in South Africa – ODIs (24 February – 12 March 2006)

On our return from Australia, we had only the usual two or three weeks to prepare before Australia arrived to start the return series. After many hours of chatting and strategising about the series, we decided to ask the head groundsmen at the three Test venues (Newlands, Kingsmead and the Wanderers) to prepare green wickets with a bit of moisture and grass on them. Our request was based on a number of factors, but primarily that we backed our seamers to make life difficult for the Aussie top order, which had scored so heavily and prolifically in Australia. We also felt it was perfectly reasonable to make any attempt to nullify Shane Warne, and with Glenn McGrath missing the tour to be with his ailing wife, it seemed to make even more sense. Finally, we backed our own top order to show both the guts and technique to make runs on wickets that were 'doing a bit'.

The tactic was, to be quite honest, a bit of a disaster!

Whereas we had thought that the selection of thirty-year-old Stuart Clark, with a modest first-class record, indicated a certain lack of depth or options in the Aussie seam-bowling ranks, he turned out to be every bit as good as McGrath and bowled magnificently well to take 20 wickets in the series. He was quite brilliant, and to make matters even worse he was a terrific bloke, too, with no interest in sledging and plenty of respect for both the game and the opposition. So he pretty much took care of the Test series.

Before that, though, we had treated the cricket-loving public to an epic one-day series, certainly the best I was ever involved in and one of the best of all time. We comfortably won the first match, in Centurion, with Graeme making a brilliant 119 not out. We were even better in Cape Town, where Makhaya produced an almost iconic performance by claiming 6–22 with the new ball, to bowl them out for just 93. Australia, bowled out for less than 100! It was actually quite difficult to know how to feel or behave. In many ways it is more emotional and exciting to win a close match than to knock your opponent out in the first round. It wasn't exactly anti-climactic, but – even for the senior players – that sort of result was unexplored territory.

Graeme and I had wanted to do something a little different in ODI cricket to manufacture ourselves an advantage, and we identified the 10 or so 'dead' overs between 28 and 40 as an area in which we could break free from convention and take a lead in the international game. Every team at that stage had a similar, if not identical, game plan: hit the sweepers on both off and leg side, drive it down the ground to the long-on and long-off boundaries against the spinners and look to score at five runs an over without taking risks while keeping wickets in hand for the last assault in the final seven or eight overs.

I reasoned that if our middle order was good enough to score at nine or ten an over for the final seven or eight overs, why weren't they good enough to do so ten overs earlier? Much was dependent on conditions, of course, but on a flattish wicket I thought teams were being over-cautious purely because that was the way the 50-over game had evolved. That was 'what you did'. But 20 runs can make a massive difference in an ODI game – at least half of games between top teams are decided by that many – so that was where Graeme and I decided to look for the extra runs.

I gave licence to the middle order guys to hit the ball out of the ground during those 'middle overs' if they felt confident and conditions were right. Although this meant you ran the risk of falling 20 runs short of a good score if things didn't go well, it also meant you could make 20 or 30 above par and put the game beyond the reach of the opposition. Do you back yourself or do you stick close to the safety of the pack? We decided to back ourselves more often than not. It was 'brave cricket', although the media were having a hard time understanding what we meant by that – and were consequently giving me a hard time. That match at Newlands worked perfectly. Mark Boucher, Jacques Kallis, AB de Villiers and Justin Kemp all played wonderful innings to set an excellent total of 289, and then we destroyed them with the ball. We were two-nil up, we'd played well, everybody was smiling and suddenly cricket was alive again in South Africa. It's amazing how quickly things change. But I was aware that Australia had a couple of key players missing for those first two games – notably Andrew Symonds – so I fully expected them to bounce back hard.

Our new tactic didn't work quite so well in Port Elizabeth during the third game, however, and despite chasing a very makeable 255 we lost comfortably. It would have been even more comprehensive were it not for a late 69 from Polly and a remarkable 29 from 13 balls from Roger Telemachus.

The fourth game at Kingsmead was a classic of its sort, with emotions and fortunes fluctuating wildly as the game reached its climax. When we claimed the eighth wicket, with 29 still required from the last two Australian wickets, we were strong favourites to win the match and series. But that man Clark popped up again, with a previously unsuspected back foot cover drive of great power and timing. I don't think it was just us who hadn't suspected that ability – I'm not sure he had. When the ninth wicket fell, there were still six runs required and it was edge-of-your-seat stuff. It was a fantastic spectacle, and just what one-day cricket should be all about.

'The 438 game' – the decider

The fifth match of the series took place at the Wanderers on 12 March. When I think of what that amazing day has meant to so many careers, I'm left struggling for words – much as I was in the immediate aftermath of the match. I believe people will still be struggling to explain, describe and understand that result in twenty years' time. There may even have been half a dozen 400+ matches played by then – who knows? Perhaps this kind of result may even become a regular occurrence if the laws of the game are changed yet again to favour batsmen, but there is also the chance that the record could remain a 'freak' occurrence between major nations if 50-over cricket is played less in the years to come as T20 takes over.

But, either way, the match will forever remain an extraordinary achievement. Unlike the four-minute mile and other iconic records in different sports, there had not been a gradual transition towards a game of that magnitude. It came almost completely out of the blue.

The first half of the match was a coach's nightmare. I couldn't watch our bowling display; it was terrible in every way possible – not only lines and lengths but also wides and no-balls, especially at the back end of the innings. Poor old Roger Telemachus – he'd bowled beautifully in the series for us until then, and he was the standout bowler once again when his first eight overs went for just 47 amid the carnage going on around him. Then his last two went for another 40 as he suffered a complete collapse and simply couldn't let the ball go. Then he couldn't run in. within the space of about five minutes, he lost his run-up, his delivery and every shred of confidence. At least, for his sake, he wasn't alone. For me, it was like watching open-heart surgery – something you would normally turn your head away from. But I couldn't. I had to watch – it was my job. By the end of their innings, Australia had racked up 434 runs.

The enormity of what happened on the day will always be remembered, but what is often forgotten is that this was the series decider. We had won the first two games impressively, Australia had hit back to win the next two by the narrowest of margins and the level of expectation going into the final match was as high as I had ever experienced. There had been a lot of media hype, and the Wanderers was packed. And we were being systematically and ruthlessly humiliated.

The Standard Bank mascot, Stan the Duck, was walking around the Bullring holding his head in his hands and looking as gloomy and pessimistic as an oversized expressionless duck can.

In the dressing room during the break, we were all in shock. Nobody said a word for at least five or six minutes. As coach, I had no idea what to say. I had already established my reputation for optimism even against seemingly impossible odds, but in this instance I didn't think it would be appropriate to launch into a table-thumping 'we can win this!' speech.

Then Kallis walked into the room, after going for a comfort break, and I think the atmosphere actually amused him. Having played more cricket than any of us, his sense of perspective is extremely well defined. Breaking the silence, he said in a firm and confident voice: 'Coach, I think the bowlers have done their job. I reckon it's a 450 wicket so they're 16 short of par.' Everybody burst out laughing, and the ice was broken. Jacques was the first to see the funny side, but there was still a sense that we had been visited by an alien. Jacques didn't believe we could win at that stage. None of us did. I'd love to pretend otherwise and say that I could see a way for us to produce the biggest shock in ODI history, but then I wouldn't be 'Honest Mickey'.

I was always a very 'structured' coach, with a big emphasis on tactics and targets and having a plan for every situation. I didn't mind if the plan changed – in fact, I enjoyed a bit of improvisation and imagination – but it was always important to me that players started off with a plan and always knew what they were trying to achieve and where they were heading. Naturally, this was a situation I had never envisaged before, so a bit of quick thinking was required.

The first line of my much-revised and recalculated tactics talk went something like this: 'Guys, we need to be around 160 after 20 overs – but we cannot afford to lose more than two wickets.' At that point I looked at Graeme Smith and Herschelle Gibbs, and, try as they might, neither of them could restrain their laughter. They giggled a bit, then burst out laughing, and I followed suit. Everyone started laughing again. So I screwed up my sheet of paper with my hastily prepared run chase plan on it and threw it against the wall. 'OK, f**k it then – targets are out the window! Just go and play, play your game and who the hell knows what might happen!' It was very much against my nature, but these were unusual circumstances.

Boeta Dippenaar was bowled, and missed out on the fun, but that just meant that Herschelle was able to get to the crease early. Watching him and Graeme bat for an hour was phenomenal. For the first hour, all I kept thinking was that at least we were going down with a fight and with some dignity and pride restored. But the key to the entire innings was that we never let the asking rate climb above eight and a half or nine runs to the over. Conventional wisdom says that you make a quick start to a big run chase, let the asking rate climb in the middle overs and then chase lots of runs in the final few overs with wickets in hand. If we'd done that chasing 435, then we would have needed 20 runs an over for the last 10 overs!

The only time the asking rate climbed a little too high was when we realised that we actually had a chance of winning it. We developed a speed wobble, which was understandable enough. Kallis and Boucher were batting at the time, and I had retrieved my screwed-up sheet of paper from the corner of the room. We sent a message out with the targets for where we wanted to be after 30, 35, 40 overs etc. It proved to be a bit of a reality check, and the guys started playing to those targets rather than just continuing as we had been doing – in other words, the 'plan' actually started hindering rather than helping us. It was a good lesson for me to learn. There is a time and a place for a plan, and that is most of the time. Very occasionally, however, there is a time and a place to just go with the flow.

We saw people leaving the stadium even before we started to bat, and even more left during the first few overs, despite the amazing start we made. I guess you couldn't blame them. But by the thirtieth over people had started coming back. It just got better and better. Somewhere between the 30th and 35th overs everyone in the dressing room started to believe that we were going to be a part of history, that we were going to have a once-in-a-lifetime experience.

Herschelle's 175 was amazing for so many reasons. Graeme and I spent a long time that morning debating whether we should select him or not. Once again, frustratingly, it wasn't a debate about his form or his ability but his behaviour. He'd been out the night before, and had had one or two too many to drink. He had probably got to bed at around midnight in a condition far less than ideal as preparation for any match, let alone such an important one. We were close to our wits' end about what to do with him. Herschelle was aware that I knew; Vinnie Barnes knew; and Graeme knew. I didn't think anybody else knew. If it had become public knowledge, we would have been forced to drop him. The drinking and late nights were almost certainly the product of nerves, but there are far better ways of dealing

with your anxiety. I was always, and will always be, very fond
of Hersch. He was extremely nervous before he went out to bat,
probably because he felt like it was his last chance – as well as
the seemingly hopeless match situation. To see him express all
his natural talent and play in such an uninhibited way was very
special indeed. Unfortunately, I think the realisation that we
could actually win the game sobered him up with a jolt and that
probably cost him his wicket! Graeme played superbly well and
Bouch was magnificent at the end.

When Andrew Hall hit the boundary to take us just one short
with four balls left, I looked around and everybody was shouting
and screaming, deliriously happy. Herschelle was sitting in the
dressing room with toilet paper in his ears so he couldn't hear
the reaction of the crowd. Graeme was sitting in the video room
tapping a stump on the ground, not watching; he just couldn't.
I was actually out on the balcony; I don't why or how because
I wasn't a great watcher during the tense times. But something
amazing was happening, and I felt as though some alien force
was in control of me.

Then my eyes met Makhaya's, and they were as big as saucers.
Honestly, he looked as though he was pulling a funny face – but
he wasn't. If you could measure the adrenaline and tension in a
human body at any given stage, then Makhaya would have broken the scale at that moment. He was next in, and whereas there
would have been few expectations if we had needed 20 from the
last wicket, or even 10, now there were only two runs needed
and everybody in the world would be expecting Makhaya to
deliver. I think he was praying with all his soul that he wouldn't
be needed. Of course, Andrew was out to the next delivery.

I swear that Makhaya turned pale with fright. He was a bit
wobbly as he got to his feet, but he was breathing deeply, which
was a good sign. It showed that he was at least trying to remain
calm and get some oxygen to his head. When he guided the first
ball down to third man for a single I felt the tears come to my

eyes. We had avoided defeat. Australia had scored 434 and we couldn't lose the game. We were going to avoid defeat. A share of the series, at least, was ours.

I know I would never have recovered if we had been bowled out for 433 and lost by a run. A bit like South Africa's semifinal exit to Australia at the 2003 World Cup and the infamous Allan Donald-Lance Klusener run-out, a piece of me would have died if we'd lost by a run.

Boucher banged the next delivery from Brett Lee back over his head for the winning runs and that was that. As he ran up the dressing room stairs I hugged him as hard as I could and yelled 'Bouch, all you needed to do was knock it for one, why the hell did you hit it in the air?!' Excuse the language, but he replied: 'Coach, the faint-hearted never f***ed a fair maiden.'

Of course we had a huge celebration afterwards. Graeme and I agreed on just about everything, but we especially believed in the importance of celebrating moments of triumph properly together. Suddenly nobody had a care in the world. We hugged each other a hundred times each and toasted each other a hundred times more. I'm not sure what time we left the changing room but it had been dark for many hours by the time we boarded the team bus. That day was one of the best in my life.

Chapter 4

From crisis to consolidation

July to August 2006

T he 2006 tour of Sri Lanka was always going to be a difficult
one for us. Sri Lanka in their country represent one of the
hardest challenges on the cricket circuit. Unlike India, however,
where off-field conditions can make touring especially challenging, Sri Lanka – particularly Colombo, the capital – can be a
pleasure to tour because of the close proximity of everything.
Travelling in the subcontinent, either by road or air, is physically and emotionally draining. But the evenings in Sri Lanka
are pleasant, with a variety of good restaurants and other leisure
options. And there are some interesting beaches to visit on the
rare 'rest' days that international cricketers get these days.

The schedule had us playing two Tests, followed by a triangular one-day series (also involving India), which was later abandoned in what some people called 'controversial' circumstances
following a bomb blast in Colombo. For us, the circumstances
weren't controversial at all: bombs and cricket simply didn't
work for us, and there was very little debate within the squad
about whether to continue with the tour.

The omens were not good when Graeme Smith and Jacques Kallis were both ruled out due to injury, leaving not so much a gap in the team as a gaping wound. After much healthy discussion about their replacements (how *do* you replace Kallis?), we decided to make Ashwell Prince the captain of the Test team and ask Mark Boucher to take charge of the one-day side. Ashwell's appointment, made completely on merit, was a milestone both for him and for South African cricket, as he became the first captain of colour of South Africa. It was a great opportunity for us as a team to celebrate transformation. Sadly, but I suppose inevitably, there was a lot of speculation – in bars as well as in the media – about Ashwell's credentials and whether he was a 'political' appointment. I can categorically state that I was instrumental in making him Test captain simply because I thought he was the best man for the job. There was no better candidate.

By and large, however, the appointment was well received, and attracted a huge amount of media attention from around the world, as well as in South Africa. I believed deeply that it was a step in the right direction. Boucher's appointment, too, was the right one on a short-term basis, as we had difficulties in fitting Ash into the one-day side. I have always been an advocate of selecting your team and then appointing a captain, rather than appointing a captain and then working out what you will do with him in the team.

From my point of view, the Sri Lanka tour will always be remembered for the emergence of Dale Steyn, who showed the first signs of the ability that would later make him world number one.

For the rest of the world, however, the tour was notable for just one thing – the world-record partnership of 624, for any wicket, between great friends Kumar Sangakkara and Mahela Jayawardena. The records just kept tumbling, one after another. When they finally passed the ultimate record, that of 576 for

the second wicket (between Sanath Jayasuriya and Roshan
Mahamana for Sri Lanka against India at Colombo in 1997), as
well as the record in all first-class cricket of 577 for the fourth
wicket (between Vijay Hazare and Gul Mohammad for Baroda v
Holkar at Baroda in 1946–47), fireworks erupted from the top of
the scoreboard and on the grass banks all around the Sinhalese
Sports Club. It was a peculiar sight to see and experience. I enjoyed it, but couldn't help wondering what would have happened if we'd taken a wicket a couple of runs earlier. Would
they have had to save the fireworks for another day? After the
game, cars were driven onto the field and the keys presented to
the two players as a reward for their feat. It was all rather hard
to imagine happening in South Africa.

Mahela was poised to break the world record for the highest score in a Test match, but was bowled by André Nel for
374, within sight of Brian Lara's 400. The partnership of 624
still leaves me shaking my head. How could so many things
conspire to allow that to happen? They batted magnificently, of
course, and deserved a lot more than fireworks and small family cars as reward, but it fascinated me that the law of averages
could be defied for so long. They must have survived a dozen
half chances each: balls bouncing over the stumps, LBW decisions going their way, catches landing inches short of the fielders. It's important to me – and I imagine it would be to Mahela
and Kumar too – for people to realise that the cricket was intense and highly competitive throughout their stand. We never
gave up. We never resorted to 'joke' bowlers. It was real all the
way through. Even when we eventually gave the ball to AB, he
charged in as though his life depended on it and actually bowled
three or four very decent overs.

The heat was something most of us had never experienced before. Players were coming off the field after their marathon fielding sessions and going straight onto rehydration drips. Boucher
looked extremely gaunt, worryingly so, and Herschelle spent a

whole session on a drip unable to recover from the amount of fluid he'd lost in the first part of the day.

We chose to bat first, and did ourselves no justice whatsoever by being bowled out for 169 in 50 overs. The irony of that first innings was that our game plan of attacking the great Murali actually looked like it was working from time to time. We had opted to attack him rather than be defensive, and it was remarkable how quickly he was prepared to move his close catchers into the infield, or even the deep, when a couple of boundaries were hit. But he finished with 4–41 in 18 overs and we were doomed.

Once Sri Lanka had declared, with 756 on the board, it was our turn again. Not many of us had much experience of batting almost 600 in arrears, and we were starting with what must rank as one of South Africa's most unlikely opening partnerships: Andrew Hall and Jacques Rudolph. Hally was always a makeshift option, but Rudolph had to move up the order because Herschelle could only bat at number seven after the time he had spent off the field. Once again, I was confronted with a situation in which I had to focus the players' minds away from what were, on the face of it, completely impossible odds.

Things started extremely well, with an opening stand of 165 in 50 overs. Maybe, just maybe, we could bat for the rest of the match and save it! But Murali was in his element. He bowled over after over, 64 of them in total, and whatever we tried he just wouldn't go away. When we attacked he backed off, and when we defended he set the field like a vice around us. And all the time he just smiled. Genius. Prince and Boucher both made good half centuries to go with the openers' efforts, and we batted almost 160 overs before eventually losing by an innings. We made them work hard but eventually it was too high a mountain to climb.

One concern I did have, though I never voiced it publicly – or even privately, for that matter – was that Shaun Pollock was starting to struggle a little bit in Test cricket. He didn't have the penetration that he normally had. I knew it was a flat wicket and there was precious little in it for anybody, but as our senior bowler I knew that he would have expected more from himself. But after an innings in which the opposition could have scored a thousand, who was I to point a finger at any individual, let alone such a great professional? Nicky Boje, for example, had bowled 65 overs, at a cost of 221, without a wicket to show for his efforts. The analysis broke all sorts of records for being the most expensive and least productive in Test cricket for South Africa (second overall behind Khan Mohammad's 54–5–259–0 for Pakistan v West Indies at Kingston in 1957–58). However, Mahela and Kumar had the good grace and decency to admit afterwards that Nicky had, in fact, bowled very well and deserved a lot better.

We came desperately close to winning the second Test, which, given the mauling we had just been given, represented a spectacular comeback. The Test, at the P Saravanamuttu Stadium in Colombo on 4–8 August, was one of the best matches I was ever involved in. Sri Lanka won by one wicket on the fifth day, but for almost the entire duration of the match nobody could say for certain who had the edge, and all three results were still possible with a day to go.

Nicky Boje once again bowled well, and but for a couple of dropped catches we would surely have won. But we dropped them, so had only ourselves to blame. But it was the emergence of AB and Dale Steyn that excited me most about the Test match and the tour. Unlike so many young batsmen early in their careers, AB showed that he was prepared to do in the middle what we spoke about and what he practised in the nets. He had the courage of his convictions. When we talked about using our feet and attacking Murali, he did it. Many young players are inhibited by the fear of failure, but AB had the *gees* to go with his talent (sometimes too much, but that was a little later in his career).

We really took care of Murali in the second Test. He could only manage five wickets in the first innings, and in the second, with the pitch turning and bouncing appreciably, we restricted him to just seven (thanks, partly, to Jacques Rudolph and Hashim Amla getting themselves run out!). On a serious note, however, it was a source of some satisfaction to me that the great man had needed to bowl 80 overs for his 12 wickets, and that we had managed to score 225 runs off him.

Steyn was electrifying at times. What was to become a regular sight years later was jaw-dropping at the time. He ran in without complaint at any time of the day, and gave everything. He was fast even at the very beginning of his career, and when conditions were right and the ball was looked after he could swing it both ways at extreme speed. He had all the attributes to become a world leader. Like all coaches, I was nervous that something might go wrong – and that I could have done something to prevent it. Thankfully nothing went wrong, and Dale would go on to become world number one and play a lead role in South Africa's greatest Test series victory.

It's hard to justify saying this when two men have scored 624 against you, but the first Test really was closer than the result suggested – honestly! The second Test, on the other hand, was extremely close. We had a first innings lead and would probably have won it easily, having set them 350 to win, if Makhaya had not been injured and unable to bowl after just seven overs. But facts were facts, and we lost the series two-nil. Painful but true.

Attention now turned to the ODI triangular series and the arrival of our one-day specialists – and India. The number of 'hangers on' attached to the Indian team made life a bit unruly and difficult in the Taj Samudra Hotel, where we were staying, so we made enquiries about moving to the Cinnamon Grand Hotel, just a kilometre away. India has a huge following everywhere they go in the world, but with Colombo being so close there were literally thousands of people hanging around the Taj Samudra. It wasn't unbearable by any means, but the switch meant your room service club sandwich arrived a lot sooner! The move was a pleasant change, and made a significant difference to our preparations.

We won a practice match pretty convincingly, but then preparations came to a grinding halt because of persistent rain. I knew we needed as much training as possible for our one-day skills, both batting and bowling, so we made the best use we could of limited facilities in an indoor centre. The batsmen benefited to some extent, but there was no way our fast bowlers could gain any benefit, so we sent them back to the hotel to rest or go to the gym. Steyn, Nel, Langeveldt, Ntini and Telemachus were all bundled into a car and whisked off back to the hotel, while the batsmen continued having throw-downs and practising their 'release' shots – sweeping and hitting the boundary fielders.

When practice had finished, and we were getting back on the bus, I noticed our security man, Faisal Nagel, in an earnest huddle with team manager Goolam Rajah. They walked quickly over to me and Bouch and informed us that there had been a bomb blast in the shopping plaza very close to our hotel (about 600 metres away). They also told us that our fast bowlers had been driven past the plaza approximately five minutes before the bomb went off. It was a chilling moment.

Emotions ran high following the incident, which occurred on 14 August. Certain players reacted more strongly than others, but we left the decision on whether to continue the tour totally in the hands of our security advisers. Faisal gathered all the intelligence he could, and kept us informed at every stage. The drive back to the hotel was even more chilling than hearing the news twenty minutes before. It was a slightly surreal reminder of what life could be like in a country during a civil war. We took a different route back to the hotel, but there was still enough carnage and chaos visible for us to confirm that the bomb had gone off very close to where we were staying. A couple of our travelling media representatives, Altus Momberg and Neil Manthorp, had been shopping in the plaza about ten minutes before the explosion. They seemed surprisingly calm – I think it was probably just relief, although journalists are a different breed! All we knew for certain was that life as a touring cricketer shouldn't involve lucky escapes from explosive devices.

Tony Irish, chief executive of SACA, was very supportive to me and the team. CSA chief Gerald Majola made sure he was personally involved, and kept us updated all the time. Eventually he made the decision to pull us out of the country, although we had to sit tight for forty-eight hours while the International Cricket Council (ICC) gave their 'blessing' and the assurance that CSA would not be financially penalised for failing to honour our Future Tours Programme (FTP) commitments.

I had a letter delivered to my room, a fax from the Tamil Tigers, telling us that the conflict was not our fight, that they couldn't guarantee our security in Sri Lanka and that perhaps we were better off not being there. That's when the reality of the situation hit home. The hardest thing for me was having to meet with so many people and deal with situations that I had neither prepared for nor had any experience in. The Sri Lankan Security Minister, the Minister of Police and a whole variety of diplomats were all urging us to stay on. All the time, I constantly had to remind myself that I was a cricket coach, not a politician, and that my first and foremost responsibility was to look after the players and take care of their fears and misgivings. It was made very clear to me what the repercussions and ramifications would be of withdrawing from the tour, and I understood them. To a degree, I was even sympathetic. But my loyalty and responsibility was to the players.

There was some very negative and uninformed media criticism of the decision to cut short the tour. What really hurt us were the demeaning and uninformed comments from people who were sitting thousands of miles away in comfortable offices or studies. There were people who said, and wrote, that they had been to Sri Lanka many times in the past and that it was a safe environment. But of course they were not there when the bomb went off. These kind of hostile remarks really affected us, but even worse were the snide and underhanded comments implying we were cowards.

It was particularly difficult being 'prisoners' in our hotel for two or three days while the situation resolved itself. Two days before we finally left Sri Lanka, one of the local newspapers ran a front-page photograph of Dale Steyn and Mark Boucher, smiling and seemingly relaxed, doing some shopping. The accompanying editorial was nasty and sarcastic, and inferred that we were running away even though there was no danger. The truth was very different. The shops were in an arcade adjoining the hotel and were patrolled constantly by police and security. We had been given clearance to go there, a fact the newspaper conveniently failed to mention. The headline ran: 'okay to shop – but not to play!'

We were in a difficult position. Family and friends back home were telling us that life was too short to run the risk of another bomb going off. They urged us to get on the first plane – and to hell with the consequences. Administrators and politicians in Sri Lanka, and even some in South Africa, told us to hang in there for the sake of the game. I fully understand the theory behind not giving in to terrorists. If you run once, then they will be encouraged to carry on terrorising. That advice is all very well when it comes from people who are safely behind closed doors on another continent. We couldn't be sure whether we would become the target of a specific threat, and it seemed crazy to stay for the sake of a couple of games of cricket. It made far more sense to return to Sri Lanka when the situation was more secure and settled.

But for all our thoughts and feelings, it wasn't up to us. It was not our decision – and it was our choice that it wasn't our decision! We had decided unanimously to leave the difficult choices to the experts, and we had all agreed as a group that we would follow instructions. Some players were far more vociferous than others. Boucher spoke loudly throughout his career, and he was adamant that it was wrong to consider staying in the circumstances. Prince, on the other hand, was a man who instinctively called for calm heads and time to reflect. But as difficult as it might have felt, we were all prepared to stay and carry on with the tour if that was the advice. But Faisal and his bosses at Nicholls Steyn & Associates (NSA) decided that the situation was too insecure for us to continue, and the decision was made to withdraw. It was a very unpopular decision among the Sri Lankans and the Asian bloc, but we felt it was the right one, and the relief amongst the players was tangible.

During the time of our 'house arrest' in the hotel, I had a lot of time to reflect on what had happened on the field. We had lost a Test series 2–0, but the emergence of several players, young men of steel and class, gave me great hope for the future. Not just AB and Steyn but also Hashim Amla. When I factored in the return calls for Graeme Smith and Jacques Kallis, I began to see the future. It's never an easy time for a coach when he realises that certain players, no matter how fond he is of them, aren't going to feature in the years ahead. We had a couple of Test series coming up, against India and Pakistan, and I was suddenly very excited about the team we would put up against them. But we had a World Cup imminent, and our focus had to be on one-day cricket. We had been desperate to play the series in Sri Lanka for exactly that reason, which makes a mockery of the criticism that we weren't interested in staying. We would have loved to have played.

ICC Champions Trophy in India (7 October – 5 November 2006)
Our preparations for the 2007 Cricket World Cup began with
the ICC Champions Trophy in India. We were drawn in a group
with New Zealand, Pakistan and, ironically, Sri Lanka. The tournament may have been perceived at that time as something of a
minor event, but we gave it all status and were seriously excited
about testing ourselves against some of the best teams in the
world in challenging conditions.

We started with a dismal defeat against New Zealand, at the
Brabourne Stadium in Mumbai on 16 October, on a dry and
dusty wicket that turned square from the first over. Stephen
Fleming made a brilliant 89 in the Kiwi total of 195, and Graeme
responded with 42 in our feeble reply of 108 all out. Given the
early history of verbal conflict between the two captains, it was
ironic that they made the only two scores of any significance in
the match. But it was always good when the two of them had
the opportunity to lock horns. They brought the best out of each
other ... and sometimes the worst!

The second game, against Sri Lanka in Ahmedabad (24
October), was a 'must win' encounter, and that's exactly what
we did. Jacques and AB anchored the middle overs and guided
us to a total of 219, which was worth about 280 on anything
resembling a normal wicket. It was treacherously slow and two-
paced, and the Sri Lankans were bowled out for just 141 in less
than 40 overs. It would be stretching a point to say that there
was an element of revenge in the air, but there's no doubt that
the victory felt just a tiny bit sweeter following the Test series
defeat. A couple of their players had also mentioned that we
were 'running' from them when we left Colombo in August, so
it was good to clear that up.

The third group game was against Pakistan in Mohali on
27 October. Once again, given the run rate permutations, it felt
like another 'must win' match. Even if we had won very nar-
rowly, there was a mathematical chance we might not qualify

for the semifinals. But we felt confident that a victory of 'normal' proportions would be enough.

The pitch was hilariously green. It was far greener and more lush than the average outfield in India. When we first walked out there at the beginning of the match, we weren't sure which strip we were actually playing on. They were all as green as each other. I didn't think there was enough water in India to grow grass as well as that. We were told by some sceptics that it was the groundsman's way of ensuring that Pakistan were eliminated, but to be honest it was such a seamer-friendly track that either side could have benefited on the back of one outstanding performance from a fast bowler. Although I felt like it could be a lottery, I talked up our chances and tried to put a smile on the faces of our fast bowlers.

My darkest fears were realised when we were sent in to bat and crashed to 42–5. A sixth wicket partnership of 131 between Boucher (69) and Kemp (64) helped us to pass 200, and confidence was extremely high given that the second innings would be played under lights and the ball would probably do even more. It did. Makhaya took 5–21 and Polly and Charl Langeveldt shared the rest as Pakistan were bowled out for 89.

Instead of finishing in second place, as had seemed likely, the overwhelming victory meant we finished top of the group and had to travel to Jaipur to take on the West Indies, who had finished second in their group. I must confess that it was an unexpected bonus, and I was not alone in feeling confident before the game, given our outstanding record against the men from the Caribbean.

But the ICC tournament jinx struck again on 2 November, and we bore the full brunt of an explosive onslaught from Chris Gayle and, to a much lesser degree, Shiv Chanderpaul. We posted a score of 258, which wasn't bad but should have been at least 20 runs better. We lost our way in the last seven or eight overs when we were in 195–4 with Gibbs and Kemp at the crease and with the likes of Polly, Boucher and Robbie Petersen to come.

Our bowling was by no means terrible, although I was concerned with the apparent inability to change plan if things went wrong. But Gayle was probably unstoppable against any bowling attack on a day like that, and with Shiv happy simply to feed him the strike they added 154 for the first wicket, and that was pretty much that. I was devastated and so was the whole squad. I am always prepared to accept criticism and evaluate the strengths and weaknesses of the team with complete honesty. Instead of instantly rejecting the suggestion that we had been overconfident or that we were unable to deal with being strong favourites, I tried to analyse whether there had been any signs of that in the build-up to the game – or even during it. If there had been any, then I had been unable to detect them. But there had definitely been a hint of 'edge' missing. I just didn't know whether it was physical or mental. Or both?

There had been some media talk of 'quotas' upsetting the balance and the mood of the camp. As is so often the case, a mountain was made out of a molehill, but the story started with a grain of truth. Everybody could see that an extra seamer was the obvious move for the Mohali match, given the conditions, and Andrew Hall was tailor-made for the job. His batting might also have been useful. There was a chance we could need as much depth as possible. But there was little or no flexibility at that stage around the target of four players of colour in each starting XI, so Hally became twelfth man. It may not have been the most obvious cricketing decision, but we were in a unique position and we had all accepted that. Perhaps a stray comment had been picked up, misinterpreted and then repeated, but there was never a suggestion within the team that we were weakened by the selection or that it would have an adverse effect on our results.

India in South Africa (November 2006 – January 2007)

My overall assessment of where the one-day team stood at that stage was far more positive than negative. We had two home series before the World Cup to fine-tune things: five matches against India and Pakistan to build confidence and a couple of matches against Zimbabwe to get into a winning habit. Eight or nine places in the XI were secure, but there was room to experiment with two or three and give the opportunity to a couple of players to force their way into the squad at the eleventh hour.

We could hardly have been more dominant in the ODI series against India (November – December 2006), winning four games in a row after the first was washed out at the Wanderers. Kallis scored a hundred at Kingsmead, and André Nel took 4–13 as India were bowled out for 91. At Newlands, we wobbled badly at 76–6 but Justin Kemp scored a century batting at number seven and added a world record 138 for the eighth wicket with Andrew Hall. Gibbs made an unbeaten 93 at St George's Park, and we won the final game at Centurion by nine wickets, with Graeme scoring 79 and AB 92 not out. All four margins of victory were enormous and completely convincing. India simply had no answer to our brand of cricket – but we were on home soil, in conditions which suited us perfectly. I couldn't help wondering how much we had actually learned, given that the 2007 Cricket World Cup would be played on much slower Caribbean pitches more similar to subcontinental conditions than our own.

Before the Cape Town match I had my first serious run-in with selection convenor Haroon Lorgat, whom I regarded for the majority of our time together as a very structured and organised man with a clear vision of what he wanted to achieve and how to go about it. But he could also be dogmatic and fixated on 'making a point' rather than on doing what was necessary to win a game. In the build-up to the Newlands game, we were struggling with injuries to Kemp and André Nel, but both were in great form and we felt convinced that everything possible should be done to get them onto the field.

Nel had a finger injury, which, although pretty painful, was exactly the sort of thing you can 'manage' with a fast bowler who was prepared to run through brick walls even when he wasn't fully fit. Kemp had something less specific in the groin or hamstring region; he said he was ready to go, and Graeme and I were happy to take his word for it. But there had been a series of incidents in earlier years when players hadn't been completely honest about their fitness, either cynically or because they didn't understand the nature of their injury, and the result was a blanket ban on 'unfit' players taking their place in the XI. It was an overreaction to a perennial problem, but Haroon dug in his heels and refused to budge.

Eventually he had his way with Nel, but we persuaded Haroon that Kemp had passed a fitness test on the morning of the match and he reluctantly backed down. When Justin scored that remarkable hundred off just 89 balls, his celebration was uncharacteristically buoyant – and aimed very much towards the President's Suite where he thought Haroon would be sitting. We all knew what was going on, but fortunately nobody else suspected anything. I'm not sure how Haroon reacted; he was outwardly very calm and assured, but he had a stubborn and hotheaded streak. Having said that, I appreciated working with him more and more once we were separated. He had some idiosyncrasies, but he was passionate and committed. On the morning of a match, however, I believed strongly that that captain and coach – in that order – should have the final say on the starting XI. The convenor's work should be done before that.

Later on, during the World Cup, I felt isolated and completely unsupported in selection because there was no selector in the Caribbean and the responsibility was left to me. I was accountable and answerable for every decision, with nobody to back me up. I may have argued with Haroon, and we had our differences of opinion, but I would have preferred to have him to bounce ideas off, and to argue with, than nobody at all.

As always during international cricket, we had to shift focus very quickly between the different formats of the game, and the resounding success of the ODI series was quickly pushed aside as attention turned to the Test series (December 2006 to January 2007). It began in horrific fashion when we were bowled out for 84 at the Wanderers. It could have been worse – we were 45–7! It was yet another extreme experience for me as a coach. These seemed relentless, almost from day one: bowling Australia out for less than a hundred, while chasing 434; Sri Lanka scoring over 700; bombs going off; and now us being skittled for 84 at the Wanderers.

The media reaction was extreme. We actually fought back pretty well, with Ashwell making 97 in pursuit of 402 in the second innings, but we lost comfortably and arrived in Durban to the sight of billboards proclaiming 'Welcome to the Mickey Mouse and Donald Duck show', with pictures of me and Graeme, who had been dismissed for a duck by Zaheer Khan after the one-day series in which Zaheer had dominated Graeme. It hurt.

The Wanderers wicket had been substandard, but I tried as hard as possible to dissuade Graeme – and all the players – from using that as an excuse. We had to accept that India had played the better cricket. We had been out-thought and, far more painfully, out-fought. Nonetheless, the hostility of the media took me by surprise. I thought it was unfair, but we had ourselves to blame.

Careers were on the line, then, as we moved to Durban for the second Test. The weather forecast was poor from the outset, and there was a major danger of defeatism setting in. But we played some really 'hard' cricket and forced the pace at every stage. We pushed at every opportunity and made sure the pressure was always on India. We declared, and set them an unlikely target of 354, having already lost a day and a half to the weather. They did everything they could to waste time on the final day in a desperate bid to avoid defeat. Zaheer took an age to change pads, completely unnecessarily, and at one point I wanted to walk onto the field and have a word with the umpires! It's never easy watching helplessly from the sidelines, but that was one of the worst moments. If we had been denied by the tenth-wicket pair, and Zaheer had gloated about the time he had wasted, I might have needed to be restrained ...

If we thought the Durban Test required us to be 'hard', the decider in Cape Town required many of the players to dig deeper into their playing resolve than ever before. India batted first and made over 400, batting until well after lunch on the second day. Not only was it a commanding total, but also a significant amount of time had been taken up. It was already looking hard to catch up. But there wasn't a murmur of concern or dissent. Everybody knew there was only one option – to win. In some ways it's easier to 'run through a brick wall' in pursuit of victory because, although it's painful, it's also quick. But sustaining that level of intensity and commitment for hour after hour in pursuit of victory is much harder. The guys ran through half a dozen brick walls for the next three days.

Life became even harder when we fell 40 runs short of their total rather than earning a lead of 140, which was the plan, but the effort put in by the bowlers to dismiss India for just 169 second time around was truly inspiring. Rahul Dravid and Saurav Ganguly added 84 for the third wicket, and at 90–2 India were looking very solid, and time was running out. It had become abundantly clear that they weren't interested in winning the Test match, and were happy just to run down the clock. In fairness, a drawn series would have been a good result for India; while I hate the idea of playing for anything other than a win, I could understand their reasoning.

As he has done so many times in his career, it was Kallis who picked the lock and opened the door. Not only does the man have almost 300 Test wickets, he has some of the most important. Statistics don't tell you how many of his 2–40s – or, in this case, 1–31s – have included game-changing breakthroughs.

Paul Harris made his debut, and, after opening his Test account with the wicket of Sachin Tendulkar in the first innings, bowled steadily and accurately to build pressure effectively from one end during the second innings. It was exactly the job Graeme and I had wanted him to do, and he rose to the challenge like a seasoned pro – which, of course, he was at the age of 29.

Steyn then smashed through the tail in a fashion that made the hair on your arms stand up, and we were left to chase 211, which we did successfully despite another four wickets from Zaheer, who caused us problems throughout the series.

It wasn't easy on the fifth day. The pitch was bouncing unevenly and turning virtually square for Anil Kumble, and there was a very real danger that we could become bogged down and overly defensive in trying to survive. Graeme batted brilliantly for his 55, but it was also the effort of Shaun Pollock, who made 37 in quick time, batting at number four, which went a long way towards getting us home. It was a gamble promoting Polly, and it could easily have backfired. No doubt the criticism would have come in tidal waves if he'd failed and we'd lost, but he didn't and we won. It was one of the most satisfying Test and series victories of my career, certainly on home soil.

Pakistan in South Africa (January – February 2007)

Pakistan arrived hot on India's heels. For once, we had enough momentum to avoid the dreaded 'first Test blues' that afflicted us so often during my tenure. In the first Test, in Centurion (11–15 January), they made over 300 in both innings, but an Ashwell century, 71 from Hashim and 94 from Herschelle bat-

ting at number six gave us a first innings lead of over 100 and
match-winning advantage. Herschelle's inclusion in the XI had
been another last-minute decision, but one which he vindicated
with one of his most patient innings in national colours. I had
always felt that he should bat at the top of the order and that
batting down the order was a cop-out. But a place had opened
at number six and he was the 'next in line'.

We paid a heavy price for a dismal batting display at St
George's Park during the second Test (19–22 January), and
proved for the umpteenth time that, almost no matter how well
you play catch-up cricket for the rest of the Test match, if you're
bowled out for 200 less than par in the first innings of the match
you can almost never get back on even terms. Things might
have been very different if the great Inzamam-ul-Haq hadn't
made an unbeaten 92 batting at number eight, as he had bruised
a shoulder during fielding practice. When we set them a target
of 191 for victory and reduced them to 92–5 it again looked as
though we might pull off an upset, but it wasn't to be. They
won – and deserved to.

Newlands was going through a pretty shabby period of its life
at this stage, and the wicket resembled much of the rest of the
place – peeling paint and patchwork grass. It will always be a
special place, of course, and Table Mountain doesn't move, so
the view doesn't change. But it was hard work playing there at
that time because you never knew what you were going to get.
For the deciding Test (26–28 January) we were served up a bowlers' delight, and the result was a five-wicket victory inside three
days, with none of the four innings passing 200. The scoreboard
suggests it was close, but there was only one moment when
I considered we weren't in control: when we slipped to 39–4
chasing 161 for victory. But, not for the first time, Jacques and
Ashwell showed how much they thrive on a good scrap, and
they took us to within five runs of victory before Jakes was
bowled.

In February, the five-match ODI series represented our last chance to prepare for the 2007 Cricket World Cup. It began reasonably enough when we made 392–6 in the first match at Centurion (4 February). As omens go, I couldn't have been happier. We came back to earth with a shudder in the next game, however, when Shahid Afridi monstered 77 from 35 balls to turn a good score into an unattainable 351–4. The third ODI, in Port Elizabeth, was washed out, but we removed any doubts from our own minds when we hammered Pakistan by ten and nine wickets, at Newlands and the Wanderers, respectively, to wrap up the series.

* * *

I was as happy as I could be about the make-up and balance of the squad, and confident that we had the talent and temperament to make an impression in the Caribbean. No, it was not just an impression; I really believed we could win it. I was confident. We were a strong, bonded unit when we left for Trinidad.

My own peace of mind and security in the job had received a significant boost after the Pakistan series, in the form of a contract extension, which gave me the freedom to keep planning ahead rather than becoming too desperate about short-term results. If we'd been dismal at the World Cup and lost in the first round, I would have done the decent thing and offered to resign anyway, but I felt I was justified in asking for an extension because we had reached the number-one ranking in the world in my two years in charge. Although our Test cricket needed plenty of work, I believed passionately that we could achieve the same success in the longer form of the game. I confess I was also desperate to have another go at Australia on their home soil. I explained that I had been new in the job on the last tour there, and that I was convinced we could become the first South African team to win a Test series down under. With a four-Test series to

England preceding the Australia tour, 2008 was going to be an epic year, and I needed to know what the administrators were thinking. Either way, I had to know whether I was going to be part of that year or whether they were thinking along different lines.

I spoke to the same panel that had appointed me, gave them a presentation and made my case. Norman Arendse was president of CSA, and I'll never forget the feeling of pride, relief and excitement when he said: 'Mickey, we have granted you your wish. You will take the team to England and you will get your second chance against Australia. Good luck.'

Chapter 5

ICC Cricket World Cup

March to April 2007

It was unfortunate that so much of the build-up to the 2007 ICC Cricket World Cup (13 March – 28 April) focused around the composition of our final XV. We had always committed ourselves to taking seven players of colour, and I was comfortable with that from the outset. It was simply an added challenge for us to get the balance right. Other countries also have to factor into their selections criteria other than batsmen, bowlers, all-rounders and wicketkeepers; it's just that their hidden agendas are never made public. Counties, states and franchises all fight for adequate representation within their national squads and, without wishing to be controversial for the sake of it, it was made perfectly clear to me during my international career that there are also 'quotas' for certain castes and creeds in subcontinental teams. It's just that nobody makes a big issue of those requirements or even, in most cases, acknowledges them. In South Africa's case, we were trying to correct an historical injustice in the sports history of our country; not only did I have no problem with that,

I supported it fully. It had been one of the cornerstones of my application for the job.

Our requirement meant that Ashwell Prince was returned to the squad as our spare batsman, having not really nailed down a place in the starting XI; it meant that Robin Peterson travelled as our second spinner; and it meant that Roger Telemachus was the fifteenth man. Roger's inclusion drew the most criticism, with many people believing he was lucky to be there and an unworthy choice. Ironically, I pushed hard for Roger's selection – I liked his *'gees'* and that he had shown a tendency to rise to the occasion when the pressure was on – notwithstanding his collapse during the 438 game! He wasn't the only man to struggle on that day, on either side. So I was particularly saddened when he reacted the way he did after the World Cup, slating the selection process and bemoaning the fact that he hadn't played a game. I had made it clear to everybody what their roles would be – that there were eleven or twelve 'starters' and three reserves who had the responsibility to stay fit and ready to step into the XI at any time in the event of injury, illness or loss of form. Most teams had exactly the same approach. I don't believe there was a single squad at the tournament that had 15 players competing for a place on an equal footing.

* * *

SAA flew us straight to Trinidad and Tobago. There was no stop in Barbados, which was a great fillip for all of us who had in the past endured the tortuous journey to the Caribbean via London (and, often, Barbados).

The build-up to the tournament was difficult. We played warm-up games against Ireland and Pakistan at the Sir Frank Worrell Memorial Ground, in St Augustine, on the campus of the University of the West Indies, where pitch conditions were treacherous, to say the least. Hazardous or even below-par surfaces can bring teams closer together, and we had to work extremely hard to overcome Ireland, which started tongues wagging and attracted negative speculation. You can talk through the night with the players about how it doesn't matter – and they all agree that it is irrelevant – but sportsmen are sensitive creatures, for all their bravado, and a small seed of doubt is sown. Getting teams to behave otherwise in such circumstances is a Holy Grail of the coach's trade.

As it turned out, Ireland was the fairy-tale story of the tournament, and a wonderful breath of fresh air. We didn't just struggle against them because of the conditions; we struggled because they were a bloody good team. There were two reasons I was pleased to see them do so well; firstly, their coach, Adrian Birrell, was one of my oldest friends or acquaintances in cricket, and it was a joy to see him succeeding like that as coach. Secondly, there had been a great deal of negative speculation about the number of minor, or minnow, teams taking part in the World Cup; my natural inclination has always been for the game to spread its wings and expand into 'untraditional' territory, so to see the Irish succeed in the way they did, and to change some perceptions, was very special.

Ironically, it was Pakistan who were eliminated at Ireland's hands. On three or four days while we were in Trinidad, I had breakfast with Bob Woolmer, who was coaching Pakistan at the time, during which we compared notes and exchanged views on South Africa, Pakistan and the cricket world at large. I had enough respect for Bob to say I was almost in awe of him, but we also shared views on a frank level and he was just as interested in my point of view as I was in his. I still shudder when I think of his untimely death in the immediate aftermath of Pakistan's defeat to Ireland and elimination from the tournament.

Conditions for our warm-up game against Pakistan were even worse – genuinely dangerous. I would honestly have been quite happy to have pulled the players off the field and abandoned the game. Bob said he would have no objection if I decided to do so, but we discussed it and came to the conclusion that a lot of tickets had been sold for the game and we had a duty and responsibility to try and make the best of a very bad situation. When Kallis was hit on the head by a good-length ball from Mohammed Sami, I thought it was the final straw, but tempers calmed down a little after that and we limped through – to a defeat, but the fact that nobody was seriously injured made it feel more like a victory. Bob and I had a chuckle afterwards. There wasn't much in the game he hadn't seen before.

But having worked so hard in the home series against India and Pakistan, and having received the number-one ranking, it did feel strange to be scratching around on a club ground with very limited facilities. There is a fine line, but a big difference, between wanting the best and lacking humility. I wouldn't tolerate players acting like 'big shots' and belittling our hosts or opponents, but at the same time I felt we deserved a little bit better.

We were in Trinidad for eleven or twelve days, but it felt like a month. It seemed almost impossible to build any kind of momentum or even get the tournament started. There was so much downtime that the players didn't know what to do with themselves. At such times, the temptation towards mischief, particularly in the evenings, is an ever-present danger! Having spoken to other coaches and managers during the tournament and afterwards, I know many of them had similar experiences.

One day in the hotel there was a tremendous explosion, which scared the hell out of us. I ran out of my room into the corridor, where I bumped into five or six of the guys all looking a bit shell-shocked. A few seconds later, we realised that our eyes were burning and it dawned on us that it might actually be some kind of deliberate attack. I am almost ashamed to admit it, but the thought had crossed my mind a few days earlier that staying in the same hotel as the Pakistan team might bring with it challenges that we could have done without. Thank goodness we were informed quite quickly that it was nothing more serious than a large gas cylinder used for cooking in the kitchen.

No excuses, and no blame apportioned. It was simply a fact that preparation had been poor in Trinidad. Nobody had advanced, or even maintained, their form. We headed off to Montego Bay, Jamaica, for the opening ceremony feeling anything but settled. It was not a great start.

Things improved greatly soon after arrival, however. All the teams stayed together in a magnificent hotel, and although that may not have suited everybody, I loved it. The opportunity to mix and mingle with friends, colleagues and opponents from all over the world was one that might come along only once in a lifetime. I loved being able to talk to coaches from other teams, but I also particularly enjoyed seeing the dynamic between the players. Watching an 18-year-old batsmen from Scotland or Holland walk up to Sachin Tendulkar and ask for an autograph brought a lump to my throat. Seeing how Tendulkar reacted, however, brought a tear to my eye. He would invariably introduce himself (just in case they weren't sure who they were talking to!) and then ask for their name. He seemed to want to make it clear that, for the duration of the tournament, they were now equals.

The opening ceremony itself, on 11 March, was a little too drawn-out and cumbersome to have the desired effect, but nobody could doubt the amount of effort that had been put into it. The whole experience was a pleasant diversion for me, although I did hear a number of players from various teams moaning already about how long they had been in the Caribbean without hitting or bowling a ball in anger.

After two or three days' training and practising on the island of St Kitts, the venue for our three group games against Scotland, Holland and Australia, our acclimatisation period resembled something from a 1930s Ashes series. And even when the serious stuff finally began, there was an element of 'phoney war' about it. Barring massive hiccups against the minnows, our first serious test would be against Australia, with both teams already having qualified for the Super Eight stage.

In the Holland game, on 16 March, we won the toss and batted first – and immediately lost AB de Villiers for a duck. After five overs we were 4–1. Just for a moment my mind wandered back to all the extraordinary things that had happened in my career – and how things already seemed to be conspiring against us here. But I could not even contemplate an upset, and, to general relief all round, we won with all the expected ease and comfort.

The match would almost certainly have faded instantly into obscurity had it not been for the 30th over of our innings, when Herschelle Gibbs hit Daan van Bunge for six sixes. We'd sent a message out to him that he could now 'give it a go', but we didn't expect a response quite like that. We finished with 350 from 40 overs. With such tiny boundaries we might have threatened 500 if we'd had the full 50! Sir Garfield Sobers made a presentation to Hersch, and he was given the freedom of the island by the then Prime Minister, an honour he later used to get married on St Kitts. Sir Viv Richards was the official ambassador for Johnnie Walker, one of the tournament sponsors, and they had offered to give $1 million to charity on behalf of the first player to achieve the 'maximum' in the World Cup. The irony of Hersch being associated with Johnnie Walker was lost on none of us, and the jokes flew thick and fast. There was talk of Hersch being given free Scotch for a year, but I'm not sure that materialised. The boys, of course, said that it was because the company couldn't afford it. That was all before he turned his life around and reformed a couple of years later.

The Scotland game, on 20 March, was far more straightforward, and we completed a seven-wicket win without a single moment of concern and with more than half of our overs remaining. It was time to start the real stuff. The Australia game was anything but insignificant because the points would carry forward into the Super Eight stage. And there were also psychological points to be won. We can all talk as much as we like about the importance of winning the big games when they really count – the Aussies are particularly good at this – but the reality is, victories and defeats between major teams always matter and always count for something.

Not only was the ground in Basseterre tiny (it actually fell short of ICC requirements), but the pitch was also a belter. There was plenty of talk about a possible repeat of the 438 game, which was still fresh in the memory. With Matthew Hayden, Adam Gilchrist, Ricky Ponting, Andrew Symonds and Mike Hussey in the top six, almost anything was possible. And Australia did not disappoint, with a total of 377–6. Six to twelve months earlier, we might have been completely despondent and hoping to escape without losing too much blood and dignity. But such had been the transformation in one-day cricket, and our expectations about what was possible, that we sat down between innings and plotted our way to victory as though we were chasing 277.

Just like at the Wanderers a year earlier, we made a flying start and were right up with the required rate; in fact, at 160–1 after 20 overs we were ahead of target. But Graeme Smith developed severe cramps and had to come off, despite insisting on about five minutes' treatment in a desperate bid to keep going. We lost momentum almost immediately, and Jacques Kallis endured one of those days when his calculations went wrong. He backed himself to hit a pile of boundaries at the back end of his innings (he had hit the last three balls against Holland for six), but this was a different calibre of opponent; small boundaries or not, it simply wasn't possible to score at 12 or 13 per over. For every game or innings that Jacques has got wrong in his career, he has got 20 right. He has won more games off his own bat for South Africa than any other individual, and just like any other individual he is entitled to a rare mistake. I was furious about the backlash against Jacques from the media and public after that game, and it took me several days to calm down. It was a bad day, yes, but the tournament had barely started.

Our next destination after St Kitts was Guyana. Our final group game finished before the other major teams, so we sat back to watch India and Pakistan join us and Sri Lanka in the Super Eight stage. That was the way the draw had been engineered, and, to be fair, it was a little daunting. Playing the three subcontinental powerhouse teams on low and slow pitches tailor-made for their style was not how we would have chosen to begin the Super Eight stage, but we had been planning for many months so at least it would not be a surprise. Little did we know just how much of a surprise we were in for.

First, India were beaten by Bangladesh, who claimed the seeded team's spot in the next phase, and then, even more shockingly, Pakistan were upset by a rampant Ireland. I watched the end of that game with an increasing sense of disbelief, and every time the cameras focused on Bob Woolmer I felt more and more sad and desperate for him. He looked tense and pale, and when he spoke afterwards on television he just didn't seem himself. Of course I did not suspect anything untoward. His team had just been eliminated from the World Cup; he wasn't supposed to be smiling or cheerful.

The sense of shock we all felt the following day is hard to describe. Initially, we were told that he had been found in his room in a coma and was fighting hard for his life. For a while at least, we believed there was some hope. But a couple of hours later it was confirmed that he had died. It was difficult to accept the news, and it hit the team exceptionally hard. Shaun Pollock, Jacques Kallis and Jonty Rhodes (who was on the coaching team) found it particularly distressing, as they had played so much of their careers under Bob's guidance and he had become something of a father figure to them. Mark Boucher, too, had begun his career with Bob at the helm. They were all devastated. When the Jamaican police announced (mistakenly, as it turned out) that he had been murdered, there was a distinct feeling that cricket, or at least this tournament, had become irrelevant. Motivation was hard to find for a good few days. Naturally, of course, it wasn't too long before somebody asked the question: 'What would Bob have wanted us to do?' And that was the beginning of our 'recovery'.

Team manager Goolam Rajah had spent almost his entire administrative career alongside Bob. Goolam spoke with great feeling and sensitivity to all the players and helped them to find their emotional equilibrium. But it was still a very disturbing and unsettling time for the whole squad. It had felt as though factors beyond our control were conspiring against us; we were a long way from home, a long way from our families; Australia had just beaten us; and now this. It felt like the World Cup should have been coming to an end, but we still had six games to go before a possible semifinal.

With everybody in pretty dire need of a 'pick me up' and an injection of energy, we faced the prospect of exactly the opposite. Twelve days in Georgetown, capital of Guyana. When most people think of the Caribbean, they picture blue skies, turquoise seas, palm trees and piña coladas against the backdrop of a golden sunset. None of that exists in Guyana, which is located on the South American mainland and is an extremely poor nation with a threadbare economy and barely functioning infrastructure. There is precious little to do to pass the time – no golf course, no cinema, no shopping centres and very few restaurants. In such circumstances, players often throw themselves into their training and practice sessions, but that wasn't possible either, because it rained almost every morning and the nets were constantly damp. I am not a complainer by nature, and am known for my tendency to always look on the bright side, but even the Pegasus Hotel in Georgetown was quite modest in most respects, and the gym could barely accommodate three or four players at a time.

The highlight of our time in Guyana was a trip up the Demerara River into the rainforest. It sounded exotic and even exciting ... but the reality was a little different. We were in an open boat and ill-equipped for the conditions. It rained from the moment we left until the moment we returned, five or six hours later! We looked like drowned rats when we finally trudged back into the hotel lobby. And we felt like drowned rats, too. Still, I'm glad we did it; in retrospect, it provided one of the few reasons to have a laugh together – although it was in spite of the experience rather than because of it.

The first game, on 28 March, was against Sri Lanka, at the Providence Stadium in Georgetown. It was vital that we finally got our campaign up and running and earned our first points. I'd like to think we were able to channel our frustrations in the right direction and that that was the reason we bowled and fielded so well, restricting them to just 209, with Charl Langeveldt claiming an excellent 5–39. Nothing could stop us from coasting to victory, with Kallis in complete and supreme control on 86 not out in a total of 206–5. We needed four runs for victory with five wickets in hand. The dressing room was a calm and happy place.

Then Lasith Malinga took four wickets in four balls and we were staring defeat straight in the face. Never, in all my time in cricket, have I experienced such a dramatic change in fortunes in such a short space of time. It's hard to explain cricketers' superstitions, but when Robin Peterson was facing what could have been the last ball in an ignominious and soul-destroying defeat, there were a dozen of us hiding in the toilets at the back of the dressing room, unable to watch. Perhaps it's a subconscious way of avoiding the immediate pain of what would have been a crushing loss. Most of us are able to 'read' what is happening in a game from the sounds of the crowd when we are too timid to watch. But when Robbie edged Malinga just past slip and down to the third man boundary, we were momentarily confused. There was a loud groan, followed by a pregnant silence, and then, a couple of seconds later, the unmistakable sound the crowd makes when the game is over. We had won by one wicket.

I still think of that game as being incredibly tense, but it wasn't. It was only the last fifteen minutes that were tense, as tense as an iron bar. For the preceding seven and a half hours, we were dominant and in control. The last fifteen minutes, however, felt like it took just as many years off my life. Although there was a certain amount of hyperventilation afterwards, we all felt that we had turned a corner and that something, at last, had gone our way. We were back on track. In fact, we were probably on track for the first time.

The next game, against Ireland on 3 April, was a scruffy affair. It was wet and grey, and nobody knew when it might clear. Right from the outset, on days like that, it becomes just about the result. Who cares what you look like or how you get the job done? Just get it done. Ireland made a decent 152 in the 35 overs to which the game was reduced, and we scratched our way home. Not pretty, not impressive – but another two points.

We had one more game to go, but the whole Guyana experience was beginning to wear thin. While the whole world was lapping up TV images of cocktail beach bars and bobbing yachts on twinkling seas, we were battling to stay dry and stop ourselves from developing 'cabin fever'.

We played miserably against Bangladesh, on 7 April. They played seven or eight left-arm spinners – OK, maybe it was three – but they all tied us up in knots and made us look seriously poor. We lacked even the basic energy required for international cricket, let alone the aggression and intensity for which South African teams are known. I know for a fact that most of our players had their minds on the departure for Grenada the following morning. They were not focused as they should have been, and they just wanted to get the Bangladesh match over and done with. As far as the result was concerned, they were happy to simply hope for the best. Nobody ever made that kind of decision consciously – it was all subconscious. As a coach, I could see the signs. I didn't know how to reverse the process, but I did all I could. I made no excuses at the time, and I have never made any since. Bangladesh were better than us on the day, they played much the better cricket, and they deserved to win.

Arriving in Grenada, we had effectively 'played four, won two, lost two', and were under serious pressure. The next game was against the West Indies, with all the hype that that entailed. The sun was shining, the hotel was on the beach and we drove from the airport through a series of thriving 'touristy' communities with steakhouses and bars – even cinemas and malls. Immediately our spirits rose, and the mood of the whole squad lifted. I met up with Yvette, whom I hadn't seen for two months, and everybody felt a sense of renewed determination and vigour. And most importantly of all, the training grounds and practice facilities on the island were excellent. It was obvious to all of us that it was time to shape up or ship out. Several hundred South African supporters had also arrived, many of them staying on cruise ships offshore, and that raised our spirits even more.

The West Indies match took place on 10 April at Queen's Park in the capital, St George's. AB de Villiers batted magnificently in reaching a century, but cramped seriously soon afterwards. Instead of slowing our progress, however, he went on a boundary binge and finished with 146, including 12 fours and five sixes, most of which came in the last third.

AB wasn't the first man to suffer cramps – Graeme was the first and most high-profile case in the game against Australia – and there was plenty of speculation as to the reasons. Alcohol intake is the easiest and most obvious reason to use. It would be foolish and naive to deny that it can be a problem. I was, and always will be, willing to discuss and debate issues provided that there is an even distribution of information. I reacted angrily and defensively when people insinuated that AB's condition had been the result of alcohol intake. They did not have any facts or information at hand. There was a lot of hearsay and gossip available, but no evidence.

I have never pretended that I got it right, or that the players were in the best possible physical condition. We had an understanding that players would not drink for forty-eight hours before a game; it was an understanding based on science rather than their practical experience or desire. Far more serious was the undertaking that there would be no alcohol consumed on the evening before a game. It was adhered to most of the time, although there were minor lapses. On one occasion I met Herschelle in the lobby of the hotel; he was wandering about, very restless. He said he couldn't sleep and asked if he could have a daiquiri to help him relax. Given the experience of the 438 game and what happened when he'd had far more than one, I couldn't see the harm. Not ideal, but it's not an ideal world. I may have been wrong, but I followed my instincts.

Fitness trainer Adrian le Roux was not happy, and we had a couple of strong conversations and exchanged some firm words. Perhaps that was the beginning of the end for him. He was adamant that he knew what was best for the performance of the team, and no doubt – from a scientific point of view – he was absolutely right. My view was that he needed to make allowances for individuals and also for the specific physical, emotional and cricketing situations in which we found ourselves. We were both inflexible. I believed that there should be some flexibility, and he believed that sporting excellence could only be achieved through strict adherence to dietary and lifestyle regulations.

There was some tension within the camp before the New

Zealand game (14 April) as a result of Adrian's frustrations about the nature of the celebrations following the magnificent win against the West Indies. There were only 72 hours between the games, and Adrian felt the guys had drunk too much. We played horribly against New Zealand, and could make only 193–7, so he would say he had a point. Hindsight is a perfect science. The scorecard provides strong circumstantial evidence for Adrian's case. But a good lawyer would be able to persuade an honest jury that there were many other factors to consider. But we had lost again and had no excuses.

That evening we were hosted by Richemont chairman Johann Rupert on his yacht, and the players let their hair down in a fairly decent way for the first time on the tour – or, at least, as far as I was aware. Following supper on the boat they went to a nightclub, and no doubt had a few rum punches. They were seen by a South African supporter who had spent a great deal of money travelling to the Caribbean to see his team win, and he felt disappointed and let down by seeing them up past midnight. The following morning he called Radio 702 and got everything off his chest. That was his right, and nobody can argue against it. From the players' perspective, however, there were many factors which might have altered his opinion, had he been aware of them.

Our performance had been good and bad up to that point. There had been some high points, but, honestly, a few more low ones. The final group game was against England, on 17 April, and it amounted, effectively, to a quarterfinal. We had three days to go until the game, which was to take place in Bridgetown, Barbados. All the frustrations could be wiped away. It was a knockout game, which would allow us to finally gauge our collective temperament under pressure. The issue of late nights and drinking wasn't going away, however, and it made life difficult for everybody. It seemed to be everybody's favourite talking point back home, and now that we were about to play England we had their tabloid hacks sniffing around and sensationalising every scrap of gossip they could find.

When we arrived in Barbados, I had a phone call from Gerald Majola to ask me what was going on. He said the story of the players drinking after midnight in a nightclub was all over the local newspapers and radio stations, and it didn't look good. It was the first I had heard of it. We had all gone to Johann Rupert's yacht together as a group and, as far as I was concerned, we left together and returned to the hotel. At least, that was what I did.

I called a team meeting as soon as possible, to find out what had happened and to try and draw a line under it so we could concentrate on the game. I took as firm a line as I could. I might have sympathised with them on a personal level, but, as head coach, I made it perfectly clear that there could be no excuses for this kind of scandal. If boozed-up members of the public want to pick a fight with high-profile sportsmen, then the sportsmen must either walk away to another area of the venue – quickly – or go somewhere else. Or don't go out. It may be unfortunate, but that is the reality. The members of a national team must represent their country at all times, and they are always in the public eye. I made it clear that it was the responsibility of the cricketer to avoid conflict or controversy. Many of them thought I was being unfair and didn't agree with my view, but it was the only way to behave, especially on a holiday island like Barbados, which was packed with tourists and cricket supporters from both England and South Africa.

There was a bitter twist of irony in the story – at least for the man who made the phone call to Radio 702. It was clear to all the players that he was exaggerating the situation and doing nothing more than causing trouble. Several days after the story broke, it was revealed that the caller was an employee of Johann Rupert. He had been around when we'd been on the yacht that evening, and had then followed the players to the nightclub.

Perhaps one of the players had refused him an autograph or hadn't engaged him in conversation. Whatever it was, he was obviously offended and had an axe to grind. When Johann found out, he fired him instantly.

The drinking episode was just another in a long list of niggles that kept distracting us as a squad – both players and management – throughout the tournament. And the next one was just twenty-four hours away. For the first time since I started the job as national coach, we had made the decision to leave Makhaya out of the starting XI for the game against the West Indies on 10 April. It was probably the first time for six or seven years that Makhaya had been left out of any team. He had become untouchable, which was healthy neither for him nor the team. He was taken by surprise, and didn't react too badly, but it became a massive and unpleasant issue when he was again left out for the game against England.

Throughout the tournament, I felt isolated and very much alone when it came to matters of selection. For some reason, there was no selector on tour with us, which meant that the buck stopped with me after every selection meeting. There are many good reasons why cricket teams are selected by panels rather than individuals. Not the least of these, in this case, was the fact that the players were constantly aware that I had almost sole power over their place in the XI. But apart from the time Yvette spent with me, I was on my own. And I certainly wasn't about to break my habit of not socialising with the players. But it was the weight of responsibility in selection that really contributed most to my sense of loneliness. Of course I called selection convener Haroon Lorgat before every selection meeting and he often had a different point of view regarding team composition. But it was always too easy for one of us to say, 'I'm not there, what do you think?' or 'You're not here, how do you know?'

I felt the pressure for every minute of the tournament, but particularly when it came to the England game. I knew for a fact that leaving Makhaya out would open a dangerous can of worms and, in all probability, lead me into previously unvisited territory where powerful people had strong opinions despite knowing nothing about cricket. I knew that, and it worried me. But what worried me more was that we would lose to England and be eliminated from the World Cup, and that a misfiring Makhaya might play a role in that. I'm not sure I was ever in a more difficult position – caught between a rock and a hard place – until the final day of my Proteas career when I was forced to resign.

I had to trust my instincts and do what was in the best interests of the team, so I left Makhaya out and then spent several hours furiously trying to soften the blow in the media by explaining that he was merely being rested and would no doubt be back in the team soon – which was actually true.

Fortunately we produced one of the most clinical all-round performances I have ever seen – from any team. I could see that the team was fired up, but was concerned about how that would reveal itself on the field. The players were under enormous pressure, and the distractions and sideshows of the last two or three weeks hadn't helped their concentration. Yet they focused their anger and frustration and aimed it straight at England. Although I had verbally agreed to extend my contract before the World Cup began, nothing was signed and I had absolutely no doubt that a loss that day would have been the end of my time in charge. But what should have been a nail-biting day of unrelenting tension was over in a flash, done and dusted two hours ahead of schedule: England bundled out for 154, and Graeme making 89 from 58 balls to chase the runs down inside 20 overs. There wasn't even time for the Barmy Army to get properly drunk. Of all the brilliant performances that day – Andrew Hall's 5–18 and Polly's 10 overs for just 17 stand out – there was one moment which revealed the mood of the team. Jacques Kallis, Mr Cool, calm, laid-back and relaxed, ran in to bowl his first ball, and it came out of his hand like a cannonball.

It normally takes a small earthquake to shake Jacques up, but this time he was steaming.

Our mixed results led to us drawing in Australia in the semi-final, which was to be played in St Lucia on 25 April. Practice facilities were poor, once again, but it's a lovely island and a good place to relax – or should have been. One day I'd like to experience what it's like to stay there on holiday without the pressures of work. But we had a series of niggling injuries, and there were problems around the non-selection of Makhaya, who was still bristling with indignation. In truth, we weren't a happy team. The perception of 'Captain's Clique' was weighing the junior players down, and several of the players of colour were miserable and feeling like spare parts after not playing. They felt as though they were just there to make up the numbers while Graeme and his 'mates' – Mark Boucher, Justin Kemp and Kallis – were running the ship. It had been a very long journey and tempers were frayed.

I have one regret about that semifinal, and it is that we didn't talk honestly and openly about how we were feeling during the team meeting the night before. Francois Hugo suggested that perhaps it was not a good idea, given the importance of the match the following day, and I agreed with him. I knew there were problems, but I was hoping that we had turned the corner with the brilliant win against England, and that the momentum gained in Barbados would sustain us against Australia. In retrospect, we should have addressed our collective emotional state, but there was a lot of bravado going around, and I sensed that more harm than good might have been done by trying to conduct an 'honesty' session. If I could have had that meeting again, I would have insisted that we talked about the fears of a World Cup semifinal and about what it meant to each player to be facing Australia in such an important game. I knew there were still scars on some of our senior players, inflicted during some critical losses to the

Aussies, and it might have benefited all of us if we had spoken about them.

Francois still talks to me about that evening, and has the same regrets. He blames himself for not being stronger and insisting that we discussed our hopes and fears, but we both thought we were doing the right thing at the time. In some ways, we can take solace from the fact that we backed our instincts. Or perhaps we just took the easy option of ignoring our doubts.

History records that we were bowled out for 149 and were thrashed. It was the lowest I've ever felt during my time in cricket, from the age of eight – when I was given out to a horrible LBW decision in front of my parents in the biggest game of my life – to the present. Everybody was gutted. There is a special kind of silence that descends on a sports changing room at moments like that; it is almost eerie. There was no shouting, screaming or crying, but you could hear the pain in the room. It was awful.

Presumably desperate for a reason to explain the wild, almost reckless approach of the top order, some members of the media concluded that it had been a team decision to 'go hard' at the Aussies up front in an attempt to unsettle them and throw them out of their routine – particularly Glenn McGrath. That was a complete figment of somebody's imagination. We never even discussed such a tactic, let alone settled on it. Sure, I had always encouraged us to be positive and to put the opposition under pressure, but we never discussed trying to hit Nathan Bracken and McGrath out of the attack with the new ball. I was as surprised as anybody to see seasoned, experienced Protea batsmen charging down the wicket and looking to hit over the top in the first few overs. I was chastised and roundly condemned for the naivety of our team approach, and I took the criticism on the chin for fear of creating another split in the camp. But it was not my idea!

Soon after our return, I was summoned to Jo'burg to face the board and explain what had gone wrong. I knew what sort of questions to expect, but was taken aback by the severity and aggression with which they were asked. We had reached the semifinal, which was the minimum requirement, but in truth it had been a poor tournament, in which we had failed to do ourselves justice and only once played to our full capability. It was reasonable, then, to expect the executive to be disappointed.

It was one thing to ask me why the players of colour hadn't been given more game time, but quite another to suggest that they had gone to the World Cup as 'waiters'. Not only was that way off the mark, but it was also deeply insulting and hurtful. I was left with the distinct impression that Norman Arendse, despite heading the panel that had appointed me and agreed to a two-year contract extension, was now beginning to lead a campaign against me. Dr Mthuthuzeli Nyoka, who was president of the Gauteng Cricket Board at the time, suggested that a complete review, and in-depth investigation, of the World Cup would be in order. Both men questioned me incessantly about why more players of colour had not taken the field, and I replied with unstinting honesty and sincerity. I was given a mandate to select the best XI players to win each and every game. I will swear to my dying day that that is what I did, and I explained that repeatedly to both men.

Eventually my patience and humility started to show signs of strain, and I attempted a pretty feeble counter-attack. I asked the board to explain what, exactly, it was that they wanted. Was it an uncompromised search for excellence on the field, or was it the ability to say that we had transformed to such an extent that we were now demographically representative? I knew that the answer was 'both' because I had been trying to achieve both objectives throughout my two years as coach. But it was often impossible to achieve a balance between the two on any given match day, so I was asking which one took priority. Typically for the board, there were no answers forthcoming.

Once again, I must acknowledge the supporting role played at that time by chief executive Gerald Majola and vice president Ray Mali. They could see the danger of their colleagues building towards a motion of no confidence, and Gerald was quick to point out that the issue of racial quotas was not on the agenda for the meeting. On a point of order as far as the CSA Constitution was concerned, our interrogator was made aware that he was not entitled to ask any question, on any subject at any time. There was an order and a structure to such meetings which had to be adhered to. Paul Harris, the independent director on the board, pointed out to Arendse that he was, to all intents and purposes, calling me a racist. It was at that moment that I first saw the ferocious temper of Norman Arendse. It was quite a sight.

I could understand the frustrations of the board members, and, in so many ways, I shared them. What we did not share, however, was a knowledge of the game that allowed us to discuss the composition and balance of a cricket team. It was impossible to talk about the merits, skills and qualities of individual cricketers, and the art of building a balanced and winning team, and then to see everything in black and white. Literally.

Chapter 6

Heading in the right direction

July 2007 to January 2008

Recovery from the disappointment of the World Cup came in the form of a bizarre trip to Ireland (24 June – 1 July) to play India and Ireland in a couple of one-dayers outside Belfast, in Northern Ireland. It served absolutely no cricketing purpose whatsoever – certainly not for India or South Africa anyway – but it made a lot of money. You could organise a game of chess with the Indian team and make millions from the TV rights. It was midwinter in South Africa, and most of our guys hadn't picked up a bat or ball for over a month. Still, Ireland is a beautiful country to visit and I was happy to go, particularly if it helped towards developing the game in that country. And I'm sure CSA found the money useful; I heard it was around R7 million.

ICC Twenty20 World Cup (11–24 September 2007)
The next major assignment, however, was the ICC Twenty20 World Cup on home soil. Yet another ICC tournament and yet another disappointment. Off the field there were the usual dis-

tractions and other factors contributing towards a sense of insecurity, but for once I can honestly say that the squad was as
physically well-prepared as they could be: good specialist batsmen, plenty of power-hitting all-rounders and specialist bowlers. It was a quick opportunity for us to turn around the disappointment of the World Cup. Playing at home was a source of
great excitement, but, as many of the players learned during the
2003 World Cup, it came with as many problems as benefits.

At a board meeting in Johannesburg, a month or so before the
tournament, Haroon Lorgat was removed as convener of selectors. His appointment had come up for renewal, and he was
voted off. I am not really sure why, and perhaps it is wrong to
speculate; perhaps he felt the position warranted more money,
but I do know that his attitude and approach to the job had
started to make a few board members feel uneasy and threatened. Sometimes it is much easier to get rid of a problem than
to solve it.

Whatever the reasons, Haroon hadn't been replaced by the
time the deadline arrived to announce our squad. As nobody else
seemed to be taking responsibility for selecting and announcing
the squad, I took the lead and presented my preferred 14-man
squad to Norman Arendse for approval, as was the custom with
the CSA president. It included the name of Jacques Kallis.

I was unaware that a couple of the remaining selectors had
already been in discussion with Arendse, and there was, apparently, already a list of 14 names in existence. It did not contain
the name of Jacques Kallis. Without a convener of selectors, it
was impossible for anybody to determine what was an 'official'
list and what was nothing more than scribblings on the back of
a beer mat. Norman decided that the first list was the official
one and that mine had come too late to make a difference. So he
used the presidential veto for my squad, and Kallis was omitted.

The decision created deep animosity and resentment between
the players and the administration. Your best players are your

best players in any form of the game, and there isn't a cricketer in South Africa who would dispute that Jacques is one of the very best – if not *the* best ever. Not having him in the team for the competition was deeply disappointing. Actually, it was a joke, but a joke in poor taste.

It was all too much for Mark Boucher, who couldn't contain his frustration and lashed out in a newspaper article. He was reprimanded and heavily fined out of all proportion to the offence, which, again, was a source of anger among the squad. I guess it wasn't his place to comment on the make-up of the squad, but he and Kallis have been best mates for a decade. When the journalist asked the question, Mark couldn't help telling it like it was.

The enforced absence of Kallis was used as a source of motivation, and our on-field preparations actually went very well. In our two official warm-up games, we lost a hard-fought encounter against Sri Lanka but beat Australia. The tournament opener against the West Indies, played at the Wanderers on 11 September, was an absolute belter, with Chris Gayle making 117 from 59 balls before Herschelle led us to a victory target of 206 with 90 from 55 balls. We won with over two overs to spare!

In Cape Town, we beat Bangladesh (15 September) and England (16 September) with such calm authority that you had to wonder just how much of a 'lottery' T20 cricket actually was, after all. Unlike the frustrations in the Caribbean six months earlier, everything looked and felt on track. There were no injuries, illnesses or 'incidents' to worry about or to distract us, and most of our key players were peaking at the right time and hitting form together.

At Kingsmead on 19 September, our form continued with another clinical victory against New Zealand. This gave us a perfect 'played four, won four' record, and, we thought, a good enough record and net run rate to qualify for a place in the semifinals no matter what happened in the final group game

against India, on 20 September. Everybody had been involved in
the game for long enough to be familiar with the phrase 'mathematical possibility', but in layman's terms it simply meant 'just
be sensible and don't stuff it up'.

We had a shocker. There was nothing too wrong with our
bowling performance, and India's total of 153 was about par
for the conditions. We needed 154 for victory, but, just as importantly, we needed 126 to maintain our net run rate advantage and qualify for the semifinals. We finished on 116–9. Gone.
Eliminated, just like that. It was cricket's version of the voyage
of the *Titanic*, except that we probably sank quicker.

My immediate emotions were more of shock and disbelief
than pain or anger, although those came later. I couldn't help
feeling that it was unfair that we could be eliminated after one
bad game in the group stages, having played the best cricket of
the tournament. Other teams had lost a game but still qualified
for the semis. But the playing conditions were there for us all
to see before the tournament started, and we all knew that this
sort of thing was possible. But it didn't make it any easier to accept when it actually happened.

Up to that day, I had preferred to believe that our continued
failures at ICC events, particularly in the 'big matches', were
nothing more than a combination of bad luck and coincidence.
But this was just too awful to be a coincidence. We had needed
126 to reach the semifinals. On a 'normal' day we could have
knocked them off batting with a stump. I accepted, with sad reluctance, that there was a BMT (Big Match Temperament) problem when it came to crunch time in world events. I wasn't sure
how to tackle it, but there was nothing I wouldn't try.

That evening, all the talk was about the new 'rebel' T20 league
that was about to start in India. Judging by the way many of our
guys felt in the immediate aftermath of our elimination, it was
hardly a surprise to hear them talking about retiring from international cricket and taking the money. Several of them had al-

ready been approached with substantial offers to join the Indian Cricket League (ICL). In fact, one player had already jumped ship and put pen to paper before we had even played our final game. Johan van der Wath told me in the dressing room, soon after the match finished, that he had signed and that this would be his last game for South Africa. Many weeks later, I was better able to understand his reasons – he was in his thirties and had his future to consider – but at the time I felt it was extremely inappropriate. It was the last thing I needed to hear at that moment. Rats jumping off a sinking ship came to mind, but I had no intention of allowing my ship to sink.

Our team manager at that time was Logan Naidoo, a decent enough chap in his own right, no doubt, but terrible for team spirit and dressing room harmony because he was clearly an Arendse man who had been 'assigned' to the team to keep an eye on us and to report back to the president. He enjoyed the trust of none of the team. His appointment came immediately after the World Cup, and I know it was meant to be a warning shot in my direction. But he was there, and that was the reality. We would have to make the best of the situation. Actually, I felt a little sorry for him. Time and time again, conversations would stop when he walked past. It was mostly polite conversation only with Logan.

Tour of Pakistan (27 September – 29 October 2007)

Graeme and I both felt that this would be a defining tour for our Test team and for the new brand of cricket that we were determined to try and implement. We had a simple plan of attack, at the centre of which were three fast bowlers who could all reach 140km/h on a consistent basis. Kallis would be our fourth seamer, and he too was still capable of bowling at serious pace at the right time and place. We also believed very strongly that it was time to properly back a spinner, over a decent period of time, and allow him to settle into international cricket. We were convinced that Paul Harris was our man. However, this meant leaving out Shaun Pollock, one of the biggest and most difficult – not to mention controversial – decisions that either of us had ever made in our cricket careers, and I had made a few more than Graeme.

We had one warm-up game before the first Test in Karachi. We had requested, and believed we had been granted, permission to make the fixture a 13-a-side match in order to allow everyone some game time. It would, of course, also allow us to start the first Test with Pakistan fully expecting to face Polly. On the morning of the match, however, we were informed that the fixture was, in fact, a first-class match with 11 players per side. It left us in a very difficult and awkward position.

I had thought long and hard about the best way to tell a cricketing legend that we were changing our style of play, and that he would no longer be in the starting XI. We were given notice just five or ten minutes before the toss that the game was to be 11-a-side. I had planned to take Polly out for dinner and tell him about our future plans in the dignified manner that such an icon deserved. But now he was in the middle of our final warm-ups and I had to find a way to get him out of the group and tell him the news that he wouldn't be playing in the warm-up game. And the implication of that was obvious. It was one of the most difficult conversations I have ever had.

Just as he was with every aspect of his game, Shaun was meticulously prepared for such a discussion and presented a strong, statistical case for his continued involvement in our Test plans. He still believed that he had a major role to play, and argued, with typical clarity, that his record offered more than sufficient evidence of his ability and importance to the team. But, ever the consummate professional, he accepted the decision and returned to the changing room and began helping the starting XI to prepare for the game. There may have been a frosty silence between us for a couple of days, but I did not expect anything less. I would have been disappointed and surprised if he had not been upset. It had been a monster decision to make, and he wasn't the only one feeling a bit shocked and bruised.

The Test match, played in Karachi on 1–5 October, went as well as we could ever have hoped – probably better. Jacques made 155 in a first-innings total of 450, and then 'Harry' bowled 36 overs at a cost of just two runs each and took his first five-for in Test cricket. Jacques scored another century in the second innings and Dale Steyn blew the home team away in the second innings with 5–56. It was a magnificent Test match victory under any circumstances, but given how much was riding on it and how easily we might have been vilified if we had lost, it meant even more. Dale was still young and a bit raw, and André Nel could be easily wound up. The worst-case scenario was that they would both feel the pressure and start leaking runs at four or five per over. How we would then have missed Polly's control. And how we would have been criticised!

Hashim Amla made a lovely 71 in the first innings, and although he made a duck in the second I was as pleased with the way he was taking to Test cricket as I was with Dale, Harry and everybody else. Although every cricketer knows how fine the line is between success and failure, in Hashim's case it was particularly stark. In the very next series, against New Zealand at home, he failed in the first innings of the first Test at the Wanderers and then edged a straightforward catch to Brendon McCullum in the second innings. He had made a difficult and uncertain start to his Test career, and everybody knew he was under pressure. McCullum dropped it. Hashim made 170 and helped us win the match. From that moment, he hardly looked back, and his Test career blossomed to such an extent that, three years later, he was ranked in the top three in the world. And if McCullum had caught it? Who knows?

Another career was supposed to have been launched in that

first Test, but Morné Morkel broke a bone in his foot and had to return home. We might have had an even more inexperienced attack if we had been able to stick to our plans. It would have been so easy to give Polly an eleventh-hour reprieve, but we stuck to our guns and selected Nel because of the aggression he brought to the attack – as well as the extra pace.

We came very close to winning the second Test in Lahore (8–12 October) as well, but the occasion was swamped by the fact that it was Inzamam ul-Haq's final Test match. In many ways, we were happy to take a few conservative options when the choices presented themselves, having done so much hard work to win in Karachi. Make no mistake, we wanted to win the second Test, but we made certain we couldn't lose by delaying the declaration a little longer than was probably necessary. Harry showed some extraordinary character in the first innings by batting almost three hours to make 46, and helping us to add a critical extra 100 runs for the last three wickets. Jacques made another century in the second innings, to complete an astonishing series, and Graeme ended a lean spell with an innings of 133. The magnitude of the achievement in winning a Test series in Pakistan was lost on none of us, particularly given the off-field circumstances.

Before the tour began, there were long and sometimes painful negotiations about security. Several players were seriously concerned before we even left South Africa, and a couple considered the option of withdrawing. But eventually, with the help of SACA chief executive Tony Irish, we agreed to stand together as a squad and be guided by the advice of our security experts. Pakistan offered to provide us with full 'presidential style' security, which gave us as many questions as it did answers. It was a relief to know that the Pakistanis would stop at nothing to keep us safe, but if the army was required to provide adequate security, surely that confirmed that the situation was every bit as serious as we feared. Also, wouldn't the presence of a large army contingent make the perfect target for a terrorist attack?

In our hotel, we were effectively under house arrest. We weren't just advised to stay within the hotel confines; there were soldiers and security officers posted at every possible exit to make sure we didn't escape! They were never aggressive and always tried to make us feel welcome – and most of them had a ready smile – but after a week or so we began to feel that their responsibilities included keeping us 'in' as much as keeping the bad elements 'out'! With so much spare time on our hands between practice and match days, it was inevitable that we pondered on the purpose of our visit. Everybody wanted to play cricket, obviously, but the circumstances in which we found ourselves were far from ideal. Personally, part of what attracted me to the life of a cricketer – apart from the game itself – was the opportunity to meet new people, see new places and have new experiences. Being in Pakistan was certainly a new experience, but the circumstances were not necessarily to be recommended.

The tour was running concurrently with the Rugby World Cup, and we were worried we wouldn't be able to see the Springboks' matches on television. However, you can always trust an Afrikaner to make a plan, even in the most adverse circumstances, and there were a good few 'Dutchies' on the television production crew for the tour. Although the satellite dish on the hotel roof had probably never picked up the SuperSport signal before, that was soon to change. Give a rugby-hungry Dutchman a screwdriver and a pair of pliers and you will be able to watch anything! Being able to watch the Rugby World Cup was a fantastic boon for all of us.

The one-day series that followed the Test series was full of all the twists and turns you would expect between these two teams; there were some great individual performances and some wonderful team ones. Herschelle and AB scored great hundreds to win the first game in Lahore on 18 October, and Mohammad

Yousuf replied with 117 to win the second game (20 October) at the same venue. Pakistan thrashed us in Faisalabad on 23 October, and we bounced back with a similarly comprehensive victory in Multan (26 October) where Graeme made 81 and Polly lapped up the opportunity to bat at number three with a brilliant innings of 90 from 84 balls.

The fifth game had been scheduled for Karachi, but yet another terrorist incident had forced it to be moved back to Lahore. Former Prime Minister Benazir Bhutto had recently returned to the country from exile, and a suicide bomb attack on her motorcade in Karachi on 18 September had made the situation unstable. Watching footage of the explosion and resulting carnage (in which 139 people died and 450 were injured) was a chilling experience for all of us. Once again, we found ourselves asking the question, sometimes privately and sometimes publicly: 'Is it really worth it?' It was quite normal for the guys with families to be more concerned about the situation than the younger, single players, but by the end of the tour even the younger guys were asking for their mums!

The night of the Rugby World Cup final (20 October) was one of the all-time classic tour stories. In the build-up to the match itself, SuperSport played a whole series of interviews with the Springboks that the team had recorded the previous week. At one point, Bakkies Botha was saying how much the players were looking forward to getting home after five weeks away, and how hard it had been for them in a foreign country, with strange food and an alien culture. And where were they? Paris! There was a moment of stunned silence as the squad wondered whether Bakkies had actually said that. There we sat, on the floor of our team room in Lahore, sipping cans of illegal beer and watching our illegal satellite feed – surrounded by soldiers wielding AK-47s. It's a good job they don't play rugby in Pakistan.

For the final ODI, when the national anthem played, the whole squad stood up, linked arms and sang it like they'd never sung before. You never see them sing like that when they're on television! Our original schedule had us leaving at 7.00 am the following morning, but given that the match wasn't scheduled to finish until after 1.00 am, it didn't take much to persuade Goolam to change the travel plans.

About a week or ten days before we were due to leave Pakistan, we were invited as guests of honour for dinner at the home of a successful and wealthy businessman. It was more of a 'function' than a private sit-down dinner, although it wasn't an 'official' event as such. There was plenty of discussion around whether we should accept the invitation, and naturally our own security advisers were a little nervous. But it was our first opportunity to get out of the hotel for about three weeks and I was very keen to take it. We had armed guards on the bus and in vehicles behind and in front. When we arrived, we saw snipers on the roof and there were more private guards with assault rifles outside the front door. But I was determined to meet some new people and see some fresh faces, so I led the way in.

Our host introduced himself to us and asked me what I would like to drink. A quick glance around the room revealed no evidence of what I actually felt like drinking, so I asked – a little nervously – what he had. He walked with me to the end of the room and pressed a button on the side of a large bookcase, which slowly turned around a full 180 degrees to reveal a magnificent, fully stocked bar of the sort you would see in the lobby of a five-star hotel. Amazing. I opted for a cold beer but later found myself sipping a glass of French Chardonnay. Here we were in the middle of Lahore – on a James Bond movie set. It was surreal.

We won the decider, on 29 October, in the most dramatic circumstances. With only a few days' notice to prepare a pitch for a match he was never expecting, the groundsman at the Gaddafi Stadium in Lahore actually did pretty well. It was, understandably, an underprepared surface, which made life awkward for the batsmen, and I thought our total of 233 gave us a fighting chance. But not so, it seemed, when the two old-stagers, Younis Khan and Mohammad Yousuf, both passed 50 and took Pakistan to within 35 runs of victory with six wickets in hand and 10 overs to spare. Most teams would battle to *think* of a way of losing a game from that position, never mind *actually* losing it. Graeme deserves a lot of credit for his tactical thinking, Albie Morkel swung the ball brilliantly and AB took an inexplicably brilliant catch to get rid of Shahid Afridi. But no matter how well the fielding side performs in a situation like that, major questions have to be asked of the batting team. It was a horrendous choke, yet Pakistan seemed strangely unmoved afterwards. I was asked some time afterwards whether I thought it was suspicious, whether, perhaps, money had changed hands. It certainly never occurred to me at the time. If I analyse every wicket and every key moment of the last 10 overs I might be left with two very thin maybes. Maybe it's just because I wanted to celebrate an extraordinary victory, and maybe it's because I still want to cherish the memory, but I believe that the game was clean. If it was proven to be fixed, however, then my reaction would be one of sadness rather than surprise. People called South Africa 'chokers', but nobody can choke like Pakistan!

Our one-day side had been solid, with plenty of options, for a couple of years, and this was reflected in our ranking. But the Test side needed work – and was still a work in progress. The series victory, however, was strong evidence that we were heading in the right direction and getting a lot more things right than wrong.

New Zealand tour of South Africa (8 November – 2 December 2007)
After the tour of Pakistan, my biggest concern was Herschelle at the top of the order. He simply wasn't consistent enough, and it felt like a gamble every time he walked out to open the

batting. It was placing too much pressure on Graeme, and I knew that we had to find him a new partner, someone who offered more reliability if not the genius or flair of a Gibbs. It needed to be done sooner rather than later, but not immediately, so Herschelle played the series against New Zealand but didn't score many runs.

The first Test against New Zealand (8–11 November) was another watershed moment for Polly. The Wanderers was green, and looked a bit uneven – a seamer's delight. I think Polly had accepted that the Pakistani wickets would not have been to his liking. He was back on familiar territory now, and I suspect he was licking his lips at the prospect of bowling at the Bullring, where he had been so successful for the best part of a decade. But Graeme and I had decided to keep our style and tactics – and therefore the team – unchanged. I always wanted to be the man who conveyed bad news (and sometimes good news!) to the players who were being left out, or included, in the starting XI. It was different for a squad announcement – that was the convener's prerogative. But I wanted to take the responsibility of informing the players when it came to the XI.

Polly was in the squad of 13, and most people expected a return to business as usual. It would have been the easiest thing in the world to play an all-seam attack, including Polly, and leave our spinner out. There were half a dozen reasons we could have used to justify such a decision. But Graeme and I felt very strongly that it was not in the best long-term interests of the Test team, and we were trying as hard as we could to plan ahead. With the greatest respect to New Zealand, they had hardly played a Test match for a whole year preceding that tour, and we expected to beat them. We wanted to beat them with the team we were hoping would tackle England in the middle of 2008 and Australia at the end of it. Polly could have played and taken a bagful of wickets – and probably would have done – but what would we have achieved as a team?

As it transpired, I'm not sure Polly would have taken a bagful of wickets, because Dale Steyn took 20 of the 40 on offer in the two Tests and pretty much destroyed New Zealand single-handedly. It was a devastating performance, and confirmed that we now had one of the deadliest cricketing weapons in the world – and he could only get better.

The West Indies tour (14 December 2007 – 3 February 2008)

The West Indies team arrived in South Africa early in December. The first Test was the traditional Boxing Day Test, which had been moved from its usual Durban location to Port Elizabeth, where it promptly rained for three or four days before the match started. There had been plenty of debate and criticism around our decision to keep the Proteas together rather than let them return to their franchises to play four-day cricket. As always, it was a Catch-22 situation. I wanted everybody to be match-fit, but I also didn't want them overworked, physically tired and prone to injury. I erred on the side of caution, preferring to keep the squad together and compromising by arranging to gather in PE twenty-four hours earlier than usual in order to put in some hard preparation work. The rain ruined that plan, and by the morning of the match I knew we were seriously undercooked – 'short of a gallop' as they say in Australia – and short of match fitness, too. I accepted responsibility for that. It is every coach's goal to achieve the perfect balance between play and rest; I'd taken a bit of a gamble, which had now backfired.

It still came as a nasty shock when we lost the Test match. I thought we might struggle, but I had never contemplated defeat. Shiv Chanderpaul scored a century and Marlon Samuels made 94 as the West Indies passed 400; we could only make 195 in reply, and although we fought back well to bowl them out for 175 second time around we were never going to chase 390 successfully. The West Indies and their supporters were all deliriously happy, and rightly so. They hadn't won a Test match for years – I recall being told that it was Dwayne Bravo's twenty-fourth Test and the first time he had tasted victory. No wonder they went crazy in their changing room afterwards. The two changing rooms at St George's Park are right next to each other – closer than anywhere else I've seen – so when a team is letting off steam next door it can really test your patience. I made all the players stay in our changing room for at least an hour after-wards listening to the booming reggae and incessant cheering. We quietly sipped our beers, but I could see the players filling up far more on thoughts of revenge than on Castle Lager.

After the Test, Graeme and I called selection convenor Joubert Strydom and the other two selectors, Mustafa Khan and Shafiek Abrahams, and requested a change at the top of the order – a new opening partner for Graeme. Herschelle had bagged a 'pair' in the Test and we felt he was as mentally fragile as he had ever been and seriously low on confidence.

Graeme and I thought long and hard over many, many hours about whom we might try. There was no ready-made opener whose form demanded a chance at international cricket. We both felt extremely strongly that the next best batsmen in the country was Neil McKenzie, and that he should be added to the squad. This was a bit of an irregular move, as the squad had been cho-sen for the first two Tests, but it was far from unprecedented. Our argument to include Neil wasn't just based on his batting and cricket knowledge. Graeme knew all too well the value that a senior player of Mac's standing and respect could bring to the team. Graeme was big enough to recognise that he could do with a bit of senior-player maturity and leadership to help him.

Our request led to another direct clash with Norman Arendse. He felt strongly that, as Herschelle had been named in the squad for the first two Tests, he should be retained. I had spoken to Herschelle at length after the PE Test and said that I believed he needed a break from Test cricket and a chance to return to the

Cobras to find some form and confidence. I believe Herschelle knew that himself.

Norman refused to sanction the change and did not appear willing or able to listen to our point of view on any level. I spoke to Gerald Majola about the issue, and, as always, he was prepared to back our judgment. Graeme and I were frustrated that the president felt it was within his jurisdiction to overrule such an important selection issue, even when the selectors understood our thinking and were, in some cases reluctantly, prepared to make the change in the interests of the team. Technically, Norman was right; the squad had been named for the first two Tests, which were back-to-back with no cricket in between, but there was no rule which stipulated that changes could not be made. We were 1–0 down, with a series to win, and we had an opening batsman who we knew, at that stage of his life and career, could only be a liability. For every hundred times a coach likes to think a player is only an innings away from coming right, there is one when he knows he won't come right. And this was one of those times.

It was the start of a miserable relationship between Norman and myself, which included increasingly unsavoury interactions on a series of issues. He was adamant that Herschelle was a mercurial talent who would come right if we backed him. I was adamant that he might well come good for a couple of innings but that we needed to look to the future, in particular the upcoming tours to England and Australia.

Eventually I got my way, and Neil Mac was included for the second Test, at Newlands on 2–6 January. It was a hard battle, and not one I particularly enjoyed fighting, but Graeme had the courage of his convictions as much as I did, and it was my duty to do the best thing for the team.

On the first day of the New Year Test at Newlands, I requested a meeting with Norman to try and clear the air. The irony then, and it remains to this day, was that I respected him for his beliefs and what he stood for, despite the bitterness of some of our clashes. He swore a lot and could be unnecessarily abusive, but at least you knew where you stood and what he believed. Although he was often accused of having hidden agendas, that was never something I experienced. But I felt strongly that he was overstepping the parameters of the presidency. What was the purpose in appointing people to various roles if you were simply going to overrule them? At least Norman had a cricketing background, which wasn't always the case with some administrators, but he was not in touch with the squad, or its challenges and requirements, and that made it very dangerous when he involved himself in operational issues. I told him that if he wanted to be involved so closely in team matters, then he needed to be closer to us and spend more time with the players. I wasn't sure whether he had the time or inclination to do so – or how the players would have felt about it if he had! But it needed to be said.

We won the Cape Town Test comfortably, and wrapped up the series even more comfortably in Durban (10–12 January). Unfortunately, though, my peacemaking efforts with Norman came to very little, and one of our nastiest and most high-profile clashes was just a few days away.

Chapter 7

Boiling point

February to March 2008

It was going to be quite a year; we had the three biggest tours in the world – to India, England and Australia – coming up within the space of nine months. I was genuinely happy with our progress in both one-day and Test cricket; we had made genuine strides on a number of fronts, and I was particularly confident that we now had the right personnel and a game plan we all understood and could work with. We had a short tour of Bangladesh to fine-tune a few things, and then just a week off before the trip to India. After that it was England, followed by Australia ...

I was fully aware that I ran the risk of being disrespectful to Bangladesh by describing the tour as a 'training camp', but in many ways it was. I know there is a long history and tradition of cricket teams paying exaggerated credit to weak opposition in an attempt to ward off bad luck and keep the cricket gods happy, but frankly it would have felt ridiculous and dishonest to say that I feared an upset. I expected us to beat Bangladesh. I expected India to provide a much stiffer test, and I didn't see anything wrong with saying that we would use the Bangladesh series to prepare for the Indian one.

Ever since my youth, I had regarded a Test cap as the ultimate reward for excellence, and never, ever to be awarded or accepted lightly. Similarly, I regarded the composition of a Test XI as the greatest challenge for a coach and selector; once settled, it should be changed only with caution and after much thought. Basically, my philosophy was 'don't mess with the Test team unless you've got a bloody good reason!' I was always more flexible with the one-day team, and prepared to experiment and see whether an individual had the technique and temperament for international cricket, but the Test team should be as settled as possible. 'Sacrosanct' might be too strong a word, but it's close to how I felt about it.

When I presented my preferred squad to the selection panel for discussion, it was agreed upon by everyone within three or four minutes. The convenor, Joubert Strydom, shared my views on the importance of continuity, although another member of the panel, Mustapha Khan, did ask whether we should be giving opportunities to fringe players given that it was a tour against 'minor' opposition. I accepted his point, but reminded everyone how important it was to build the team towards the England and Australia tours, and that opportunities for fringe players could be found on SA 'A' tours and ODIs against minor opposition. I genuinely believed it would be a formality. Years later, that belief may seem naïve, given how things transpired, but I actually thought we were all striving for the same objectives.

I heard the first alarm bell ring when Mustapha started talking. Norman Arendse was never shy to share his opinions, on anything, with whoever was listening, so I had a very good idea on what his thinking was regarding selection. It was very hard to avoid the conclusion that he had identified Mustapha as 'his man' on the selection panel, and had invested a good deal of time in getting his views across. Nothing that 'Mushy' said during that meeting (it was actually a teleconference) had been said before by him, but they correlated exactly with what I had heard about Norman's thinking. Evidently, things might not be as straightforward as I had thought – and hoped.

Joubert Strydom had convened the teleconference, which included his fellow selectors Mustapha, Shafiek Abrahams, myself and Vinnie Barnes, the latter always providing a critical sense of balance and perspective. Once the team had been agreed upon, protocol demanded that Joubert should dial up the president and have the team ratified. At that stage of the CSA constitution, the president still had a unilateral veto over any squad. I was still hoping, even expecting, a relatively smooth process, if not an instant rubber stamp. Norman rarely gave a rubber stamp to anything!

When Joubert dialled him into the conversation, it was obvious that Norman was agitated, to say the least, and he quite soon became aggressive. He clearly had prior knowledge of the squad he was likely to be presented with, and he was very unhappy. Joubert read the team out. Believe it or not, I was still hoping for a presidential 'tick'. Perhaps his bad mood had nothing to do with squad selection. It was wishful thinking.

He angrily said that he refused to sanction the squad. There was a long and awkward silence while nobody dared to speak. I assumed that Joubert would pick up the conversation and explain the rationale behind the composition of the squad. Eventually he did, but Norman was having none of it and stated categorically that he would neither sanction the squad nor release it to the media. All I could think at that time was cricket logic; the squad had won five consecutive series and we had three iconic series to come following the Bangladesh tour. I was struggling to believe what I was hearing. To compound my sense of disbelief, Joubert then said: 'OK, we'll have to do some thinking and resubmit a different squad to you.'

At that point my patience snapped and I jumped in, having

maintained a diplomatic silence until that point. 'I am not prepared to rethink the composition of the squad and I am not prepared to jeopardise our chances of success. This is the best team
and it is getting better – we must keep it together and maintain
our continuity and progress,' I said, or words to that effect. I
was animated, and took my tone from Norman. If he was lib-
eral with his language and demeanour, then I saw no reason
why I should not follow in the same vein. I asked him what his
reasons were for wanting to break up such a successful squad.

He replied that it was his right, and duty, to transform the
team as much as possible, and that, against weak opposition
such as Bangladesh, it was an opportunity to give fringe players
experience of international cricket. I told him that I understood
his reasons, but that, given the circumstances of consecutive
tours to India, England and Australia, it was essential for our
credibility as leaders and administrators that we maintained a
sense of order and trust amongst the players. If individual and
team success on the field counted for nothing when it came to
keeping your place in the team, then we would lose our credibility among the players, and transformation would once again
be seen as nothing more than window-dressing and quotas.

Norman was not prepared to budge. He was not prepared to
listen, and the concept of compromise never entered his head –
at least, that was the way it sounded. At that point, it began to
get ugly. He was shouting at me and accusing me of all sorts of
prejudices. He said I was being just like Springbok coach Jake
White and refusing to give black players an opportunity. He said
that Jake 'talked the talk but then only picked two black wings'.
I replied that Jake White had won a World Cup. I told him that,
from the moment he had assumed the presidency, he had acted
as though Cricket South Africa was all about him and his ide-
als. I told him he was treating CSA and its people as though
they were his personal property – and that he was acting like a
control freak.

It was unpleasant but, unfortunately, probably unavoidable. I didn't know whether to be angry, sad or amused when he accused me of lacking sincerity when it came to transformation. I was certainly pretty emotional, because as far as I was concerned my record on transformation was there for all to see; it was one of the reasons I had been given the job. It could bear the closest scrutiny that anyone cared to give it. I had always been prepared to force the process of transformation in our ODI team, and in every other team at every level, but not the Test team. That had always been my position from day one, and I could not change that principle. I believed then, and I still believe today, that youngsters of all colours and creeds are far more likely to be attracted to a winning team and a winning sport than to one which 'looks' right.

After three or four minutes of Norman's rant at me, I heard Vinnie Barnes say: 'I'm not listening to this shit any more', and he slammed his phone down. A few moments later, Shafiek Abrahams also put his phone down. I'm not sure whether Mustapha Khan was still on the line, but he wasn't saying anything. As convenor, I guess Joubert was obliged to stay on the line but he wasn't getting involved.

The gloves were well and truly off now, and the language deteriorated further. There was no greater insult Norman could have thrown at me than accusing me of being racist and not wanting to play black players. I was furious, seething with rage. Thank God it was a teleconference and we weren't in the same room. I dread to think of how Vinnie and Shafiek would have kept the peace if we'd all been together, as sometimes happened.

It might have been different if he had engaged me in a debate on my conviction that the Test team needed to be kept together for the sake of the next twelve months, which, I believed, had the potential to be an iconic year for South African cricket. But he refused to even listen to my point of view, let alone discuss it.

His belief was that we should drop Neil McKenzie, André Nel

and Morné Morkel from the proposed squad, and among the replacements should be Herschelle and Charl Langeveldt. Nobody
was a bigger fan of those two players than me, but the irony of
their inclusion in the name of transformation would be lost on
nobody. They were the two oldest nationally contracted players!
What would have been transformed if they had been included?
It would have been deeply insulting to both men if they had
been included in the squad on the basis of anything other than
their form. Shortly before the 'conversation' ended, Norman
had his habitual rant about Kallis and Boucher, saying they were
'over the hill' and not worth their places. I was becoming used
to that line. These were two of the greatest cricketers in the
world, never mind South Africa, and he would slag them off at
every available opportunity. I had to smile. Eventually I put the
phone down. The whole exercise was pointless and unpleasant.

Norman then sent me an e-mail letter, charging me with insubordination and threatening to have me suspended unless I
apologised before the end of the day. I thought about it many
times, but each time dismissed the idea. The whole incident
had been very much out of character for me, and it would have
been very much in character for me to try and make peace afterwards. But I could not allow myself, in any way, to let Norman
believe that I was backing down. He had started with the aggressive attitude and name-calling, and, if anything, my reaction
had been self-defence! I knew I was right about the selection
process, and I believed equally strongly that he should not be
playing an active role in choosing teams. I could not apologise.
It would have been insincere and meaningless.

Instead, I responded to his letter with one of my own in which
I accused him of showing complete disrespect for an employee.
I then called Gerald Majola to tell him what had happened so
that he was not caught unawares. I explained exactly what had
happened during the teleconference; I was as impartial as possible, and admitted that I was completely wrong to have stooped

to Norman's level and engaged him in gutter talk. As always, Gerald was extremely supportive and concurred with the view that the CSA president should not be playing an active role in team selection.

The support from the players was almost overwhelming, and SACA chief executive Tony Irish was in constant contact to advise me about the best way forward. The stalemate on the announcement of the squad, meanwhile, was causing difficulties both for the players, who were trying to get on with their lives, and for the CSA travel and logistics department, who needed to book tickets and get visas in passports.

I spoke to very few people for the first two days, and barely answered my phone. After forty-eight hours I didn't answer it at all. Tony and others had advised me to 'lie low' while they dealt with Norman, so I gave Tony, Gerald, Joubert and Graeme Smith the number of Yvette's mobile and headed for the bomb shelter.

Norman's next move was to call an extraordinary meeting of the board, again via teleconference, at which he reiterated his accusations of dissent and insubordination and pushed through a motion to have me removed from the selection panel, with immediate effect. When I pointed out that my contract clearly stipulated that I was a member of the selection panel, and that Norman's motion was a clear and direct breach of my contract, he was obviously angry and embarrassed. The board members, too, were embarrassed – especially at having been railroaded into making their decision with undue haste.

By this time the whole scandal was public knowledge and deeply embarrassing for CSA. The only thing that could have compounded the situation was if the threat of a player's strike had ever made the media. There was still no official squad, of course, but the senior players – Smith, Kallis and Boucher – said they would not board the plane for Bangladesh without me, and would persuade the other players to do likewise. I appreci-

ated the gesture, but was under no illusion, at any stage, that
I was more important than the team, or that an international
tour would be put on hold for Mickey Arthur! No player – and
certainly no coach – is bigger than the game!

From time to time during this immensely difficult period I
couldn't help wondering how and why Norman was so completely prepared for the 14 names we had proposed. Before he
descended into foul-mouthed abuse, he had been so quick to
rebuff certain names that he was almost saying 'no' before they
were read out. Then I remembered a short and seemingly innocent conversation I had had with Logan Naidoo during the fifth
one-day international against the West Indies on 3 February. As
I mentioned, we never spoke about very much in any depth – it
was mostly polite chit-chat – but he had made a point of saying how well things were going, and asked what my thoughts
were on the composition of the squad to tour Bangladesh. I was
watching the game at the time and gave my answer very little
thought. Why should I? 'If it isn't broken, why try to fix it?' I
replied. I guess it was all the warning that Norman needed to
prepare his onslaught.

I must stress again that Logan was an entirely decent person
during his time as manager; in a different era and under different circumstances, he could have played a very worthwhile
and well-received role. But his association with Norman, and
willingness to be used as a pawn and messenger, negated the
positives he offered. It was obvious to everybody that he really
wanted the job of team manager, but when the players realised
for certain that he was providing a direct hotline to the president and his boardroom, they lost all respect for him and the
relationship was doomed.

Although I have always been prepared to roll up my sleeves
and get my hands dirty, both as a player and coach, I am a natural mediator and have never been drawn to conflict as a way of
resolving difficulties. The head-on, and very public, clash be-

tween myself and the CSA president caused me many sleepless nights, and I developed a knot of anxiety in my stomach. The fact that it came so soon after our first spat over the relegation of Gibbs, and the promotion of McKenzie, made it all the worse. I often thought of backing down in order to keep the peace, but that would have involved handing in my resignation. I could not operate as a puppet. But I was so committed to the team, and excited about the future, that the thought of resignation turned me cold. I had no choice. If I was to fulfil my dream, and help this team realise its potential, I had no choice but to fight on.

In the heat of the moment, I would be convinced that Norman did not have the best interests of South African cricket at heart. But when the dust had settled, and I was able to reflect on his actions, I had to conclude that he believed in what he was doing and that it was the *right* thing to do. He believed that you could transform the Test team by changing its colour overnight. I believed that you could transform the Test team on a long-term and sustainable basis by making it the most successful one in the world.

By the time the squad for the Bangladesh tour was finally announced, they were already calling the flight at OR Tambo International Airport. Things were a bit of a rush. As I sat on the plane, there was no sense of victory or triumph, just a bewildered sense of confusion that something I saw as so simple and straightforward had spiralled so quickly, and so badly, out of control. I wasn't aware of all the details after we left, but I think there was a vote of no confidence in Norman by the board, and I know that Tony and Gerald worked extremely hard on my behalf. I asked them to keep me up to date purely on a 'need to know' basis. I wanted to concentrate on cricket! My future was still uncertain when we began the tour, but I felt at peace because I was prepared to lose my job over the principles that were at stake. I desperately didn't want to lose my job, but I was prepared to accept my fate. About a week into the tour, Logan came to my room and asked whether I would be prepared to drop my charges against Norman; he said that Norman was prepared to drop the disciplinary action against me. Only at that moment was I prepared to believe that I would still have a job in a couple of months' time, and that I would, at least, be taking the team to England.

Tour of Bangladesh (17 February – 14 March)

In the first Test, in Dhaka on 22–25 February, everything went very much according to plan. Steyn and Morkel shared eight wickets to bowl Bangladesh out for 192 – until we were bowled out for 170 in reply. At 148–4 in their second innings we were under pressure on a difficult pitch, until Kallis suddenly found some swing and took 5–30 to end the innings in a hurry, and we reached the victory target of 205 with few worries. It was just what we needed: a decent workout in unforgiving subcontinental conditions.

Graeme and Neil Mac combined for a world-record first wicket partnership of 415 in the second Test in Chittagong (29 February – 3 March), and Steyn was once again outstanding. But far more important than the individual performances was the way the team was gelling, with a deep and clear understanding of exactly what their roles were and what was expected of each other. I could see a formidable Test squad developing, and I felt fully vindicated for making my stand, although far from smug or triumphant.

About halfway through the tour Logan was required to return to South Africa to testify at a special meeting of the parliamentary portfolio committee on sport, chaired by Bhutana Komphela, and specially requested by Norman. Piecing together the evidence of what was said, from at least half a dozen first-hand accounts, it was hard to avoid the conclusion that Norman was metaphorically throwing his hands in the air and telling the politicians: 'I am doing my best to transform cricket but I am being resisted at every turn. I need your help.' I subsequently read some of the transcripts of that meeting, which was held in a committee room in Parliament, and was shocked by the language and tone of what was said. At one point somebody says: 'Whatever the whites did to us, we will do back to them with interest.' Sentiments like that are understandable, given the decades and generations of neglect and abuse under apartheid, but are worrying when coming from a parliamentary committee.

When Logan returned to finish the tour, he was ostracised completely. He was running with the hare and hunting with hounds. Even the polite conversation between him and the players dried up. But even worse was to come.

With the India tour following so soon after the Bangladesh tour we were obliged to pick our Test squad just before the three-match ODI series (9, 12 and 14 March). Having already been through an emotional hell to get the team ratified, I hoped – even expected, naïvely – that it would be a formality the second time around. Far from it. I conveyed my feelings to Joubert, and hoped the selectors would concur. But when the squad was announced it contained the name of Charl Langeveldt in place of André Nel. I respected 'Langers' enormously as both a cricketer and a person, and had championed his cause on numerous occasions for the job he could do for us in one-day cricket. But there were doubts about his Test credentials, particularly his ability to perform a sustained role as the third seamer, given that our brand of Test cricket involved having three quicks who could bowl at 140km/h. Nel was our backup in that department behind Steyn, Ntini and Morkel. Langers had different skills – a stylish away swing and the ability to hit the block-hole, but not the sustained pace and hostility we were looking for in Test cricket.

I had discussed the strategy on numerous occasions with Joubert and the other selectors, and felt that there was a common purpose among us. I was dismayed at the change in the squad, and realised, with even deeper dismay, that the political machine was operating at full pace back home.

I went to Nel's room on the evening before the second one-dayer, and conveyed the news that he was not going to India. I always tried to ensure that players were given the right messages when receiving bad news, but on this occasion there was nothing I could say. There were no good cricketing reasons for his exclusion. I had assured him that he was an important part of our plans for the next six to twelve months, and now he was gone. And I had nothing to say to console or reassure him. It was an immensely difficult conversation.

I then went to Charl's room to convey the good news and congratulate him. As I said, he was a damn fine bowler, so it wasn't as if I was trying to justify the inclusion of a 'nobody' or a has-been. But we had a hierarchical system in the squad, which allowed everybody to know exactly where they were in the pecking order if they weren't in the starting XI. If we had two bowlers competing for a place, or even for the position of first reserve, they would always know which of them was the next cab off the rank. Langers knew that he had jumped the queue, and was immediately uncomfortable. His first words to me were: 'This is Arendse, and it's political, isn't it?'

I replied: 'Yes, it is, sorry about that.' That was the truth. Charl was an intelligent man, and would have been insulted by lies. He just laughed. Not the laugh of a man who was amused, but the resigned laugh of absurdity.

All this was happening at 9.00 pm on the night before a one-day international. I often despaired at the insensitivity of administrators and their complete lack of knowledge or understanding of how an elite sports team operated. If they had even an inkling of how the dynamics worked, I would never have been put in that position and neither would the players.

André was very emotional indeed, and Graeme and I spent a

lot of time with him in his room that evening. We encouraged him to call as many of his friends and closest confidants as he wanted. His instincts told him to say 'to hell with it' and sign a Kolpak contract with an English county side. He was entirely ready to walk away from South African cricket at that point. Graeme and I urged him to be calm, and to take a few days to let things calm down and think about the way forward. I promised him that, as far as I was concerned, he still had a big part to play in our future plans and I would do all I could to ensure that he was still involved. I asked him whether he felt able to play in the match the following morning – ironically, alongside Langers, because we had decided to rest Steyn and Morkel. He said he wasn't sure, which I respected, and asked whether he could decide on the following morning.

A short while later, Charl came to my room and said that he was not prepared to go to India. He admitted that he had already received an attractive offer to play for Derbyshire as a Kolpak signing, and that it was a far more attractive proposition than being used as a political pawn in South Africa. At that moment I felt a strong mixture of deep respect and deep sadness for Charl: respect for his honesty and decency as a person, but sadness because he had been made to feel like a pawn. He wasn't one. Or shouldn't have been. He was always good enough to play for South Africa, and his record is testament to that. For him to be made to feel that the colour of his skin was suddenly more important than his ability was a slap in the face – a disgrace, in fact.

My last port of call, before a sleepless night, was to Morné Morkel's room. I told him he was on stand-by for the game, after all. He looked quizzically at me, but on seeing the look on my face decided against asking why.

The following morning, André said he wanted to play. He bowled beautifully, and was named man of the match. At the post-match presentation, Graeme went up to receive his award on the pretext that Nella wasn't feeling well. In truth, all the emotions of the previous night, and the fact that he had just made his point about his worth to the team, were too much for him. Even if he had wanted to go and collect his trophy, I would have been concerned about what he might have said or done. I was happy for him to make a silent protest. The problems behind the scenes had started to become public knowledge, and the last thing André wanted was to be asked questions in a public forum.

As things transpired, neither Charl nor André went to India, but at least they both knew exactly where they stood in the 'food chain', and that was a source of some comfort to both them and me.

Despite all the unpleasantness of the background situation, we had won the Test series two-nil and the one-day series three-nil. A few of the senior players, Kallis and Boucher amongst them, had been sent home to rest before the India series. On the field, things remained very much on course, with Alviro Petersen batting in the middle order – and making a very good impression – and AB de Villiers keeping wicket.

The epilogue was that Norman was voted out as president of CSA in September 2008. He was replaced by Dr Mthuthuzeli Nyoka, a man who had transformed himself from a firebrand rebel into a peacemaking settler of disputes – or so he had persuaded the cricket community.

Out of the frying pan and into the fire.

Chapter 8

Tour of India

March to April 2008

We had won six Test series in a row, but plenty of people were quick to remind me that New Zealand, West Indies and Bangladesh represented the basement, rather than the penthouse, of the Test-playing world. The trip to India in March–April 2008 represented a far more accurate litmus test of our ability.

It was a Test tour only, which excited me and allowed all of us to focus our energy in the same direction without the distraction of an ODI series. However, there was immediate consternation and criticism from some 'experts' at home about our decision to do without a warm-up game before the first Test in Chennai (26–30 March). Even more sacrilegious, as far as the traditionalists were concerned, was the fact that we actually used the six days between tours as an opportunity to return home rather than simply cross the border and play a two- or three-day game to acclimatise and prepare for the tour. How much more acclimatising did we really need?

My views on the matter were clear, and my thinking was

straightforward. In a sense, the critics were right; we didn't play a warm-up game before the Test series – we had just played a warm-up month! Touring Bangladesh can be emotionally draining, though, and I didn't want any of our key players moving straight to India already suffering from 'cabin fever'. It was a simple choice between the negative effects of ten or twelve hours in an aeroplane cabin, offset by the enormous benefits of three full days at home with friends and family, or moving straight from Bangladesh to India without the chance to refresh mentally. I knew how I responded to having just a day to relax and unwind at home. Having consulted with all the players, I knew for certain that it was the right decision. I was convinced that, once we arrived in India, all the players would still be acclimatised to the heat and cricketing conditions after a month in Bangladesh. After three days of hard practice, the major challenge would be getting our mindset right for the challenges of Test cricket.

The first Test was in the debilitating heat of Chennai, and it was a great relief to win the toss because the pitch looked flat. The bowlers certainly enjoyed the chance to put their feet up on day one.

An opening stand of 132, which lasted until well after lunch, settled everybody's early nerves. Graeme and Neil batted beautifully, but it wasn't just the runs that were so satisfying, it was the way they *looked* as an opening partnership. There seemed to be an intuition between them, an understanding that went beyond merely playing together, it was more instinctive than that. Everyone joked that it was a King Edward VII School thing, and maybe there's something in that ...

Hashim was outstanding value for his 159 – the most calm and composed innings of his career up until that point – and Bouch made a good 70. With a total of 540 on the board, I felt we were in an excellent position to put India under real pressure despite what was a faultless batting pitch. I never, ever contem-

TOP: Graeme leads the singing of the team song after spearheading the team to victory with a brilliant century in Kolkata. He still has his pads on!

ABOVE: South African team in India.

LEFT: It's a terrifying thought, but there were people sitting up there a couple of days later. It could only happen in India.

ABOVE: Adrian le Roux leads the warm-up drills at the World Cup while I keep a close eye on the opposition, looking for signs of team discord or a clue to their final XI.

ABOVE: RIGHT: World Cup, Super Eights vs West Indies, Grenada. Me, Vinnie and Shane. I've just caught sight of the dancing girls warming up ...

BOTTOM RIGHT: Despondent and miserable after World Cup semifinal defeat to Australia in St Lucia in April 2007.

TOP LEFT: Francois Hugo played a significant role in our success. You can come up with all the names you like, but psychologists are always going to be called 'shrink' by someone!

TOP RIGHT: Mixing with the rich and famous – chatting to Laurie Dippenaar and Jeremy Ord aboard Johann Rupert's yacht in the Caribbean.

LEFT: With Graeme and Loots Bosman at the launch of the 2007 Cricket World Cup in Jamaica. I really wanted Loots there. I believed in him, especially in this format.

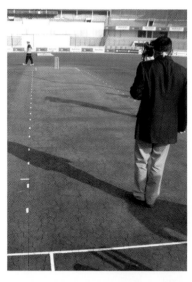

LEFT: Bangladesh National Cricket Stadium, Mirpur, Dhaka. When you are told that cricket is played on grass, don't take it literally. Not a blade of it anywhere near where the match was played!

RIGHT: Never too old to get into the nets and show them how it's done!

LEFT: Waiting for the post-match presentation in Bangladesh. 'Nella' was man of the match, but in no state to collect the award.

RIGHT: Makhaya loved Graeme and Neil Mac's world record opening partnership. It meant he could relax like this for two days.

CENTRE LEFT: On the subcontinent, any milestone worthy of the name is celebrated with a cake. They were generally better for photographing than for eating.

BOTTOM LEFT: I don't know. I have no idea what's happening. You can't explain fast bowlers. Maybe it was the heat. (Steyn, Morkel, Ntini)

BOTTOM RIGHT: One of the 'loudest' team buses we ever had. Look at those tasselled curtains! I'm taking yet another call from the media.

Our security man, Faisal Nagel, forms a working relationship with the elite Pakistani police.

I enjoyed Geoff Lawson's company immensely. It was a brave move taking over from Bob Woolmer as coach of Pakistan, and he deserved a longer run in the job. The players respected him.

Graeme, me and Logan at the fines meeting after we drew the Lahore Test to win the series in Pakistan (October 2007). Beer was available, unlike after the Karachi Test, which we won. It was Ramadan.

LEFT: A series win in Pakistan. Jacques had a phenomenal run, with three hundreds in four innings. Maybe he should grow the beard more often.

The Arthur clan in the bowels of the MCG, shortly after the series win!

Fahmida Moosajee, Poppy Rajah, Yvette Arthur and Debbie Barnes. Just so that everybody knows they really did join us in the changing room after victory in Perth!

TOP LEFT: Christmas lunch, Melbourne 2008. Very, very happy memories ...

BOTTOM LEFT: Christmas lunch, Durban 2009. Never happier than when we're all together.

BOTTOM RIGHT: Yvette and our daughters Brooke, Kristin and Ashton. *(Yvette Arthur)*

TOP: In the dugout at the T20 World Cup. Jeremy Snape, Vinnie and me. It was going so well ...

ABOVE: Lord's may be the home of cricket, with the most famous dressing room balconies, but that doesn't mean to say they are the most comfortable!

TOP: Worcester Cathedral. The game against Bangladesh in Worcester in July 2008 was possibly the lowest-key match I ever presided over as coach of the Proteas.

CENTRE LEFT: Our corporate seats for the big game at Wembley: Kallis, Smith, Boucher, Arthur, Barnes and our host and liaison man for the T20, Wayne Bently.

ABOVE RIGHT: Meeting the South African High Commissioner in London, 2008.

LEFT: Ashwell and Lopsie carry on the singing for the short – but late – bus trip from Edgbaston to the hotel after winning the series in England.

TOP LEFT: National anthems before the Adelaide ODI on Australia Day. There weren't enough mascots to extend to our entire management team!

TOP RIGHT: About to win the ODI series in Adelaide. Can you feel the excitement? Lopsy and Vaughn van Jaarsveld taking pictures, Bouch hugging Albie ... look at Jacques's face!

CENTRE LEFT: Vinnie and I celebrate a 4:1 ODI series win at the WACA, in Perth. It would become my new home barely 18 months later ...

CENTRE RIGHT: Arthurs, Moosajees and Rajahs. The little man is Luke McKenzie, helping us celebrate the record run-chase in Perth.

LEFT: Amazing what you can say with one hand while talking on the phone with the other. This means 'OK, see you in the lobby bar for a beer in 10 minutes as soon as I've done this radio crossing.'

BELOW: More team celebrations in Perth.

ABOVE: Rossco Barrat, keen follower and agent for kit suppliers Albion, arranged a cruise for me and Vin in Sydney Harbour.

LEFT: Smith, Arthur and Barnes strategising on the Swan River soon after arrival in Perth.

BELOW LEFT: Unique memorabilia: the first shirt ever signed by a victorious SA team in Australia.

BOTTOM LEFT: For once, Bouch won't be needed at the death of a run-chase. Moments before victory in Perth, everybody starts to relax.

BELOW: Proof that we really did chase down 414 to win the first Test in Perth (December 2008). I hope future generations will never forget what is possible ...

ABOVE: Impressive photo of a floodlit Lord's, but there was nothing impressive about our cricket during the ODI series in England in 2008.

LEFT: A tearful Jacques after winning the Test series at the MCG. JP says 'What's the fuss? Easy game!' After years of pain and suffering against Australia, Jacques could finally savour the moment he had been waiting 12 years for.

BELOW LEFT: Amazing ODI win at the MCG: Albie Morkel destroyed the Aussies in the batting power-play just when they thought they were in control of the game.

BELOW: Victorious at the MCG, long after everyone else had gone home. Everyone except the media, that is!

SOUTH AFRICA		Runs	[B]	[M]
		1	3	6
AMLA	b. TAIT	22	28	32
GIBBS	b. HIL'HAUS	41	49	69
KALLIS	b. CLARKE	71	93	131
DUMINY	c. WHITE b. BRACKEN	63	80	106
MCKENZIE	c. PONTING b. HIL'HAUS	0	1	4
BOUCHER	b. TAIT	4	8	8
VAN JAARSVELI	Run Out	40	18	40
MORKEL		12	18	35
BOTHA				
MORKEL				
STEYN		18		
EXTRAS	(8wd, 10Lb)			
TOTAL		7 for	272	

TICKET.COM © VBTOPTICKET.COM © VBTOPTICKET.COM © VBTOPTICKET.COM

ENGLAND	1986	DEC.	B.C. BROAD	112	ENGLAND
ENGLAND	1988	DEC.	R.B. RICHARDSON	122	WEST INDIES
ENGLAND	1990	JAN.	IJAZ AHMED	121	PAKISTAN
ENGLAND	1990	DEC.	D.I. GOWER	100	ENGLAND
ENGLAND	1992	DEC.	P.V. SIMMONS	110	WEST INDIES
ENGLAND	1995	DEC.	A.P. GURUSINHA	143	SRI LANKA
ENGLAND	1997	DEC.	J.H. KALLIS	101	STH. AFRICA
STH. AFRICA	1998	DEC.	A.J. STEWART	107	ENGLAND
ENGLAND	1999	DEC.	S.R. TENDULKAR	116	INDIA
ENGLAND	2002	DEC.	M.P. VAUGHAN	145	ENGLAND
ENGLAND	2003	DEC.	V. SEHWAG	195	INDIA
ENGLAND	2004	DEC.	YOUSUF YOUHANA	111	PAKISTAN
ENGLAND	2008	DEC.	J.P. DUMINY	166	STH. AFRICA

1990	DEC.	A.R.C. FRASER	6/82	ENGLAND
1991	DEC.	KAPIL DEV	5/97	INDIA
1996	DEC.	C.E.L. AMBROSE	5/55	WEST INDIES
1997	DEC.	A. DONALD	6/59	STH.AFRICA
1998	DEC.	D. GOUGH	5/96	ENGLAND
1998	DEC.	D. HEADLEY	6/60	ENGLAND
2003	DEC.	A. KUMBLE	6/176	INDIA
2004	DEC.	SHOAIB AKHTAR	5/109	PAKISTAN
2004	DEC.	DANISH KANERIA	5/125	PAKISTAN
2007	DEC.	A. KUMBLE	5/84	INDIA
2008	DEC.	D.W. STEYN	5/87 & 5/67	STH. AFRICA

TOP: Dale Steyn's match-winning heroics at the MCG, recorded forever. Pity his 76 doesn't go up there as well … But JP's 166 certainly does!

CENTRE: Graeme hits the Lord's Honours Board – for the second time!

BOTTOM: Three first-timers for the Lord's Honours Board. Justifiably proud!

TOP: Action during the the Test series at The Oval. The iconic gasholders can be seen in the background.

CENTRE, BOTTOM LEFT AND BOTTOM RIGHT: Proud recipients the Basil d'Oliveira Trophy and the sponsor's trophy.

TOP: Outside the Northern Ireland Parliament Buildings, Stormont.

CENTRE: On tour in Ireland.

LEFT: Royal Portrush Golf Club, County Antrim, Northern Ireland. Clearly, I cannot wait to get started!

TOP: Champagne at the SCG ...

CENTRE: The victorious Test squad at the Sydney Cricket Ground. The only time I wasn't distraught about losing a Test match, the team having won the series.

LEFT: Me and Vinnie with the Test series trophy at the Sydney Cricket Ground.

TOP: When Madiba asked to meet the team so early in my career, I thought I might be peaking a bit too soon! Here we are outside his home in Houghton.

CENTRE LEFT: Graeme and Neil Mac after batting for the entire first day of the second Test in Chittagong. The world record would have to wait until the following morning.

ABOVE RIGHT: The legendary Goolam Rajah, tireless worker. Except when he's tired and having a little nap.

LEFT: The management team celebrate another trophy: me, Shane Jabaar, Adrian le Roux, Vinnie Barnes, Gustav Obermeyer and Goolam Rajah. I'm on the phone – again!

TOP LEFT: To many people, it must just look like a random series of names and numbers, but to me the '438 game' scoreboard, well after sunset, is a work of art.

TOP RIGHT: Vinnie and I visited Middlesbrough FC during the 2008 England tour to experience different management styles. Here we are briefed by manager Gareth Southgate.

CENTRE LEFT: Jeremy Snape passes Jacques a 'forfeit' drink during the fines meeting at Edgbaston after we won the Test series in 2008.

ABOVE RIGHT: Everybody supports a Premiership team, it seems. But I was happy with the shirt I arrived in! (Prince, De Villiers, Smith, Arthur, Ntini, Kallis, Steyn)

LEFT: Makkie with his son, Thando, about to lead the team onto the field at the start of his 100th Test match.

plated that we might get a little nervous ourselves later in the match. But that's what happened, following the most extraordinary Test innings I have ever seen.

When a cricket person looks at the scorecard of a match, it is like reading a book: it tells a story. Often it won't tell the whole story, but certainly you get the gist of what happened. Very, very occasionally, though, you see a scorecard with an entire chapter written in a different language. Despite having witnessed every delivery he faced, I still cannot believe some parts of Virender Sehwag's innings. He scored 319 off 304 deliveries. Some of the 50s came off 25 or 30 balls, and I think his third century came from 84!

Every single thing we tried, he countered. He had an answer for everything. When we changed our tactics, he changed his; he was always one step ahead of us. I was wracking my brains for a solution to the puzzle, but by the time I'd thought of something else to try, he'd scored another 70. I thought we might see the world record. The way he was going, he had the time to score 500! At the close of play on the third day, he was 309 not out. A teatime declaration on day four would have given him plenty of time to reach 500. It seemed completely ridiculous to speculate about such a possibility, but no more ridiculous than what we had already seen.

Overnight I tried to come up with yet another plan. I thought he might be vulnerable to the short-of-a-length delivery early on – not the bouncer, but the back-of-a-length, chest-high delivery. Perhaps it was a complete fluke, but Makhaya caught him early, trapped on the crease early next morning, and he never got onto the front foot again for the rest of his innings, which didn't last much longer before he nicked one. Actually, he didn't get onto the front foot much for the rest of the series. Whether it was a chink in his armour or not, it worked for us. He certainly didn't score any more triple hundreds against us, anyway.

A supposedly dominant first-innings total of 540 suddenly

seemed a bit shaky in the face of India's 627, and we all knew
that two or three early wickets on the final day with a deficit of
87 runs might make life very awkward for the last few hours.
But we responded magnificently, with Hashim adding 81 to his
first-innings century and Neil Mac, to the delight of the changing room, atoning for his first-innings near miss (94) with an
unbeaten and chanceless 155.

It was a batsman's wicket and a batsman's match, which is
why Steyn's performance stuck so firmly in my memory afterwards. He'd bowled five or six spells of eyeballs-out effort for
no reward as Sehwag was running riot, but he never gave up
and never gave less than 100 percent. Towards the end of the
innings, Graeme threw him the ball and asked him to do it all
over again. He responded, as always, without complaint or even
a frown, and his reward was four quick wickets at a cost of very
little to finish the innings with 4–103. A draw was not a bad
return for almost two days' work!

Throughout the five days, the entire management team sat
just behind the boundary rope in a show of solidarity for what
the players were going through in the extreme and relentless
heat. The conditions were, without a doubt, physically dangerous. Naturally we were too sensible to sit in the sun *en masse*,
but we did take it in turns to spend a session out there. It was
brutal. I could not have been wetter if I had walked straight
from a shower after one of my two-hour sessions. The changing
rooms were air-conditioned, though, and the contrast between
inside and outside was extraordinary. It's probably not healthy
moving between such extreme environments, but, to be honest,
nobody gave a damn during those five days. We just wanted to
be as close as possible to the air conditioning.

The second Test, in Ahmedabad on 3–5 April, must rank
among the most perfect ever played by a South African team.
To win inside three days, in India, is almost unprecedented, but
the way we did was extraordinary. There had been so much

media hype around the impending first season of the Indian Premier League (IPL), and it was dominating column inches in most newspapers. There had also been a lot of negative reporting about the fact that many of the Indian superstars had been required to do photo shoots and other PR engagements for their IPL franchises in between the first and second Tests rather than concentrate on preparing for the Ahmedabad fixture. The irony of India being bowled out in exactly 20 overs, before lunch, on the first day, was lost on nobody.

Steyn was unplayable, and both Ntini and Morkel weren't far behind. But the Indians were awful, and all the talk about their minds being elsewhere was obviously true. They were spineless and distracted. That might have been understandable from some of the junior players, but not the seniors, who were already millionaires. It was significant to me that Sachin Tendulkar was missing, due to injury. I don't think some of the batsmen would have played the way they did in his presence. To be bowled out for 76 was pathetic.

It was very important that we built a significant first-innings lead because it was obvious that batting conditions would not improve – not that they were ever bad in the first place. But none of us had any idea just how benign was the surface. Jacques worked hard to reach the iconic landmark of 30 Test centuries, and AB finally proved his ability to dominate for well over a day with his unbeaten 217. Halfway through the second day, there was a completely unseasonal and violent thunderstorm, complete with destructive rains and high winds, which washed out the final three hours. It forced Graeme's hand as far as the declaration was concerned on the third day, but I believe AB could have threatened 300 if he had been able to bat the 'stolen' time.

Facing 494–7, the hosts faced a mountain just to make us bat again. Actually, it was more like a mountain range. Saurav Ganguly made a fighting 87 and MS Dhoni made 52 in reply, but the three quick men – Steyn, Ntini and Morkel – shared an-

other eight wickets, making it 18 out of 20 in the match, to conclude a crushing victory. One of the traditional questions that
is asked of a losing team in such circumstances is: 'What are
the positives you can take from this match?' At the post-match
press conference, Harbhajan Singh replied: 'None. Nothing at
all. Maybe just that we all arrived on time for the start.'

The third and final Test (11–13 April) was in the 'infamous'
city of Kanpur. Every international cricketer who has ever played
a game in Kanpur has had the same experience – and it's not
good. The only accommodation of international standard is the
Landmark Hotel, famous on the international circuit for having
the hardest beds ever made. You would be more comfortable on
a concrete bench. I could never see what made the hotel a landmark, but at least it offered a refuge from the desperate poverty
of the streets and from the local security forces, who were so
intent on keeping us away from innocent fans and autograph
hunters that they created far more problems than they solved.

I was desperately sick before the Test match. In a city like
Kanpur, it's sometimes difficult to know whether illness is
brought on by the wretched pollution in the air – or just by the
thought of it! It made no difference. I was coughing, retching
and heaving for forty-eight hours before the match even began.
Maybe it was something I ate. Actually, maybe it was everything
I ate. Kanpur is the leather capital of India, and the 'rotten egg'
smell of the tanning factories is everywhere. I felt dreadful, and
could not eat anything apart from a few pieces of dry bread for
three or four days. I did everything I possibly could to be positive and constructive, but I felt as sick as most of the dogs on the
streets of Kanpur looked.

The pitch at the Green Park Stadium was terrible. I had never
before seen a wicket so underprepared for the first day of a Test
match. As we were leaving the ground after our final practice
the day before the match, India arrived to start theirs. I had a
quick chat with Gary Kirsten, but was careful not to say too

much about the pitch – he'd seen a good few more than me in his 101 Tests. But my verdict was instantly endorsed: 'Worst first-day pitch I've ever seen,' he said simply. We both laughed. At least it would make for an interesting match.

It was dry and cracked before the match even started, and it would obviously get much worse – and quickly. Whoever managed to earn a first-innings lead would probably win the match; it really was that simple. By days three and four we felt conditions would be nigh on impossible for the batsmen, and by day five ... well, we all hoped to have left Kanpur by then! The only positive thing I can say about the Green Park Stadium (named, presumably, in irony) is that the practice facilities were also completely awful, so they gave you a chance to get used to match conditions.

India were desperate to level the series, and someone had obviously issued an instruction to prepare a pitch that would help their spinners. I'm not sure, though, whether it was supposed to be quite such a lottery. I know Gary and the senior players would have preferred something a little less extreme.

As it turned out, we won what should have been a decisive toss – at that stage India were already 20 percent behind the game, and their gamble seemed to have backfired. By the time we had reached 152–1, India were comfortably odds-on to lose the series 2–0. Neil McKenzie ran down the wicket to try and hit Piyush Chawla over the top after an opening stand of 60, but Graeme and Hashim played as well as possible on such a surface – actually, they were brilliant. In complete desperation, India turned to Yuvraj Singh's left-arm spin. Almost inexplicably, the change of angle momentarily confused Graeme and he popped a catch to short leg off his glove. After that, the innings folded pretty quickly and we finished with 265 – not bad under the circumstances, but we all felt it was 50 or 60 short of what we needed to be confident of controlling the game. Nonetheless, nobody was too disheartened. We could have been bowled out for 150 – any team could have been. It was the kind of wicket that you had to cash in on once you were 'in' because it was extremely hard for the new batsmen to feel settled in any way.

Sourav Ganguly batted brilliantly when India replied. It was incredibly frustrating, because he gave the bowlers a chance with just about every delivery, backing away and exposing his stumps and playing the ball a long way from his body, but he knew exactly what he was doing. His 87 made all the difference, although we were also hurt very badly by one of the most unlikely 10th-wicket stands I've ever seen. India's lead was just 14 runs when Ishant Sharma came out to join Sreesanth at the crease. They added just nine before the close of play on the second day, and we believed that if we could end the partnership early on the third morning the lead would be inconsequential. But somehow they took their stand to 46 and an overall lead of 60, which was worth double that on a decent wicket, even a half-decent wicket. It was very hard not to feel deflated.

During our second innings, Harbhajan Singh was as close to unplayable as any modern spinner has ever been – no wonder he took the new ball! Graeme made a fighting 35, but nobody else had a clue. Ashwell Prince received some criticism for finishing 22 not out from 87 deliveries. Could he have done more to farm the strike and protect the men at the other end? Ideally, yes, but it was all he could do to survive, and I wasn't about to climb into him for doing that.

India needed just 62 to win, and, as predicted from the start, the game ended on the third day. The behaviour of the younger players in the aftermath of victory was absolutely extraordinary, and that's putting it kindly. They ran around screaming, shouting and cheering as though they had just won the World Cup. Perhaps what made me cringe was the shock of seeing a celebration style so different from our own, but I found the practice of spraying each other with Coke and Fanta very hard to understand. But, then again, why should that be so different to our custom of using Champagne?

But it was the lack of grace and humility that I found most galling. It's hard to control your emotions at the moment of triumph and in the immediate aftermath of a Test victory because so much emotional and physical effort goes into it. But four or five minutes later it's important to acknowledge that your vanquished opponents have also expended a lot of effort, and that it takes two teams to produce a contest. It was notable that Sachin, along with other senior players like Rahul Dravid, MS Dhoni and Ganguly, were not involved in the cacophony. But the youngsters simply couldn't calm down, and seemed to work themselves up into an ever-greater state of delirium the more they tried to rub our noses in defeat. I asked as many players as I could to watch the commotion, rather than to avert their eyes, and to remember it the next time we played.

Despite the defeat, I left India in high spirits, convinced that the Test team was on course to create history. I have always been an optimist, but I am a realist too, so I knew I wasn't kidding myself. I was absolutely certain that we had both the skill and the attitude to make history by winning in England and Australia.

Chapter 9

Tour of England

June to September 2008

It was the fulfilment of a dream. Ever since I was a small boy, collecting and avidly reading copies of the *Wisden* magazine and immersing myself in English cricket, I had imagined that one day I would see and experience English cricket for myself. When I played in the garden and in school nets, I would dream and imagine that it was Lord's, the home of cricket. Of course, I was playing for South Africa, not England!

I will never forget the day I walked into the headquarters of cricket as coach of the South African national team. Fortunately it was three or four days before the first Test match, so it didn't matter whether I was overawed or not. Actually, I wanted to be overawed. I wanted every single ounce of cricketing history, respect, culture and ethos to wash over me, and momentarily drown me, while I came to terms with the reality of where I was and what I was doing. I recognised immediately that I needed to get the whole Lord's thing out of my system well before the Test match, and I tried to manage the situation in a similar way for all the other Proteas' 'first-timers', of which there were a few.

We had a couple of months off between the India tour and our departure for England, which gave us time to reflect on our progress as individuals and as a team, but also to reaffirm our collective commitment to becoming the number one team in the world, with all the sacrifices that would entail. There was no room for bullshit. Fortunately, the senior players from the last tour to England, in 2003, were still smarting about losing the final Test at The Oval and being forced to share the series, and they were thirsting for revenge.

As epic as this tour was for me, however, it was still part of the journey towards Australia, where no South African team had ever won a Test series. In no way did that demean the importance or significance of our time in England – far from it. But Graeme and I had spent 18 months planning for 2008, and we had certain yardsticks by which we would measure our success towards the ultimate goal – winning in Australia. It is important to remember that Graeme and I were still hurting after the last tour to Australia. We disguised it well, and never spoke about our obsession to win there, but we had started planning for the next tour on the plane back from Sydney. It had occupied a significant part of our thoughts for three years.

As usual with itineraries to England, we had a couple of warm-up games before the first Test match and plenty of practice days to acclimatise. In years gone by, touring teams used to play seven or eight county games before they started the 'real' stuff, but we felt perfectly happy with two three-day games, against Somerset and Middlesex. On that basis, I decided that our pre-tour camp should have very little to do with cricket or training but a lot to do with all the other forms of preparation that are so crucial to any international sports team.

We convened at the luxury resort of Pezula, near Knysna on the Cape south coast, and spent significant time doing the things we all loved doing, mostly playing golf. But we also ran together

on the Knysna Heads, rode mountain bikes and played all the
fun sports, from table tennis to darts. Most importantly, however, we spoke as a squad about any issues, problems, doubts or
resentments that may have existed among us. It was vital that
we had 'clear air' within the touring party if we were to succeed
in England. It was never a case of forcing people to become 'best
buddies', but it was important that everybody understood the
other person's opinion and that there was mutual respect. You
didn't have to like, or agree with, everything your teammates
said or thought, but it was important that you understood their
points of view. It was, I must admit, very interesting to observe
the ferocity with which certain players attacked others during
the paintball sessions. Afterwards, we subtly manoeuvered ag-
gressor and victim together and encouraged dialogue to prevent
future violence!

We had some fantastic meals together in the evenings, and
enjoyed a few glasses of quality wine, but most of all we really
enjoyed spending time in each other's company and talking in
a way we didn't often get to do – honestly, without fear of re-
crimination or grudges. We spoke about where we wanted to be
and what we wanted to become in the future, both as a team
and as individuals. It was reassuring, even heart-warming, to
hear players, young and old, express their dreams and ambitions
without inhibition. Many of them were to tell me later that the
time spent at Pezula was one of the major reasons we stuck
together so effectively, through thick and thin, in both England
and Australia.

I'll take some credit for having the idea, but I think it's very
important to have experts on hand to facilitate and organise
events like this. Once again, I was grateful to be able to call upon
the services of Francois Hugo. I had also made the decision to
bring former England international Jeremy Snape on board in
a full-time capacity as our performance coach. Basically, he became our sports psychologist, but nobody seemed very keen on

using the term 'sports psychologist'. He was also responsible for bringing in new ideas and best practice from other sporting codes, and would join up with us in England.

One of the more successful tasks initiated by Francois involved a giant noticeboard bearing the names of all the members of the team; under each name, the players were required to write something positive and something which needed improvement. Once again, it was an eye-opener, but the thing that made it so satisfying was the lack of defensive or protective behaviour among the squad. If there was a perceived criticism, even an unexpected or potentially harsh one, then the response was generally positive rather than negative. Players were prepared to look at themselves and make honest assessments once their 'lists' had been written on the noticeboard. Perhaps one or two players may have felt slightly upset, but they didn't show it, preferring to take Francois's advice and look for the positives. Only our physiotherapist, Shane Jabaar, became a bit agitated. Many of the players made similar observations about his demeanour. He did not enjoy the comments and felt the assessments were unfair. Shane was brilliant at his job, but there is so much more to creating a happy team environment than simply doing your job. I was concerned about the situation and knew I would have to keep a close watch on progress. We needed everybody in the squad to be givers and creators, rather than takers, of energy. Shane had perhaps reached that point in his career when he needed new inspiration and a change of direction.

The start of the tour was an especially happy time for me personally because it was during school holidays, and we were able to go over as a family. The fact that our first warm-up match was against Somerset, in Taunton on 29 June – 1 July, made it even more special, because our middle daughter, Kristin, had spent six months as an exchange student at Millfield School, in the nearby town of Street. For her, the trip was something of a homecoming! She spent lots of time with the girl whom she had stayed with, and we were all invited around for supper to meet the family, who were wonderful people. Our youngest daughter, Ashton, later also went on an exchange programme to Millfield, so we knew exactly where she was staying and what she was doing. I loved that first match – but mostly for the evenings during which we were able to spend quality family time together.

We played pretty well against Somerset without doing anything special, but Graeme came in for some uninformed criticism about the scratchy nature of his innings in our second match, against Middlesex at Uxbridge on 4–6 July. Graeme was returning from yet another injury, and needed as much time in the middle as possible, so that is exactly what he did – bat for minutes rather than runs. We were both very happy with his innings. It rained at the end of the Middlesex match, but, overall, I was pleased with our preparation. We were as well set as we could have hoped to be as we travelled to London for the Lord's Test match (10–14 July).

The first day of the build-up was all a bit dreamlike for me, though not in the rabbit-in-the-headlights sense. I was extremely conscious of where I was, what I was doing and exactly what was going on around me. I enjoyed every step I took walking across the nursery ground towards the indoor centre, I stared in wonder at the Honours boards in the dressing rooms, and I loved doing my press conferences in the Lord's Museum. It was all such an honour and privilege, and I was conscious of it every minute.

For the first couple of days of training I encouraged everybody to bring their cameras, their videos and iPods – anything and everything that they might want to record on – and to get it out of their system as much as possible. By the time the first day of the Test arrived, I wanted everybody to be over their Lord's 'awe'. It was a good idea in theory, but any major stadium is a vastly different place when it is full of people, and there is a particular atmosphere at Lord's. Unless you have some experience of the 'buzz' at HQ, especially on the first morning of a Test match, then you are bound to be affected. I don't think it's possible to prepare anybody for such an experience, and it undoubtedly contributed to our apparently lacklustre performance on the first day. The bowlers were anything but lacklustre, of course, but that's the way they appeared – certainly Steyn and Morkel. The hype with which the English media had built them up also didn't help. Honestly, some newspapers made them sound like Malcolm Marshall and Joel Garner instead of two very talented, but very young and inexperienced, fast bowlers with plenty of potential.

There were an incredible number of South Africans at the game. My mother and father had flown over, as had my great friend Mike 'Doc' Doherty from Griquas, Robbie Muzzell ... in fact, so many old friends were there it was difficult to keep up. And the same applied to many of the players, who had parents, siblings and a myriad of old school friends asking for tickets. We used up our allocation (three per squad member) within minutes and the hunt was on for spares! For the majority of the squad, the level of excitement before the Test was unprecedented. With that excitement came a weight of expectation, as well as a desperation to perform. We wanted to live up to everyone's hopes for us as individuals and as a team.

We won the toss and chose to bowl first, a decision based on research and careful thinking, although it didn't look like that when England batted for most of the first two days and put 590 on the board! Kevin Pietersen scored 152, and celebrated with an ostentatious recommitment of his soul to England and all things English, and Ian Bell made a very good 199. Denying him a double century was probably our sole success in two days of hard toil. Just when we thought we might have an outside chance of getting back into the game at 422–6, Stuart Broad made 76 down the order to put us out of the game. By the end of day two, there was only one team that could win. Facing three days of match-saving attrition is one of the hardest situations you can face in the game.

We needed to bat for as close to two days as possible, save the follow-on and then kill the game on the fifth day. That plan didn't work either. Despite a brilliant century from Ashwell Prince, we were bowled out for 247, with Monty Panesar taking four wickets with his left-arm spinners. Now we were really, really under pressure, following on 346 runs behind. Very few people gave us a chance of saving the game.

On the third evening, Graeme and I spoke in very strong terms to AB de Villiers about what it meant to be an international cricketer and what 'taking responsibility' actually meant. He had batted perfectly, and without any difficulty, in reaching 42 before chipping a tame and soft catch to mid-on. Graeme began the conversation by telling AB that he was not doing justice to his talent, and that he certainly wasn't justifying his place in the team. These were very strong words, and I contributed many more of my own. AB didn't take it very well at all, and felt he was being picked on when so many others had also failed. But it needed to be said; he needed to know that stylish 40s were of absolutely no use in Test cricket, and that we knew he had the ability to score big hundreds. And now was the time to start delivering them. In the second Test, at Headingley, when AB made 174, he raised and pointed his bat almost aggressively at the two of us, who happened to be sitting together on the tiny balcony. Point made. Point taken. On both sides. Although Graeme and I felt far more vindicated than he did!

But we still had a mountain of work ahead of us to save the first Test. It was critical that we did not go one-nil down in a four-Test series. We had spoken so often about how important the first result would be in deciding the fate of the series, so we all knew what was at stake. And we hardly needed reminding of how many people had invested significant amounts of time and money to be there and to share the occasion with us. There was a determination in the changing room that was hard to describe. You could feel it. Everybody was very calm; there was no loud noise and no chest-thumping speeches. If we were going down, it was obvious that England were going to have to fight harder than they could imagine.

There was nothing I could do, practically, to help save the match. It was the usual coach's dilemma: you plan, you strat-egise, you organise and you facilitate, but when the job needs doing, you can't do much but sit on the sidelines and encourage. And hope.

At one point during the first three days, I met my dad at the pavilion entrance and took him upstairs to see the chang-ing rooms and the balconies on the top floor where the MCC Members made themselves as comfortable as they would in the own homes. Then we walked downstairs to the Long Room and gazed at the portraits on the walls, just soaking it up. We didn't say much until the end, but it was so obvious how proud he was that he was being shown around by his son, the Proteas' coach. The only stronger emotion in the world at that moment was the gratitude I felt towards him for encouraging me to pursue my dreams from such a young age, for throwing balls to me for thousands of hours and for holding my head up when I felt like dropping it. It was a powerfully emotional time. But although we acknowledged – to a degree – how we felt, the 'typical male' in us kept it simple. I'm not sure how it would have gone down amongst the Members in the Long Room if we'd had a good old back-slapping hug.

When I returned to the dressing room, I felt like I would have gone out to bat without gloves or pads, and kept every ball out with whatever part of my body was necessary, to make sure we moved on to Leeds with the series still level. I'm not sure the players had any idea of how passionate I was feeling, but what-ever determination they shared was more than matched by my own.

I genuinely believed that we could save the Test match, but I must confess I imagined a nail-biting, bitterly tense finish on the final afternoon, with bad light looming and our last couple of wickets hanging on for dear life after an epic two-day struggle. I could hardly have been more wrong. Graeme, Neil and Hashim all scored centuries at the top of the order, and my predicted rearguard action never happened; it wasn't needed. Although things were never entirely relaxed on the balcony, there was never a moment when any of us felt we were in trouble.

We spent some time on the third evening reiterating what we had agreed at Pezula – that it was the top six batsmen's responsibility to score 300 runs between them, and that it was Boucher and the tail's responsibility to find another 100. It was a non-negotiable fundamental that everybody had agreed upon, and now was the time to put it right.

After saving the match, which ended in a draw, my abiding memory is of our own awards ceremony, which involved placing the names of the four centurions on the Honours Board, written in koki pen on masking tape. Cricket is a team game, something which teams have been reminding themselves of for centuries, but no other team game offers more opportunity for individuals to shine and to play for themselves – in the name of the team and its best interests. Neil McKenzie's innings was a classic example of self-denial. He limited himself to perhaps 30 percent of his shot repertoire and batted for nine hours. To the vast majority of those who watched, it was intensely dull, and for England supporters very frustrating and depressing. But it was also an exhibition of supreme concentration and skill, and his reward was to see his name (in official lettering a few weeks later) in the place where future generations will see it for years to come. The same reward, of course, went to Ashwell and Hashim – and, for the second time, to Graeme, following his monumental 259 five years earlier. When we put those four names on the board, to be enshrined in history, I could not have been more proud.

When we left the following morning to drive to Leeds, there were two reasons for us to feel positive – one emotional and one physical. England had been buoyant for three-and-a-half days, perhaps even four, as they looked forward to victory. For a similar period of time, we had been mindful and concerned about the possibility of defeat. It is no wonder, in those circumstances, that one team is much happier than the other with a draw.

Practically, with the first two Test matches being played back-to-back, and a break of just three days in between, we were convinced that the England bowlers would suffer repercussions from bowling 260 overs in very nearly three consecutive days in the field. We all knew how we would feel if the roles were reversed. Three days might seem like sufficient time to recover, but there are always stresses and strains that bowlers carry into matches or pick up along the way, and they usually require a week or ten days to recover. Even if there were no injuries as a result of such a sustained workload, we found it impossible to believe that they would be firing on all cylinders by the time the second Test started at Headingley.

To have played really ordinary cricket for the first two days at Lord's was disappointing, but, at the same time, to have emerged unscathed felt almost like a win. England, on the other hand, had played very good cricket – perhaps even as good as they could get – and had failed to win. We knew we had come nowhere near our potential and were all excited about the prospect of doing so. No wonder we arrived in Leeds full of optimism.

The Headingley Test (18–21 July)

In my time as coach, we played two or three near-perfect Test matches, but this was as close to the perfect '10' as we got. No doubt England were immensely relieved to win the toss and bat first, but we simply overpowered them with Dale and Morné both taking four wickets as we bowled them out for just 203.

There was a headline-grabbing moment, for the English any-way, when Andrew Strauss edged a ball to AB at slip. He dived forward, felt the impact of the ball on one hand, turned his head away as he completed the dive, and emerged after a bit of jug-gling with the ball in his hands. He never claimed the catch – he was genuinely uncertain about what had happened and wheth-er the ball had bounced off his arms or chest when he lost con-trol of it. We watched the incident immediately in the changing room and could see very clearly that it had bounced. AB had raised the ball as a question – he was shouting 'I'm not sure, can we have a look at it?' On television, it looked unmistakably as though he was claiming the catch. The umpires later confirmed that he wasn't, but by then the tabloids had done their work and AB was well and truly labelled as the villain.

At lunchtime, England captain Michael Vaughan walked into the communal dining room and snarled at me: 'Coach, is this really how you want to play the game?' He then tore into AB and called him all sorts of names, 'cheat' being one of the kinder. I must say that Michael was a man who enjoyed the complete respect of our entire team. He was a gentleman, an ambassador and a bloody good bloke. So while it may have been inappropri-ate and mildly embarrassing for him to make such a scene in the shared forum of the players' dining room, it was easily and quickly forgiven. But we could see that he was under intense pressure, both as captain and batsman, and that this outburst was symptomatic of the fact that the whole England team were feeling the heat. There is a time and a place for a captain to stand up for his team – physically and verbally, if necessary – but this was just a mad rant. It probably didn't help their mood that one member of the XI, Darren Pattinson, was a British-born Australian whom half the England players had barely met before.

Things deteriorated even further for Michael towards the end of the day; Hashim drove a ball to mid-on, where Michael dived forward to take what he obviously thought was a clean, low catch. Watching on TV, we were all certain the ball had bounced. I ran to the players' viewing area and frantically gestured for Hashim to stand his ground, while Graeme, who was in the changing room below me, raced out to the edge of the boundary to make sure Hashim didn't get anywhere near crossing the rope. The decision duly went to the third umpire, and although nobody could claim the evidence was conclusive it did not look good for Michael. Hashim was given the benefit of the doubt, and finished the day 18 not out in a total of 101–3 in reply to England's 203.

I am, and always have been, a very strong believer in self-regulation and 'natural justice' in the game of cricket. I've seen evidence of it so often that it just has to be true! Anybody who takes the game for granted, or tries to take advantage of it, will get their comeuppance at some point – often sooner rather than later. I felt Michael Vaughan was out of order at lunchtime, but just four hours later the boot was on the other foot. I can only imagine how close to boiling point he was. I made a careful point of not going up to him and asking whether claiming catches on the bounce was '... the way he wanted to play the game'. However, I did make a comment to the media, during the press conference after the day's play, to the effect that 'Mother Cricket' has a way of reminding players that she is the boss, and of making sure they remember that. Michael was obviously miffed when he read the papers the following morning, and we had a discussion to clear the air.

One of the funny things about the cricket world is the frequency with which you bump into people you are trying to avoid, or who are trying to avoid you! If you are on tour together, you will invariably walk into a lift with that person in the team hotel. If you are at a function, you will inevitably end up in a corner of the room with that person. So when I walked out to the middle to have a look at the wicket on the second morning, it was almost preordained that Michael's timing would be identical to mine. Typical of the man, he didn't allow the time to become awkward and spoke immediately, asking whether we could have a chat. He thought that certain things should remain 'private' and that I was wrong to have said what I did. I agreed with him that 'certain things' should, indeed, remain private, but that it was my duty to defend my players when they came under attack and that his behaviour was unacceptable. But I took his point. Graeme joined the conversation towards the end, and also had some strong words to say. Michael responded firmly, too, but by the end of it I was certain that we all understood each other – genuinely – and that the matter had been laid to rest.

All of this was unfolding against the background of a very confused and unhappy England camp. Graeme and I had seen it extremely clearly on the first morning, and had spoken about the possibility of a 'meltdown' among the hosts. The selection debacle around Pattinson would have been hilarious if it wasn't so ridiculous. If things had been different within the England squad, then I'm sure Graeme and I would have taken a far more lenient line, but we weren't about to make life any easier for Michael or his misfiring management and selection team.

I always watched the opposition very closely during preparation and warm-up on the morning of a Test match. I reckon I was pretty good at interpreting body language and gestures – they weren't too different from our own, after all. It was clear and obvious to me on the first morning that Vaughan and coach Peter Moores were having major 'issues'. I could see from Moores' actions that he was being 'firm' and refusing to swallow some pride and adopt a conciliatory or compromising approach. As head coach, you are in charge, but on the morning of a Test match your captain has a lot on his mind and is under pressure – sometimes you have to say 'yes, skipper, of course you're right.' And then talk about it later in the day. Moores and

Vaughan appeared to have locked horns. And I'm afraid to say, as uncharitable as it sounds, I was delighted.

You always hear the opposition line-up well before the toss, very often the day before. However hard some teams try to keep it a secret, it's impossible. But even though we had heard a long time earlier that Paul Collingwood might be left out, it was still a massive surprise to see it confirmed. It was an amazing decision. When things got tough for England, it was Collingwood who fought hardest. He never gave an inch, and never asked for one. When England omitted him, they handed us a significant advantage. Every player can fail on any given day, but when England said 'we don't need our gutsiest player', we smiled with delight. He may have been scratching for runs at that point, but he was an integral character, and every successful team needs their characters. Perhaps they felt that Andrew Flintoff's presence would be good enough – but he was barely fit and obviously out of form.

Collingwood walked past me in the players' tunnel, having finished his warm-up, and I said: 'Hard luck, sorry you're missing out.' He replied with something along the lines of: 'You give your guts to the team for this long and this is how you get treated ...' At that point I knew we had an enormous psychological advantage and it was just about whether we could capitalise.

Having bowled them out cheaply on the first day, we needed to throw a mountain of runs at them, and to really impose ourselves. It wasn't just the Test at stake; it was the series. The most obvious feature of the partnership between AB and Ashwell was the discipline they showed – ruthless, faultless and uncompromising discipline. Every single ball that needed to be left, they left. Every ball that needed to be defended, they defended. And every ball that could be scored off, they did so without mistake. It's hard to describe the effect that such discipline has on the opposition. Bowlers need to be given a 'teaser' every now and then to keep them interested. It's actually easier to bowl at Virender Sehwag while he scores 300 than to bowl at Jacques Kallis – or Prince and De Villiers in the mood they were in during that stand.

The lead of 319 was too much for England to recover from. It was always going to be too much, despite the coach's tendency to ask (with uncommon regularity) 'what if?' We looked like winning by an innings and plenty, which would have been nice, but even Flintoff's late flurry, and 67 from Stuart Broad at number nine, couldn't change anything. We needed nine runs to win, and did so by ten wickets. It was profoundly rewarding.

I was prepared to do some 'shepherding' that evening, some guiding of the players. I fully expected them to celebrate with gusto in the changing room and then to have a couple more drinks back at the hotel. After escaping from Lord's with a draw and coming to Headingley for an exhilarating and overwhelming victory, the need to let off steam was compelling and understandable. I wanted to celebrate, too, but I was keen, if possible, to 'manage' the situation.

My concern was completely unnecessary. Nobody showed the slightest tendency to over-celebrate. Graeme and I felt strongly that each and every win should be properly commemorated, that the team should spend some quality time together and that those who enjoy a beer should feel free to have three or four, but on this occasion I wanted everyone to remember that this was just the beginning. We had talked for so long and prepared at such length to win the series, not just a Test match. Clearly that was exactly the mood of the players. The traditional post-game music was quieter than usual, and, while the smiles were all there, there was no shouting and cheering. There was a feeling of deep satisfaction about the way the team had performed, but also a strong sense of a job half done.

The next fixture, on 25–27 July, was almost from a parallel universe. I don't suppose many teams have toured England over the years and found themselves playing Bangladesh 'A' in the middle of a Test series, but there we were – in Worcester. But I wasn't negative about the fixture in any way; it was an opportunity for all our reserves to play and for some of the stalwarts – like Ashwell, who had scored back-to-back centuries – to have a well-deserved rest. I expected it to be a 'soft' fixture, and I was happy about that. The last thing we needed was another white-knuckle game against opponents determined to fight for every inch.

Our only concern before the game was the fitness of Dale Steyn, who was nursing a badly bruised finger, having fielded a hard return drive from Jimmy Anderson on the final day at Headingley. At least, we thought and hoped it was just bruised.

The pitch at New Road, Worcester, was flat, and the sun was beating down. The Bangladeshi bowlers were unthreatening, to say the least, and we scored a mountain of runs, with Robin Peterson and JP Duminy relieving some of their frustration at not playing on tour so far with quick hundreds. Never mind the quality of the bowling, they actually both batted beautifully. We bowled the Bangladeshis out cheaply, but then found it much harder to dislodge them a second time, and the game drifted off to a tame draw.

Sadly, I will remember the game for what happened on the second day, and it was off the field rather than on it. Dale had gone with Shane Jabaar to a local clinic for an x-ray on his finger. When they returned, Shane requested a meeting with me, Graeme and Dale. It would have included our new team manager, Dr Mohammed Moosajee, but it was a Friday and he was at mosque. I instinctively wished he had been available for the meeting. I had a sense of foreboding, and could have done with Doc's level head. He had met all of my expectations since becoming team manager – surpassed them, in fact – and there was hardly a day on tour when I didn't give myself a little pat on the back for having the courage of my convictions and pushing for his appointment in place of Logan Naidoo.

Shane explained that the x-ray revealed a break in a finger on Dale's left hand, which ruled him out of the third Test at Edgbaston. Just like that. No discussion, no debate and no opinion sought. Shane had never got a fact wrong in all the time I'd known him; in fact, I'm not sure he ever got an opinion wrong either. But at that moment he was talking to the captain and the coach, who were as desperate as each other to put the strongest team on the field to try and win the series, and he was sounding more like a member of the opposition than one of our team! We had so many questions, the most obvious of which concerned the fact that the broken finger was on his left hand. We didn't care if he couldn't bat, and we were happy for him to stand down at fine leg with a splint on his finger. We were prepared to do anything. And so was Dale, by the way. But Shane simply blanked us. The disappointment and anger was hard to swallow.

Graeme finally asked whether there were any other options or possibilities, and Shane said 'no'. I then asked whether we could postpone the meeting and resume when Doc was back from mosque. Shane exploded with rage and accused Graeme and me of not trusting him as a physiotherapist. This couldn't have been further from the truth, but at that point he appeared to lack care or compassion, either for the team cause or for individuals. He had been becoming steadily grumpier for a while, but when I was made aware that players had started feeling very uncomfortable about going to him for treatment, the dynamic changed completely. Whereas his demeanour had never affected his performance in the past, it seemed that it was now. Every time Graeme and I asked a question, completely innocent questions, it seemed that Jabs would take it personally. We just wanted our best players on the field; we were no different to any other captain and coach in that regard. Anyway, Steyn had his finger put in a cast and was out of the last two Test matches.

Edgbaston Test (30 July – 2 August)

I had played several seasons of league cricket in Birmingham, so it was a delight for me to return and catch up with old mates I hadn't seen for years. I had become familiar with the Edgbaston ground, its staff and facilities, and the changing rooms felt like a home from home to me.

It was bad enough losing Dale before the game, but it seemed, right up until the morning of the match, that we would have to do without our captain as well as bowling spearhead. Graeme's back was in a terrible state, and he was unable to bat in any of our practice or net sessions. Shane worked round the clock to try and get him better, but by the evening before the match the prognosis was still gloomy, and we officially put JP on stand-by. I refused to even consider ruling Graeme out of contention until the last minute. He would have a fitness test the following morning. It was an uncomfortable and nervous night for many of us.

Graeme still looked pretty glum at breakfast, and was walking like an old man. At the ground, Shane helped him through a series of harsh stretching exercises, and he managed – just – to complete a rudimentary net session lasting about fifteen minutes. And now we had to decide whether he had 'passed' his fitness test. Shane was dead honest; he gave us his opinion and then said he needed to be removed from the decision-making process. He said he thought Graeme had 'a chance' of getting through the Test match, and that he would do everything he could to keep him on the field, to keep him mobile and to limit the possibility of aggravating the injury. Very clearly, Shane's medical training indicated that Graeme was not fit to play. Equally clear to Shane was that his opinion, at that moment, was not one we wanted to hear. He said that Graeme and I would have to make the decision, and that he would do his best to back us up.

Tough as nails as always, Graeme took the decision to play,

despite being in considerable pain and discomfort. The irony, of course, is that he would never have taken such a decision had he not completely trusted Shane's ability as a physiotherapist.

We bowled first, and did a very good job in keeping England to a total of 231. André Nel did a fine job stepping into Steyn's place, although his antics in reacting and playing up to the infamous Edgbaston crowd were a gamble we could have done without. He may have thought he was in control, and that a bit of by-play with the spectators helped him raise his game, but he was not as in control of the situation as he thought he was, and it was a distraction that some of his teammates didn't appreciate. But the important thing was, he was there. It was exactly the kind of scenario that I had wanted to plan for when I insisted that he come to Bangladesh. I wanted a squad in which everybody knew their place, and knew who was next in line. When Steyn went down, Nella was ready to step in. No doubts, no insecurities – just a straight swap.

We should have done a lot better than 314 in our reply, and might well have done had it not been for the infamous 'sight-screen-gate' scandal, which cost us two wickets. When Andrew Flintoff was bowling from the pavilion end, his hand, at the point of delivery, appeared to extend just above the sightscreen into a much darker area, making it impossible for the batsmen to see some deliveries until it was too late. Before play on the third morning, I went to speak to umpire Aleem Dar, who listened with the utmost courtesy and agreed that there was a problem. He also pointed out, however, that any of my suggested solutions would have to be agreed to by England. My cool relationship with Michael Vaughan made that unlikely, although, to be fair to him and England, only a single delivery – from Morné Morkel to Ian Bell – had been 'lost' by an England batsman during their entire first innings. Flintoff had bowled dozens of 'invisible' deliveries to us. As it turned out, Michael did not agree to my proposal to extend the sightscreen a little higher – and I wouldn't have done so either if the roles had been reversed!

We had England in all sorts of trouble in the second innings. At 104–4 they led by just 21. Then Collingwood joined Pietersen and the game began to change, slowly at first but very surely. Pietersen was in his pomp, while Colly was scratching around in a desperate attempt to save his career. Our bowlers were weary, and when their partnership reached 115 there was a sense that the game might have been slipping away from us. Victory might have looked like a formality two hours earlier, but now, with Pietersen on 94 and Collingwood having dug himself in as surely as a soldier in a trench, we were struggling.

We had spoken about Pietersen's ego and how to play on it, if and when the opportunity presented itself. Mostly we decided to ignore the strutting peacock, but just occasionally we thought we might tempt him. Sure enough, the prospect of one crisp hit bringing him a century was too much to resist. He hit Paul Harris straight to long-on. Another hour of Pietersen at the crease could have buried us. The game was there for him to control. Two or three balls later, 'Harry' got one to fizz out of the rough and Flintoff was gone, caught at short leg. It wasn't just the turning point of the Test match; it was the turning point of the series. England's two most dangerous players were gone within five minutes.

Harry had come in for a lot of unnecessary and unfair criticism during the series. Geoffrey Boycott had started it with some puerile commentary. I guess he had to live up to his reputation as being controversial, but the cricketer in him could surely see the value of the job that Harris was doing for the team. He kept things tight in the first innings, applied pressure and allowed us to rotate our seamers. In the second innings, with a bit more assistance from a deteriorating pitch, he was a wicket taker as well.

Having looked like chasing 100, our target was revised to

around 200. But that didn't take into account the tenacity of Collingwood, who had now really found his feet and gone on to make a career-saving century and eke out another 140 runs from the tail. When we finally took the last wicket, we needed 281 to win the match and series. Having looked like being over before the end of the fourth day, the match now seemed destined to extend well into the fifth.

We had a decent opening partnership of 65, which settled the nerves before Neil Mac was LBW to another ball from Flintoff which he never saw. Hashim went quickly, LBW to Monty Panesar, and when Jacques was 'done' by another ball from Flintoff which he never saw, he was distraught. I'd never him so upset before. It was hard to believe we could win. Our chances were slim at 93–4. I have an emotional brick wall when it comes to thinking negatively, so at times like that I develop an impenetrable membrane of optimism and keep talking positively. But deep down, in my subconscious, I do hear the little voice saying: 'we're in shit here, Mick.'

We took tea at 111–4. I will never forget, for as long as I live, the way Graeme was when he came in and sat down. He was calm to the point of serenity. He was completely at peace, unfazed by anyone and anything. Nothing could invade the space around him. He spoke calmly and quietly drank his energy drink. He said a couple of basic things to the backup team, and then said to me, very calmly: 'Coach, you have to get someone to stay with me. If someone can stay with me then we will win this game. I will make sure of that.' He said it with such conviction, but with such calm control, that I honestly, honestly believed him. It was almost trancelike.

When they walked out to bat after tea, Graeme quietly implored AB just to stay with him for a significant period of time. Through sheer bloody-minded determination, they added 78 to stop the rot and give us hope once again. Then AB nicked Panesar to slip, and we still needed 110 to win as Boucher stood up. The game was in the balance for everyone who was watching, and everyone who was playing, for that matter – except for Boucher. His attitude throughout the run chase had been defiant and determined to the point of insanity. He had been on two previous tours to England and failed to win, and he hated that. He and Kallis had sworn several months earlier that they could never be happy with their careers without a Test series win in England. When he walked out to bat, he gave the impression that it would take the military to stop him.

And they did win it. They won it in magnificent style. Graeme's unbeaten 154 will always rank as the greatest Test innings I have seen. The circumstances, the pressure, the prize at stake – and the fact that Panesar was turning the ball square from the rough outside his off stump – were almost overwhelming. Physically, emotionally and psychologically – as captain of your country, too – it was a performance that even Graeme found hard to explain.

At the start of Graeme's partnership with AB, I moved to the gym that overlooked the ground and decided to work off some emotional energy on an exercise bike. Cricket superstition dictates that nobody moves from where they are when the game is going well, and so my intended twenty-minute session turned into an hour and a half. I was not allowed to stop pedalling. I felt like I'd done the Tour de France when AB was finally out. Similarly, having made the mistake of sitting rather uncomfortably on the arm of a chair when Bouch and Graeme started their partnership, I wasn't allowed to move. With 10 runs to go, when I finally stood up to applaud I was violently hauled down again by Morné Morkel. It was a small price to pay for the unbridled joy that swamped us all when Graeme hit the winning boundary. I had never experienced such happiness in cricket before, and wondered whether I would ever experience it again.

The team poured onto the field to embrace Graeme as he walked off. Despite the difficulty of controlling your emotions at a moment like that, I was proud that our celebrations weren't too over the top or embarrassing. Everyone managed to shake hands with an England player and thank them for the game before dancing and collapsing in an emotional heap of joy. As soon as I could, I phoned Yvette to share the moment with her and the girls. I just wanted to say that all her years as a 'cricket widow' had been worth it, just for this moment. My only regret was that none of my family, immediate or extended, was there to share the moment with me. Dad had been with me at Lord's but not at Headingley or Edgbaston.

Shortly afterwards, I had a wonderful phone call from Gerald Majola, who had been such a pillar of support throughout my tenure. Graeme had a quick word with him, too, and we both said with complete conviction that we dedicated the Test and series win to him.

During our celebrations in the changing room we had a traditional fines meeting which everybody always enjoys. At one point Graeme came forward and presented me with his man-of-the-match medal. He said he wanted me to have it for everything I had done in the build-up to the game. I was shocked, and thought he was joking, but he insisted that I should have it. It remains among the most treasured items of my cricketing memorabilia.

It was close to midnight when the bus took us on the short ride from the ground to the hotel, but there was just time for a spontaneous and impromptu rendition of the national anthem, sung with full force and at full volume. I'm sure it sounded appalling, but to me, at that moment, it sounded like a bus full of Pavarottis.

Some of the guys went for a nightcap at the hotel bar, and some of the braver, younger ones hit the town to carry on celebrating. But I was physically and emotionally spent and headed straight for my room, where I lay on the bed and contemplated what a day it had been for all of us and for South African cricket: the first team to win in England since 1965 and the first in the post-unity era. I thought about the doubts I'd had before taking the job, and in the first few months as coach. Could I be successful? Was I really up to it? I thought about all the selection issues, the unpleasant clashes with Norman Arendse, the names I had been called and the things I had been accused of. And all of them faded away to nothing when I remembered that we had just won the series, a Test series, against England. With a game to spare. I slept magnificently that night, at least until the hotel fire alarm went off at 6.00 am. Nobody could be certain whether it was a genuine accident or a particularly unpleasant form of revenge from a disenchanted England fan. Some of the players looked terrible, having had very little sleep. Two or three, who shall remain nameless, felt so bad they just pulled their pillows over their heads and went back to sleep.

A little later on, after a long shower and a good breakfast, I started answering my phone and many, many requests from the media. Some of them tipped me off that Michael Vaughan was about to resign, but I did not believe them. I hoped it wasn't true. But it was. I felt incredibly sad as I watched him tearfully bow out of a position he had filled with great dignity and such success. I knew I had contributed to his demise, and had put the boot in when he was on the way down, but I'm sure he knew that was purely professional – not personal. The humility he showed in the immediate aftermath of Edgbaston was quite extraordinary, and the speech he made there had a lasting effect on me. He commanded the respect of the cricket-playing world, and he deserved to retire as captain holding a trophy, or a little urn, not at a hastily organised press conference. Graeme and I both sent him messages to wish him well and to say what a fine job we thought he had done for England and world cricket.

Kevin Pietersen took over as England captain, which surprised me but made sense given the lack of candidates. In fact, given that selection chairman Geoff Miller wanted one captain for all three formats, KP was the only option. He would undoubtedly have a different philosophy to Michael – 'street bling' taking over from 'city style'. It was a heck of a gamble England were taking. I was fascinated to see whether they could pull it off, whether enough of the key players, both on and off the field, would be able to put their own thoughts on hold and do things the 'KP way'.

But I failed as a coach in the days after the Edgbaston Test. I took my foot off the accelerator, and was never able to get the tour going again. I had never discussed the possibility of winning the series and achieving a lifetime's ambition with a Test match still to play, let alone had a plan for what to do if it happened. The players were clutching at anything, real or imagined, to get fired up for the last Test, at The Oval (7–11 August), but nothing was sticking. On reflection, I know I should have pushed the boys harder physically, and I take a lot of responsibility for the lacklustre display during that match. Our preparation was not what it should have been. I may have had limited experience of how to prepare players mentally for that situation, but that was no excuse to compromise on our physical training.

There was plenty of discussion around whether to play the 'reserves' and get some fresh legs involved. Monde Zondeki, Robin Peterson and JP Duminy could have played, or at least two out of the three. The fact that they didn't would come back to bite me later in my dealings with the board. When they wanted evidence that I was not giving sufficient opportunity to players of colour, they would cite the Oval Test as an example. With the perfect vision of hindsight, I wish we had made changes to the team, but mostly because our performance was flat and we were well beaten. But to imply that the decision to keep the team unchanged was made randomly or arbitrarily, or had any-thing to do with racial bias, is grossly irresponsible.

There were many things going through my mind. Our next se-rious Test assignment, with respect to Bangladesh, was against Australia, and I thought it would be a good idea to keep our victorious Test XI together. Besides, nobody in the Edgbaston XI was putting their hand up and volunteering to be 'rested'. I also didn't particularly relish the idea of being accused of 'insulting' England by playing a 'second XI' in the final Test. I can still imagine the headlines if we had done that. And finally, as much as all three would have loved to have played in that Test, and were in the squad on merit, the prospect of telling them that the team was being changed on the basis of colour was unpleasant for a number of reasons – chiefly because of the risk that they would feel like political pawns, as Langeveldt had in Bangladesh. Still, they should have played. It was my mistake.

Not having my family with me to share the series victory was disappointing, but at least I had my very best friend with me for the final Test. Wayne Schonegevel made a huge commitment to be there for all five days, and, as someone I had bounced ideas off and shared my innermost thoughts with all my adult life, it turned out that I needed him. The emotional after-effects of Edgbaston, so quickly followed by the defeat at The Oval, took some talking through. Wayne provided the shoulder to cry on – metaphorically, anyway – and constant reminders about what the team (and the coach) had achieved, and what we were still going to achieve.

Sadly, the Oval Test served as a precursor for what was to come in the ODI series, which was pretty much a disaster from start to finish. We started with no momentum, and never managed to gather any. Flintoff was back to his best, and everybody seemed to fire around him. Graeme finally lost the battle with his elbow injury, and returned home after the second game, in which we were bowled out, humiliatingly, for 80-odd at Trent Bridge on 26 August. It was a day-night game, or was supposed to be, but it finished before they could turn the lights on. It was awful.

Although we played extremely average cricket, a good deal of the blame must lie with our strategic planning, which left many of our one-day specialists – Herschelle Gibbs, Albie Morkel and

Vernon Philander – arriving in England from the middle of the South African winter, having played no cricket of any consequence for months. I was part of the strategic planning group and, once again, I accept responsibility for our lack of preparation. Things might not have been quite so bad had we been able to play all of our warm-up games, but the English weather took care of those. It seemed to rain non-stop for ten days (which would have been a very long time even in good weather) between the Test series and the one-day series. Spirits had flagged significantly even before the first one-dayer, at Headingley on 22 August.

There was a highly significant day for me, personally, before the third one-dayer, which was played at The Oval on 29 August. I met with Gerald Majola in London to sign a three-year extension to my contract, which had been in discussion for some time. We were both very satisfied with the terms agreed, and I felt able to refocus on the years ahead without worrying what might happen should the tour to Australia, in four months' time, not go according to plan.

By this stage of my career, it was fair to say that I was nervous about the CSA board and found it extremely difficult to second-guess what they might be thinking and how they might react in a political context to purely cricketing decisions. We had left an out-of-sorts Makhaya Ntini out of the one-day team, and I knew there would be repercussions and ramifications in the future. It was made clear to me that some members of the executive would never be sympathetic to such a decision, and would never forgive me. I was told to mind my back because retribution would never be far away.

After the ODI series wound up, we had two or three weeks to recover and relax before preparations began for the arrival of Bangladesh in South Africa. This would be our last chance to fine-tune things before we left for Australia. However, that time was anything but relaxing for me.

Chapter 10

Triumph down under

October 2008 to January 2009

Much of the talk before the Bangladesh series (5–28 November) was about how weak their team was, and how inadequate they would be as preparation for the tour of Australia which was to follow straight afterwards. This was missing the point; there wasn't a hell of a lot we could do about who our opposition were. We needed to make the best of every opportunity to rectify our horrible one-day series in England and to get the Test team into the best possible frame of mind for Australia. We needed positive thinking, not pointless carping about something we could not control.

For the second time in the space of a year, we were using a series against the minnows from Bangladesh as a training camp, and once again I saw no reason to deny or apologise for that. Prior to the Bangladesh series, though, there was a two-match ODI series against Kenya (31 October and 2 November). These matches presented chances to get our combinations right in 50-over cricket and to be thorough and clinical in the two Test matches.

Once again, Makhaya didn't make the one-day side but remained an integral part of the Test line-up. Hashim Amla made a huge impression with a brilliant century in Benoni during the second ODI against Bangladesh (9 November). We won all three ODIs, as expected, and both Test matches. With respect to Bangladesh, they gave us plenty to think about at various points in the Tests, and although they never threatened to win either, we were grateful for the competitive spirit with which they played.

My only significant worry was the form of Morné Morkel, who was all over the place in the Test matches, bowling no-balls and wides and being smashed for five or six an over while the other bowlers were, largely, making merry. Morné's biggest problem, ironically, was that so many people cared about him and felt empowered to give him advice. And being such a well-brought-up and well-mannered human being, he felt duty-bound to listen to everybody – not only those who were qualified to comment, but to every Tom, Dick and Harry as well. He was completely confused. It's hard enough to bowl a cricket ball in a straight line at 140km/h while nothing is going through your head, but it becomes impossible when you are thinking about three or four different things and trying to fix another two or three aspects of your technique all at the same time.

Graeme and I decided to back him 100 percent and not to add any extra pressure or worries about his place in the team or whether we still believed in him. We gave him nothing but positive affirmation and encouraged him to relax, believe in himself and remember what got him selected to the national squad in the first place. Vinnie Barnes was excellent with him, gently helping Morné to find answers for himself rather than seek them from other people. We both believed that he could, and would, play a crucial role in Australia – but not if he had doubts in his mind. I was thrilled (and felt thoroughly vindicated) when he came right in Australia.

The issue of Makhaya's absence from the one-day team had started to become nasty. Ever since I had known Makkie he was always at the forefront of protests against picking teams with a racial bias. 'The best team must play,' he used to say. 'You can't pick people because of the colour of their skin, it's as simple as that.' It was always reassuring to hear such statements from him – an icon of South African cricket who was prepared to take the rough with the smooth and never expected any preferential treatment. The trouble is, when he was saying those things he was a fixture in every team. Sadly, when he finally lost form, and was left out on form (or lack of it), he was quick to change his tune. That was when I lost a bit of respect for Makhaya, and saw a side of him I never suspected existed. Everybody, especially senior players, is upset when they are dropped, but I was desperately disappointed when Makhaya started telling influential administrators that Graeme and I didn't want black players in the team. I refused to believe what I was told, and dismissed it as vicious rumour-mongering.

But after the Bangladesh series I was 'invited' to a breakfast meeting with Doc Nyoka, Ray Mali ... and Makhaya, in East London. Makhaya was obviously upset about his continued absence from the one-day team. Doc and Ray made it clear that there had been political ramifications at government level and that they were under pressure. With no black African in the squad, the game's administrators were being made to feel extremely awkward. They were being told that cricket was letting the country down.

I could understand that Doc Nyoka and Ray felt that they had been placed in a difficult position, and I could sympathise with them. It was a tricky balancing act, with me trying to win games and them trying to appease politicians. It had been, and continued to be, frustrating for both sides. But when Doc apologised to Makhaya for being left out of the team, with all the inference that it had been unfair, unjust and ill-considered,

I was stunned. Ultimately it amounted to a concession that Makhaya might have had a point about racial prejudice in selection. I was flabbergasted, and I felt my anger rise. I had loved Makhaya in all the years we had known each other, and had only followed the principles that he had always advocated. At the time, I thought how ashamed Makkie would be in the years to come when he reflected on the way he had behaved.

Doc Nyoka then gave Makhaya an assurance that the situation would be rectified before the next series, which was Australia. The controversial presidential right of selection veto had been dissolved with the departure of Norman as CSA president a couple of months earlier, but here was his successor guaranteeing a place in the next squad for a player who was struggling for form and had been left out by an appointed panel of selectors. Never mind how undermined and belittled I felt – what about the constitution of CSA and the application of its procedures? So that was it. Makhaya would be selected for the one-day squad for Australia, no matter what the coach or the selectors felt was appropriate.

This was all preceded by Herschelle Gibbs' 'meltdown' the night before the Twenty20 match against Bangladesh (5 November). I had flown home that afternoon to be with my family. One of our daughters was undergoing a minor operation; although it was nothing serious, I never made any secret of my dedication to my wife and daughters and would take any opportunity, when possible, to repay their faith and love. Vinnie took the practice session that afternoon while I headed back to East London.

That evening Herschelle had attached himself to the hotel bar a little earlier than was polite – certainly for an international sportsman. He took way too much fuel on board, at indecent haste by all accounts, and became involved in a series of embarrassing altercations. The hotel management had attempted, unsuccessfully, to encourage Herschelle to leave, and resorted to calling Graeme and Vinnie for assistance. The captain and assistant coach finally got the job done, not without a few threats, and finally the embarrassment came to an end. The details aren't relevant here, but, for the tabloid-minded, Hersch was, apparently, making inappropriate comments about the attire and attractiveness of the wives accompanying a group of businessmen attending a function in Sandton. It may sound humorous, but it was in fact offensive and embarrassing.

When I returned the following morning, Graeme and Vinnie briefed me in full. I felt deeply disappointed; like the parent of an errant teenager, I had waited patiently in the belief that the 'good' side of Hersch would pull through. But this was too much. Something had broken, and we all knew it. We just didn't know how it would affect his career. There wasn't much we could do about it right then and there, so we let him play the T20 game but resolved to tackle the situation immediately afterwards. A real resolve this time: no more half-measures, no more soft touches just because he was 'lovable Hersch'.

After the game, in which he scored 18 off 10 balls batting first, Doc Moosajee and I took him into the gym under the Wanderers changing room and told him that his time was up. There were no more warnings, fines or reprimands left for him. Doc explained that he needed to undergo a full rehabilitation course – not a token 'tea and biscuits' session, but a full alcohol addiction programme. This meant he would play no cricket for five or six weeks. Naturally, it was a massive shock to his system. But it didn't sink in until Doc announced the decision to the world at a press conference later the next day. It was an extremely hard thing to do, but the relief we felt told us it was the right thing. I knew that if Hersch stuck to the course and made progress, he could be available for the ODI series in Australia in January 2009. I really wanted him there. Some people make the mistake of thinking we were throwing him out after a decade of service to the nation, but the opposite was true. We were trying to save him from himself, and to prolong his career.

If he bucked the system and failed to conform, we would not select him again. That was made crystal clear. Clearer than it had ever been made to him before. Very early in my coaching career, I learned that you coach individuals; you coach people, and not just cricketers. With the help of Doc Moosajee that day, I was finally coaching Herschelle Gibbs. The person.

He was angry and resentful about being discharged from the squad and sent home, but he had very little to argue against. He returned to Cape Town and spent two or three days incommunicado. But finally, in consultation with his agent Donné Commins and others close to him, he made the decision to book himself into a programme. I felt incredibly proud of him. Nobody knew whether it would be successful or not, but at least he had made a positive commitment to address a very serious problem that was threatening to end his career prematurely. He could point fingers at other people, paint himself as a victim and deny the reality, or he could face his own situation and come back a better person, a better cricketer and a much better team asset. Only those who have been through a similar situation can appreciate the courage and honesty it requires to do what Hersch did. It was little short of heroic. On the other hand, there were many people whom he had let down in his career who would have said 'it's about time.'

So the build-up to the Australia tour was anything but the quiet, calm and determined period we had hoped for. At least the commotion and controversy was off the field rather than on it. As far as the game between bat and ball was concerned, I was very happy and very confident that the near miss of three years ago could be reversed.

Tour of Australia (11 December 2008 – 30 January 2009)
We flew into Perth ten days before the first Test match. A long and well-planned build-up had worked successfully three years earlier, so it made sense to repeat it. Perth is an attractive city, and the winding Swan River is a real tension-soother. There are thousands of South Africans living in the city, so the hospitality is special; we get as many invitations to braais as the Indian team get to curry nights in Durban. It's practically the only city in Australia where we are not heckled and abused during a net session.

The ten-day schedule leading up to the Test was very carefully organised and planned – even our time for freedom of expression and spontaneity was well organised! We had a strong emphasis on skills training and conditioning, working on particular shots that would be required in certain conditions and against specific bowlers, while the seamers practised getting the ball to swing, particularly in unhelpful conditions. And given that we had dropped a total of 12 catches in the last series in Australia, we did a lot of catching practice.

Former England coach Duncan Fletcher was with the squad during the entire build-up period, specifically to work with the batsmen – and chiefly with Jacques Kallis. I was always willing to involve anybody who could make a positive contribution to the squad or to an individual. It sounds almost heretical to say it about such a brilliant player, but Jacques was going through a bit of a difficult patch. I knew we would need him to be at his very best for us to have a chance against Australia. Jacques had worked with Duncan since he was a teenager, and Duncan had coached him at Western Province. It made sense to get them back together again.

But apart from getting Jacques back to prime form and confidence, I asked Duncan to work his magic with the tailenders. Throughout his coaching career, Fletch had shown a Midas touch with batsmen of 'limited' ability. Rather than identify a host of problems and then try to correct them, Duncan would pick on something – even if it was just one thing – which a tailender could do well, and then work on it until the player had complete confidence in that shot. With an improved and tighter defence, at least he knew he could score in one area. From there, he could work outwards and expand the shot repertoire. We had a long tail, and I knew we needed plenty of improvement in that area if we were to meet our target of 100 runs from the last four batsmen. You need only glance at the scorecard from the second Test in Melbourne to see how Fletcher's work paid off in that department, and how crucial it was to the result of the series.

Performance coach Jeremy Snape also played an important role during this preparation period. I asked him to spend time in one-on-one sessions with all of the players to discuss exactly what they needed to do to beat Australia. I wanted them to dissect and analyse their own games and be honest about how they reacted in certain situations – and how they wanted to react. Apart from individual sessions, we had group workshops in which honesty and constructive criticism were highly encouraged.

At the start of one of these sessions we were all required to write down our greatest fears or concerns about performing in the series ahead. We then placed these pieces of paper on the floor and, through a process of team discussion and analysis, removed the least serious and easiest to deal with until we were left with the five greatest concerns. Through team discussion we were then able to reach a consensus on the four most important and relevant qualities we needed, as a group, to tackle our concerns. These were: honesty with ourselves and with each other; pride in our team and our country; total focus on the immediate task at hand and not thinking too far ahead; and refusal to be overawed by the Australian media or public – an ability to filter out distractions like the inevitable crowd hostility that we would encounter.

The Perth Test (17–21 December)

The level of expectation and excitement before the first Test surpassed anything I had experienced before. One of the reasons, I
suspected, was because many Australians actually believed that
their team could lose. That had not been the case for a decade
or more, but now their team had changed and lost many of its
superstars. We had arrived with very few superstars but a collective purpose and determination that some people had picked
up. We made no bold statements and gave the tabloid press very
little to work with. But instead of being wary and cautious of
the media, we were friendly and open. We were honest. South
Africa had never won a Test series in Australia. We were hon-
oured to be given another chance, but although we were confident history was against us.

I had never lost a game at Perth, and I was acutely aware of
that. I had an incredibly strong and powerful sense of home
and belonging. Saying that as I do now, from the comfort of
my office in Perth, as coach of Western Australia, it may seem
'convenient', but it is nonetheless absolutely true.

We were as well prepared for that Test match as any other
we had ever played – better, in fact. As we wrapped up the
final net session, Ashwell said he would like to face 'just
a few more deliveries'. It was a great sign: one of our most
important players wanting to put the final, finishing touches to
his preparation. Makhaya then said that he would like to bowl
'just a few more balls'. What could be better? Two of our key
players having a final five minutes together. The very last ball,
literally, that Makhaya bowled to Ashwell reared off a length
and smashed into his hand. It instantly looked very bad. As a
coach you instinctively know when something is serious, and I
feared the worst. X-rays confirmed the break a couple of hours
later. It was a massive blow, literally and figuratively.

For all our 'game breakers' – Smith, De Villiers and even
Kallis on occasion – Prince had become the rock around which

we built partnerships. For a dozen Test matches, he had been the foundation on which we built our recovery if we ever lost two or three wickets cheaply. And now he was gone. Most teams in that situation would have had good reason to panic, but we had steadfastly stuck to our methodical system of selection, and there was no doubting the succession system. JP Duminy had toured the world with us for a year and a half, patiently waiting for his chance, and now it had come. He was ready. He had been systematically prepared to be ready for fifteen or so Test matches, so this was not a breath-catching moment for him. He was ready.

Two days earlier, I had chatted to him about how he was feeling, physically and emotionally. It can be very hard being a reserve for such a long time. Jeremy Snape had worked very hard and specifically with JP, making sure that he was ready to take his chance whenever it presented itself. Snapey said that he had no premonition, but he specifically worked on preparing JP for this Test match. When I spoke to JP two days before the game, he said: 'Coach, I think I'm going to make my debut here. I dreamt it.' We both had a chuckle about that. He had been waiting a long time for his chance. I said: 'Maybe not this time, JP, but it's not far away. It'll happen when you least expect it!' The main point was that, while the Australians and many neutral observers may have felt that losing Ashwell on the eve of the game was a catastrophic blow, we were all confident that JP would slot in with the minimum of fuss. It was an example of how our planning was successful and why continuity was so important. There was plenty of emotion when Graeme presented JP with his first cap on the outfield moments before the Test started. Everyone was sorry to lose Ash but extremely pleased for JP, who had waited so long, and so patiently.

Some basic homework and planning on the Australian top order paid immediate dividends. I would never, ever claim to have 'worked out' Matthew Hayden, Ricky Ponting and Michael

Hussey – three of the all-time greats – but all I can say, with all sincerity, is that our plans worked. We thought we might have seen a vulnerable area early in their innings, and they were all dismissed in the manner that we had discussed. It was probably coincidence, but it felt great.

Simon Katich and Michael Clarke then added 150 to bring us back down to earth, but Paul Harris earned his worth in exactly the way we had hoped, and believed he could, by bowling tightly and with great discipline, frustrating the batsmen and eventually persuading both Clarke and Andrew Symonds to hole out at long-on. Symonds was another player, like Kevin Pietersen, who we termed an 'ego player', one who could be susceptible to a bit of provocation at the right time. Nobody was better at that than Harry. Because he was so easy for batsmen to underrate, they often thought they could take a liberty against him as revenge for something he had said – he was very clever at goading batsmen into playing inappropriate shots.

One of the most significant differences between this tour and the previous one was the way the team reacted to the abuse and hostility of the crowd. Three years earlier, we had reacted angrily, as South Africans often do, and we were always resolving to 'take them on' and 'give it back to them'. This time, the players just laughed and compared notes on what had been said to them. It was like water off a duck's back. Even the really personal stuff didn't affect them. The team was in a good place, having matured emotionally and psychologically.

Australia's 375 was a good score but not an insurmountable one. It was a fabulous batting pitch, and at 234–3 halfway through the second day we were both comfortable and confident of earning a first-innings lead. Then disaster struck. Or rather Mitchell Johnson struck. In an astonishing spell of fast bowling, he took five wickets in as many overs at a cost of just two runs. One of those dismissals was especially harsh: JP caught behind off his helmet. He was desperate about his failure, but very significantly blamed himself and not the umpire. Accepting responsibility for your score, whatever the circumstances, is a sign of maturity. By the close of play we were 243–8. We were shell-shocked. We were devastated. The silence in the changing room was deafening. We honestly believed that we had earned the first-day honours, albeit marginally, and by three-quarters of the way through the second day we believed we were on top. Then, very suddenly, we were 132 runs behind with only two wickets left.

Most of the time my optimism comes naturally; it requires no thought or 'planning'. This time, however, the dramatic nature of our collapse and the shock it left behind required some careful thought. Several hours later, we had a chat. The first requirement was for Bouch and the tail to make another 20 to 30 runs. Then we had to bowl as well as we ever had done before. The pitch was superb for batting, and I had been told by a number of local experts that it would remain so for the rest of the match. We had to believe that a target of 300, even 330, would be possible on the fourth and fifth days.

Graeme's team talk was superb. He reinforced all of the positives in our play, our approach and attitude during the last fifteen months. He encouraged everyone to remember what they had achieved as individuals and what our team goals were. It was a very bad day, an awful day, but did we want to let all of the hard work of the last year and a half go to waste? We had to dig deep, deeper than many of us had done before.

Boucher helped the last two wickets to add 40, and once again we bowled superbly to reduce Australia to 162–7, a lead of 'just' 258. We were very, very much back in the game. Then Brad Haddin belted a superb, counter-attacking 94, and before we knew it our target had gone significantly past the 370 which I thought was at the upper limit of our capability. The target, eventually, was 414, which made it the second highest fourth-innings run-chase in history – if we got there. Even so, I couldn't help believing that it was a possibility. The pitch was still perfect, and nobody believed in our batsmen as much as I did, not even themselves.

When Graeme Smith plays well, South Africa play well – and mostly win. His century at the top of the order was a brilliant innings for so many reasons. He had never done himself justice against Australia, and the local media were relentless in reminding him of that fact. Although he averaged 50 in his career, he averaged only 22.5 against the Aussies. We were never far away from an article – newspaper, magazine or online – suggesting that our captain was brutal against the minnows but seriously lacking against the big boys.

Kallis, too, showed big-match temperament at the end of the fourth day. It always gives me goose bumps when I remember it. It had been a long, long day, which didn't finish until 8.00 pm. The bowlers were exhausted and desperate to get off the field. But instead of closing up shop and waiting for the next morning, Jacques decided to make a move – a massive, game-changing move. With well over 200 runs still required and the game feeling very much in the balance, he ripped into off-spinner Jason Krejza and Peter Siddle and scored 27 from the last three overs of the day. It was an extremely unusual finish to any day's cricket, let alone one in that situation, and coming from a player who was regarded as conservative. Suddenly, within fifteen minutes, the game had shifted from 'finely balanced' to South Africa, needing 'just' 170 more with seven wickets in hand, being favourites.

What struck me about the following morning was the calmness with which everybody set about preparing for the day's play. Perhaps everybody just took their cue from Jacques, who prepares for a day's Test cricket as though he's in a cathedral library. He's completely unflustered – at least, that's the impression he gives. It was a very different attitude to what I'd seen in many other high-profile, high-pressure situations. Graeme was extremely relaxed and quick to remind everyone that, sometimes, these things can be taken out of your hands by a bad decision here or moment of bad luck there. He reminded everyone that the only way of guaranteeing ourselves the best chance of making history was to be relaxed and play as 'normally' as possible.

Jakes was out with the total on 303, with 111 (a 'Nelson'!) still required. JP had a couple of overs to survive before lunch. Both teams knew how critical that short period of play might be. When he returned to the changing room, six not out with the total on 322–4, I looked for him to ask how he was feeling. I couldn't find him anywhere. Eventually Doc Moosajee located him in the toilets, vomiting away the tension. It had been a very, very tough little session. But he'd survived it. Nobody needed to tell him anything. Nobody was more aware than him of the magnitude of what was at stake.

The way that he and AB and went about winning us the Test match in the penultimate session will always rank among my favourite memories of any match, any time, anywhere. They had played with and against each other for years, right from early schoolboy days. They were happy and comfortable in each other's company – they trusted each other. AB was the senior partner, but there was nothing 'senior' or 'junior' about the way they batted or treated each other. As far as AB was concerned, it was business as usual, just as it had been for the last seven or eight years. As far as JP was concerned, it was the chance he had been dreaming of for all that time, and waiting for over the last eighteen months.

I sat with Paul Harris and Dale Steyn right at the back of the changing room, almost in the showers, with none of us able to watch. Every time there was a cheer, or a groan, one of us would run to see the replay on the television. Jacques's girlfriend, Chamone, had given him a small teddy bear as a good luck mascot, and he sat with it on his lap from the moment he was dismissed. As usual, ordained by centuries of cricket superstition, nobody moved from their positions while the going was good.

But with 20 runs to go, somebody broke ranks and walked outside to sit on the balcony, and the rest of us followed quickly. When JP stroked the winning runs through the covers to move from 47 to an unbeaten 50, with AB already boasting a century, it was hard not to feel that God had a soft spot for cricket! It's tempting to say that our joy was uncontained and our celebrations had no boundaries, because that's how we all felt, but both statements would be untrue. Both batsmen shook the hands of the opposition, and the umpires, before allowing themselves to hug each other, and the rest of the players took their time and made the effort to behave with a bit of dignity and humility as they poured onto the field.

Even in the privacy and sanctity of the changing room, where cricketers can notoriously celebrate, commiserate and throw their bats without fear of recourse, there was an amazing air of maturity. Wives, girlfriends and families joined us in what is generally a male preserve. I sat with Yvette and our girls, Brooke, Kristin and Ashton, and shared a bottle of wine. (Obviously the girls were on Cokes!)

But before everyone joined us there was a team 'moment', during which we shared the experience and what it meant to all of us. Reflecting on it two years later, I swear there was a quantum shift in attitude and belief on that day. We had all talked a good game; I was very good at saying the right things, and players invariably responded with the 'right' words. But here, now, this time, we had really done it. And I thought, very clearly at that moment, that our victory would change South African cricket for decades – forever, in fact. I hope that proves true. I still believe it will. Now future generations will always be able to look back and say: 'Well, they did it in Perth in 2008 – why can't we?'

Having said that, it was incredible that the senior players –

Graeme, Bouch, Makhaya and especially Jacques – were all saying that the job wasn't done yet. It's fair to say that, for all of them, winning a series in Australia had become an obsession, sometimes an unhealthy obsession, but they had the presence of mind to remember what they had come to Australia to do, and that they hadn't done it yet. We had just chased 414 to win a Test match, the second highest run-chase ever, but there was still more work to do. That was the way they saw it.

After an hour or so of the most 'grown-up' celebrations I've ever experienced – particularly to commemorate such a defining victory – it was time to let our hair down for the next hour with the traditional 'fines meeting'. The girls all went back to the hotel and held their own fines meeting, which amused us all no end.

I have often wondered what it is about the fines meeting which is so integral to the routines of teams around the world. At its crudest and most base level, it is (or was) about downing beers and getting a bit drunk. But while there are plenty of players who happily tolerate that aspect of it, the South African team had a couple of non-drinkers (Hashim Amla being the most obvious example) and several more who enjoyed a couple of beers but no more. So drinking wasn't the focus.

A fines 'committee' oversees the process, but fines are issued by any player against another player or member of management. Fines are often an expression of appreciation or are designed to draw attention to something beneficial, amusing or mildly irritating that a player has done which may have been missed by the majority of the rest of the squad. Somebody could be fined for 'compromising his time by being too concerned about the wellbeing of every other player'. In other words, it's a backhanded way of saying 'thank you' but 'take care of yourself, too!' They are very, very popular meetings – especially when you have just won.

When we arrived back at the hotel it was obvious that the

girls had enjoyed a few glasses of wine and their own version of
the fines meeting. But everybody was still in good enough shape
to go out for dinner and continue the celebrations. Yvette and I
went to an excellent restaurant; as we looked at each other over
the candlelight, she told me how much it meant to her to share
in a moment like this, how she appreciated how much work and
dedication I had put into my career, and now the national job,
and how proud she was of me. I struggled to reciprocate for fear
of bursting into tears and sobbing. The sacrifices I had made
were nothing compared to hers. At that moment I felt I owed
everything to her. All the years of sleepless nights, crying kids,
broken locks and green swimming pools. All that I had missed.

The Boxing Day Test

As we had experienced three years earlier, there are few sporting events quite like the Boxing Day Test at the Melbourne
Cricket Ground. Unsurprisingly, we were in a buoyant mood
after Perth, but the prospect of playing a match to win a series
in one of the planet's greatest cricketing amphitheatres left us
all buzzing with adrenaline. To have our partners and families
there made it even better.

It was an interesting period for the team management. Most
of the time you are faced with the challenge of raising your
team's demeanour and lifting their belief after a defeat or
allowing them time to 'come down' after a victory, but this time
our efforts were concentrated on 'maintaining' the team spirit
and keeping things on an even keel. There was no need to try
and 'lift' the players. Most of them were chasing the greatest
prize in their careers. Kallis had gone on record as saying that
a Test series win in Australia meant more to him, and was a
far greater achievement, than winning the World Cup. And I
agreed with him. And there was no point in trying to 'lower'
them. You couldn't ration the adrenaline flowing through their

bodies. So the task of management was about trying to help them 'manage' themselves and make sure they didn't waste too much emotional energy.

A couple of days before the Test started, Mark Boucher came to me for a chat. We were in the middle of all the hype of Christmas, and the local media were running amok about Australia's inadequacies and our perceived strengths. Bouch's reading of the game is remarkable; his aptitude for tactics and emotions, during play and between it, is second to none. His acuity, prized by his captain and teammates, is often underrated by administrators, who have no idea of the contribution he makes to winning games outside of the catches, stumpings and runs. I will never forget the hostility I had to face from board members regarding his selection, and how often I had to fight for his place: one of the greatest wicketkeeper batsmen of all time, and I was forever defending him. Every time the team performed poorly, it was Boucher they wanted to axe. He did himself no favours, of course, being cantankerous, argumentative and bullish, and by his refusal to make polite conversation with the men in suits who could ultimately decide his career.

Anyway, this time he came to me and said: 'Coach, the Aussies are going to bomb the shit out of our tailenders. They have seen a weakness and they are going to expose it like an open wound. We have to work on it – hard.'

He was right, of course. He had been at the other end trying to make things happen in Perth; nobody had got a closer look at how the tail was coping. And nobody had heard more clearly what the Aussie quicks were saying. So I agreed immediately – and put him in charge of making the last two days an absolute hell of bouncers and short balls for the men who came behind him in the batting order. And so he did.

For hour after hour he took Steyn, Morkel, Ntini and especially Harris into the indoor nets as soon as they had finished their bowling stints, and he bombed them mercilessly.

The last thing we wanted was for them to be blown away again, and we wanted to know that we had done everything possible to prepare them. Duncan Fletcher had done a magnificent job with the groundwork, but the period of his consultancy contract meant he was no longer with us. Bouch took on a critical role and carried on with the work. The other players looked at what was happening and wondered whether Bouch was taking his new job a bit too seriously. Some of the batsmen even thanked their lucky stars that they weren't being subjected to this barrage. As always, Bouch may have taken things a bit further than necessary, but he was driven by a belief that it was essential.

It's easy to turn the bowling machine up to 150km/h and feed balls into it, but he did more than that. One of the best exercises was to serve tennis balls at the tailenders for them to practise their evasion techniques. At least we didn't run the risk of putting them out of the Test match with a serious injury! I left him to it – but kept a very close eye on proceedings, too. Bouch was always on the edge of potential disaster when he was sufficiently 'driven'. He is the kind of person who needs to know, from experience rather than from a textbook, where the 'breaking point' is! Fortunately, everybody was still healthy enough to enjoy an excellent Christmas lunch.

We do things a little differently on tour at Christmas time; at home, we would have dinner on Christmas Eve and then spend Christmas morning with our families before an afternoon practice. Overseas, we would have a big traditional Christmas lunch with all the families together after training in the morning – the more wives and children, the merrier. The religious aspect of the festival was always underplayed and left to the individuals. For us it was more about celebrating our togetherness as a team, and that was never better illustrated by the fact that Goolam Rajah, one of several squad members who didn't even celebrate Christmas, was instrumental in organising a fantastic occasion, right down to having a Santa Claus arrive to present everybody with a gift – with extra ones for the kids.

Lunch was followed by a quick team meeting, and then the rest of the day belonged to the players and their families. Our hotel, the Hyatt, was located close to the MCG and right among all the festivities on the Yarra River. It was tempting to forget, just for a moment or two, that we had the biggest Test match of our lives the next day. One of the perks of being coach – or captain, I might add – is the tradition of being given a suite, rather than a standard room, at most hotels. I'm not sure Graeme always needed his, but, with a wife and three teenage daughters, mine was especially useful in Melbourne! One of my favourite memories is of sitting in the executive club on the top floor, enjoying the panoramic views of the city at sunset and sharing a glass of wine with Yvette. We were there for business, serious business, but one of the foundations of my coaching style has always been to appreciate the surroundings and to remember how fortunate and privileged I was to be doing this job.

The atmosphere on Boxing Day morning was everything I remembered from three years earlier: seventy or eighty thousand people making their way towards the stadium from trains, trams, taxis and mostly, it seemed, on foot. Painted faces and waving flags for those who would populate the terraces, but also a higher than average percentage of jackets and ties for those lucky enough to be invited to one of the many corporate and executive suites. Not unlike Lord's in that regard – just twice the size.

Ricky Ponting was dropped at second slip by Neil McKenzie and went on to make a brilliant century. I regularly thought back to Kallis's dropped catch three years earlier, and wondered whether we would be haunted by something similar this time around. But we bowled superbly and never gave up, never let them escape. At 280–6 by the close of play, I thought both teams had enjoyed a good day. There was nothing in it. Even when

Michael Clarke and a resilient tail took the score to 394 shortly before lunch on day two, I was pretty confident that we could earn a first-innings lead. By the close of play, though, I could hardly have been more wrong. Or thought I was. It was 198–7 and we had only just avoided the follow-on! JP was 34 not out and Harris had survived to be unbeaten on eight.

I left the team pretty much alone at the end of the day. There was little to be gained by holding a team meeting or dwelling on how far we had let the match slip. I knew it was better for everyone to have a good meal and a decent night's sleep. We could address the situation the following morning. Everybody knew we were in terrible trouble, and nobody needed me to point that out. Graeme said a few words to a couple of individuals, but circumstances like that often call for personal reflection.

The following morning I was crystal clear about our plan. I always had a blackboard in the changing room on which I wrote quotes, facts, figures and targets – anything that needed to be reinforced and used as a potent reminder or motivation. I learnt very quickly in my career that the sound of the same voice too often causes players to 'switch off'. And there is rarely, if ever, a good time to catch all of the squad in a 'switched-on' mode. So I would write things down and allow the players to peruse the day's targets on a regular basis as the day unfolded.

The first goal was to bat for 30 overs. This placed a great responsibility on JP in his second Test, but Harry, Dale and Makhaya also knew what was required of them. It was a big ask, a very big ask, but it was desperately needed. There is an old-fashioned school of thought that bowlers should not be held responsible for scoring runs if the batsmen have failed to do so, but that has changed as the game has become more and more professional. Besides, I wasn't necessarily asking the tailenders to score runs; I was asking them to bat for 30 overs. If they did, I reckoned we'd have 90 runs and therefore be trailing by around 100, hopefully a few less.

The final parts of the plan were to bowl magnificently, dismiss them for around 250 and then chase down 350 for victory. That was probably too many. Conditions were different in Melbourne than in Perth, and the pitch had started to deteriorate. We had chased 414 two weeks earlier on a pitch that was as good on day five as it was on day one. This time it had started to deteriorate, and everybody knew that my 'plan' was a long shot – a very, very long shot. But better to have a plan than none at all. For some reason, I was passionate about the need to bat for 30 overs. I had a slightly bizarre fixation that batting for a session might have such a negative and deflating effect on the Aussies that something unusual, anything, might happen. They were in such a dominant position in the Test match that I thought they might, perhaps, be subconsciously inclined towards 'cruise' mode. Perhaps we could make that backfire. Perhaps ...

JP was calm. Everything depended on him. In retrospect, I placed an unacceptable amount of pressure on his young shoulders, yet he looked as though he was preparing for a net session. With all the specialist batsmen, and Boucher, all dismissed, perhaps he felt the task was beyond the team. Or that he had nothing to lose. Either way, he was very composed.

I still laugh loud and long when I remember what the signs around the changing room were telling him. Jacques, who loves spending as much time as possible in shorts and T-shirt, prepared for the day by dressing in whites and taping up his toes in preparation for bowling. Even worse, Bouch taped his fingers and prepared himself as though he would be 'keeping in 20 minutes' time! Fortunately, JP was too absorbed by what faced him to notice.

So we took our various positions in the changing room, some of us down below in the underground section watching on TV, the braver ones upstairs in the viewing gallery. And we sat. And we sat, and we sat. And we sat. As Harry and JP hit the 20-over mark, we actually began to believe that we might make our 30-

over target. But then Harry was out for 39. He'd added another 53 on the morning. If Dale could just hang in there for another 10 overs, a few more, we could still make the 90 or 100 runs we'd set ourselves.

We sat for almost the rest of the day as Dale made an heroic, career-best 76 and JP went on to score one of the finest centuries in South Africa's Test history. The only time I left the underground changing room was when JP reached 98 or 99 and we all charged up the 70 steps to get to the viewing area. It was at that moment, as I reached the top, that I vowed to return to my playing weight and get my fitness back. (And I'm glad to say that I subsequently did!) It is always a moment for huge celebration when a player reaches a century, but this was euphoria we had not experienced before. A century in your second Test match was cause enough to celebrate, but the match circumstances made it unique. I am proud, rather than embarrassed, to say that several of us had tears in our eyes when JP ran the ball to third man to reach 100. We had absolutely no idea of how much more there was still to come, but at that point we were thrilled beyond belief.

That day remains one of the hardest in my career to describe, because everything after lunch was uncharted territory, like exploring the moon. My target of batting 30 overs had been achieved by lunchtime, with the loss of just one wicket, and that was just about possible to accept. But after lunch it was all brand new. JP and Dale batted the entire session between lunch and tea, adding 95 to take us into the lead. If Peter Pan and Tinkerbell had made a guest appearance, none of us would have been surprised. There was an element of fortune in that Brett Lee was injured and couldn't bowl during that time, but that should not detract from the determination and application of JP or Dale. Nonetheless, when they walked into the changing room at tea time and finally realised what they had done, they both burst out laughing. It was a spontaneous recognition of the bizarre nature of what they had achieved. I think they were in a mild state of shock.

Against the greatest odds I have ever witnessed, we had earned a first-innings lead of 65 runs. We felt like millionaires. We could not have felt more confident if we'd had a lead of 265.

Dale was incredible in the second innings. He bowled with his usual pace and hostility, but also with a magnificent sense of 'nous'. He looked like an educated, thinking bowler to go with everything else. Morné Morkel, too, bowled with such control it was hard to believe he had been so wild and erratic just three weeks earlier. He bowled some of the quickest spells of his career in that innings.

Ricky Ponting made 99, to go with the 101 in the first innings, but fell to a moment of inspired genius from Graeme, who put himself in at short cover a couple of balls earlier and then took the catch. Mitchell Johnson delayed us with a fighting knock of 43, but the fourth innings target was 'just' 183 and we were extremely confident of getting there provided the new ball didn't do any serious damage among the top order. A good start was vital, and was duly delivered by Graeme and Neil Mac, who all but won the game with an opening stand of 121. The captain's aggressive 75 from just 94 balls was typical of the man when faced with a match-winning situation: ruthless and decisive. An hour after lunch on the final day, Hashim clipped the winning runs away to finish 30 not out with Mac on a patient 59. Hardly a moment had gone by over the last twelve months when I hadn't thought about the battles I'd had with selection – particularly with Neil. Every run he scored, every game he helped us win, was just that little bit more rewarding.

We hadn't just won; we'd won by nine wickets. It was a thrashing. After two days of the Test most people would have agreed that there was a thrashing on the cards, but not this way around.

The first South African team to win a series in Australia.

Ever. In over a century of trying. I'll forever be proud of the way we managed to maintain our decorum in the immediate moments of triumph and live up to our motto of being 'humble in victory', despite the enormity of the achievement. But this time – as soon as the duties and formalities were over, there was a general acceptance that it was time to celebrate. Euphoria and an organised pandemonium broke out.

But just as we had behaved in England, so we behaved in Australia, and it was noted. Some of my most prized and cherished newspaper articles are those highlighting the grace with which we accepted victory. We were not, I am the first to admit, a team of cherubs. It was hard, and sometimes very harsh, in the heat of battle, and our players said and did things which nudged the boundaries of decency – as did the opposition – but when the game was over there was no excuse for anything but decency, respect and humility. The absolute minimum I expected from every player was to interact on a personal, social level with at least one member of the opposition.

There had been some less than complimentary talk about the Australian team's behaviour in the aftermath of their victory against India the preceding summer, and there was more negative media speculation about their demeanour. Steve Waugh's 'Unloveables' were mentioned as predecessors to Ricky Ponting's team. But I was struck by their graciousness in defeat and by their willingness – even desire, in some cases – to share some time with our team and even to join in the festivities for a short time.

Initially, however, it was very much a family affair, just as it had been in Perth, with wives and girlfriends joining us in the changing room for a few glasses of wine and cold beers. They had all had a pretty good time in Perth, it seemed, so they were only too happy to leave us alone again after about an hour and return to the hotel to carry on with their own party. Left to our own devices, we partied long and hard into the night, just as we

had done at Edgbaston, this time to celebrate an even greater
Test series triumph. It's not often in a game that has been
played for over 130 years that you get the chance to achieve,
and celebrate, something unique. And we weren't about to let
the occasion slip by.

The messages of congratulation poured in thick and fast for
all of us, and our message boxes were soon full. It took days for
many of us to return all the calls and SMS messages we received.
I called Gerald Majola very soon after the match to share the
moment with him; as far as Graeme and I were concerned,
the victory was as much his as it was the team's, given how
much support he had given us, often under pressure, during the
preceding two or three years. I told him that I hoped this result
made it all worthwhile.

Because the match had finished at lunchtime, it felt as
though it was late at night after our fines meeting, but in fact
it was only about 6.30 pm when most of the boys weaved
their way out to the middle of the MCG, formed a huddle
and sang our team song at lung-bursting capacity. Some of
the boundary fielders ran to corners of the ground where they
had received abuse during the match and yelled all the things
they had felt like saying at the time but weren't able to! It
was hilarious.

The ground was virtually deserted. There were a few security
guards around who didn't seem to appreciate or share in our joy.
They did, however, seem to enjoy telling a couple of the boys to
put their cigars out because the MCG was a non-smoking venue.
That was even more hilarious. A 100 000-seater stadium, empty,
but no puffing of a celebratory cigar allowed! Fair enough.

There was one room in the enormous venue that was still
full, a rather important room to which none of us had given any
thought: the press box. It would have been easy and, for the
tabloids, very tempting to write disparaging things about the
team's behaviour. Having behaved like gentlemen in the public

spotlight, were we now showing our true colours? Fortunately, not a single reporter took that line, and by all accounts we put a few smiles on their faces as they battled away to meet their deadlines.

The bus ride back to the hotel was awash with emotions, which varied from player to player – depending on how many times they had played Australia and tasted defeat! On the one extreme you had JP: played two, won two, 50 not out and 166. Easy game. On the other extreme you had Kallis and Boucher, who had been battling the Aussies for over a decade and carried the mental scar tissue to prove it. At one point Jacques's floodgates opened and he started crying, completely unashamedly. That set Boucher off, and before you knew it they were both crying like babies! The reality was only just beginning to sink in. All those years of hoping, desperately wanting to win. And all the disappointment. And now a victory – the greatest victory. It was a strong mixture of emotion, adrenaline, Victoria Bitter and Champagne!

Following the victory in Perth, I had made the team a promise that if we won in Melbourne then I would swim in Sydney Harbour on New Year's Eve. As was the case three years earlier, a boat had been arranged to take the squad out into the harbour to watch the fireworks. Before the show began I duly changed into my pink board shorts and dived into the water. A promise is a promise, and I wanted to make certain that everybody knew that my word was good.

New Year's Day was spent resting and recovering – a couple of the guys had a few throw-downs, but that was all. We did have a team meeting in the evening, however, at which we discussed the importance of our approach to the rest of the series. Everyone still remembered the disappointment of the way the England tour finished once we'd won the Test series, and there was a serious determination to prevent that from happening again. We still had the third Test to play, followed by the five-match one-day series. We weren't just determined to finish strongly in Australia; there was an added feeling that we were also playing to atone for the feeble way we finished in England.

Chapter 11

Reaching number one

January 2009

New Year in Sydney is a special experience. The party on New Year's Eve involves a million people! It was very special, something the first-timers would never forget. But it was just as special for those who were experiencing their fourth fireworks display and party.

I was guilty, sometimes, of *hoping* the mood was right before a game rather than believing it. Sometimes you have to try and convince yourself in order to convince the players that everything will be OK on the day. It was like that before the Oval Test in August 2008. I said the right things to the media, and then again to the players, and they said the right things back. This time, however, I *knew* we were in the right frame of mind. An extra day's preparation had been scheduled before the start of the Sydney Test (2–7 January), and the party mood was well and truly over by the time we started work.

Although we had won all of our Test series for a couple of years, the only previous experience we had of playing a 'dead' Test at the end of a series was in England, and we cocked it up.

This time there was energy and passion. The talk among the players about the possibility of winning the series three-nil was almost (but not quite) as exciting as it had been about winning the series.

There was a surprising amount of interest in the match, considering the series had already been decided. We attracted a great deal of interest from the media, who had become obsessed with what made this team different to the others which had arrived before with such high hopes, and failed. They even appeared to quite like us! Graeme's performances and leadership had been written about a lot, and, given his record against Australia before this tour (averaging 22.5, with one 50 in eight Tests and none in his previous seven), it was unsurprising that he was attracting so much attention.

Australia batted first, and batted very well. Michael Clarke scored an excellent century and, although there were several chances for us to get back into the game, Mitchell Johnson and Nathan Hauritz scored 60 and 40 at numbers eight and nine to take Australia to a total of 445. It was always going to be difficult from there, on a pitch which notoriously dried and cracked quickly as the match progressed.

We fought hard to make 327 in reply, Bouch typifying our spirit with a gutsy 89, but it was a big deficit. The big story of the innings, of course, was Graeme's broken finger, sustained against Johnson early in our first innings reply. It was a bad break, necessitating a flight to Melbourne to see a top specialist midway through the Test match. Not only was he definitely out for the rest of the match, but he would be returning home immediately afterwards to start the healing process and would miss the one-day series.

With all chance of victory gone after three days, it was a case of fighting to preserve our two-nil series win rather than losing the Test.

We began the final day on 62–1 with Neil Mac and Hashim

Amla at the crease. Despite a pitch which looked like crazy paving, and prospects for survival which were rated by locals as somewhere between slim and non-existent, we were confident of giving Ricky Ponting's bowlers a damn good run for their money. To be honest, I think we believed we could do anything after the first two Test matches. But at 110–4 after 40 overs, with approximately another 75 to survive, our optimism was waning quickly. Graeme was a dejected figure. Apart from the broken hand, his tennis elbow condition meant he was in constant pain, and now he was facing the prospect of finishing the tour on a double downer. We limped into tea at 198–7, but with Harris and Steyn at the crease we didn't expect to survive for long afterwards.

But as history will forever record, the resilience and guts displayed by the tailenders led to one of the most dramatic finishes in Test history.

When Harry and Dale had batted for about half an hour, but there were still somewhere between 25 and 30 overs to go, with Makhaya still in reserve, Graeme began to think about 'it' for the first time. He was sitting outside the changing room in his shorts and vest, and there was Makkie alongside him, staring intently out to the middle and tapping his spikes. Graeme recalls that he felt like he was letting his team down. If Harris and Steyn could fight so hard, and even Makhaya was so intense and focused in the face of what still seemed like impossible odds, at least he could think about batting. What if it came down to the last over?

It wasn't just the fighting spirit in the middle and the sight of Makhaya that influenced him; it was also the gathering storm clouds and the prospect of a thundershower coming to our rescue. But he hadn't even brought his kit to the ground. His coffin was there with bats, gloves and pads etc, but no clothes.

He first went to Doc Moosajee to ask for a medical opinion, but he already knew the answer to that. Not a good idea! From a cricketing point of view, I said I thought it might be a very good idea, and from a psychological point of view Jeremy Snape said that whatever decision he made, he had to be 100 percent committed to it. No umming and ahhing. We left it up to him, although it was pretty obvious which way the three of us were all leaning. Well, we would, wouldn't we? We didn't have a broken hand or chronic tennis elbow. But we all agreed that there was absolutely no room for indecision, and that we would back him up and endorse whatever he chose to do. Typically, after a moment's final thought and a couple of 'air shots' without a bat, he said: 'Let's do it.'

We needed to agree on a precise cut-off point for when he would go out there, and then stick to it. Nobody knew how long he might be able to survive, or even how long he could hold a bat with one hand, but we needed to make an educated guess. We decided that if the innings was still in progress with 20 overs to go, or less, when the ninth wicket fell, then Graeme would bat. It was crazy in hindsight. It felt pretty crazy at the time, too, especially when he started borrowing clothes – trousers from Morné, a shirt from someone else and Harry's burger-stained sweater. Neil Mac and Doc took charge of adapting his batting glove to fit over the cast on his hand, which was a surgical operation itself. It's very hard to describe how, or why, it was so important for us to try and draw the game. We'd won the series and we were risking Graeme's long-term career. Another blow on the hand and he could have been out for six months to a year. But we just did. We were desperate to avoid defeat and deny Australia victory.

With 20 overs to go, Graeme came and sat right at the back of the changing room out of public view. We didn't want Australia to know. Besides, it allowed us to change our minds at the last minute if we wanted to! Then Dale was dismissed and there were eight overs remaining. Graeme stood up and walked quite slowly towards the pavilion doors, at first not looking at anyone. He seemed quite calm but later said he was just deep in thought about how he was going to try and play each delivery with one hand. He had already made up his mind that he was going to have to take certain bouncers on the body because his movement was limited. The other concern was yorkers; it wouldn't be easy digging them out with one hand, especially not at Mitchell Johnson's pace. Just before he walked through the doors, he looked at me with a half-smile and said: 'My mum's gonna kill me for doing this.'

I still get goose bumps when I remember the sound that the crowd at the Sydney Cricket Ground made when Graeme walked through those doors. The cheering for the wicket had quickly given way to an excited and expectant buzz as neither the team nor the spectators knew whether Australia had won the Test match. Then there was silence, or it sounded like it. Then the noise picked up again, rising and rising to a crescendo as more and more people caught sight of him and realised what was happening. He walked to the wicket to a standing ovation. The same man who had been heckled and ridiculed by the SCG crowd just three years earlier had turned that attitude into a deep respect, perhaps even a touch of affection. No, that would be too un-Australian. But certainly they had warmed to him in a big way.

In some ways it would have been easier for everybody to accept our fate if Graeme, or even Makhaya for that matter, had been knocked over immediately. But the skipper was obstinately determined, and Makkie was playing the most disciplined and impressive Test innings of his career. I don't believe anybody had any expectations with 50 balls remaining, but with 30 left we wondered, and with 20 left we dared to hope. With 10 left we all believed it could be done, which is why it hurt so much when Johnson produced a magnificent delivery to bowl Graeme out. It was a source of marginal consolation that it was, at least, a 'jaffa', which might well have bowled him at the very peak of his powers.

Australia were cock-a-hoop, and deservedly so. They'd made a couple of big changes to their team, with debuts for Andrew McDonald and Doug Bollinger, and in many ways the Sydney Test was the beginning of a new era. But the fact that we had fought so hard and come within 10 deliveries of saving the game was also a source of significant pride for us. We'd banished the memories of The Oval, we'd won the series and achieved what had been a career-long ambition, not just for us for but generations of South African cricketers.

It was funny afterwards in the changing room and back at the hotel. A cold beer still tasted good, but we'd done our celebrating in Perth and, especially, in Melbourne. That evening, it seemed more appropriate to have a good meal with teammates and friends and reflect on the journey we had been on since the last tour to Australia, how we had changed and what we had achieved.

The ODI series (January 2009)

It was a very big decision to appoint Johan Botha as the one-day skipper. It would have been much easier to use Jacques, yet again, as the fallback option, but I felt certain that we needed to look ahead and think about the future rather than treading water and waiting for Graeme's return. Besides, I wasn't in the slightest bit worried about the senior leadership around Johan, with Jacques, Bouch and especially Neil Mac all there to offer advice and support. Neil had been retained to replace Graeme, and, once again, it wasn't an entirely smooth or easy process. Just because Norman had objected so strongly to Neil's inclusion a year earlier, it seemed that his place in the squad was continually being questioned. I'm delighted to say that Neil again proved his worth even more than we could have hoped for.

Wayne Parnell was introduced into the squad, and Lonwabo Tsotsobe was retained from the Test squad – two young players with immense potential and a tremendous attitude. As far as I was concerned, it was no more than a happy accident that they happened to be good for the politicians as well.

Herschelle was back, too, having completed his rehabilitation programme. He had played virtually no cricket for a month and a half, and his selection could easily have been interpreted as controversial, as indeed it was by a few critics. And, let's be honest ... it was a controversial selection. All the old rules about selecting on form and not on reputation were still relevant, but on this occasion a very rare exception applied. When Doc Moosajee and I had read the riot act to Hersch a couple of months earlier, we made it clear that if he could make the commitment to the team to sort his life out, then we would reciprocate by recommitting the team to him. He was a very rare and special talent, and had given over nearly a decade and a half of his life to the Proteas. Too many cricketers have been tossed aside once they aren't needed any more, or make a mistake in the twilight of their careers, and we didn't want to do that with him. Despite making a fool of himself and getting into trouble on a regular basis for all those years, it was felt by everyone that he deserved a shot at redemption if he made some serious and long-term changes to his life. Which he did. So he was back.

Albie Morkel's inclusion was also, potentially, a make-or-break selection. There was never any doubt about his devastating ability with the bat, but was he good enough to command a place in the top six – or was his bowling too unreliable for him to play as an all-rounder at number seven?

The series began on 11 January with a T20 match in front of an almost packed MCG, where David Warner announced his arrival on the international stage with an amazing innings of 89 from 43 balls. It wasn't just remarkable from his or Australia's point of view, it was the moment (or one of them, perhaps) when the world realised that Twenty20 cricket was a different animal to the other forms of the game. Warner hadn't even played a first-class game by then!

We were well beaten again in the second T20 at the Gabba in Brisbane on 13 January, despite a second consecutive half-century from JP, who continued to exude the class and style he'd shown in the Test series. Despite the omens not looking good for the ODI series, we refused to panic. I would not stand for any negative talk, and was quick to speak with any player who I thought might be exuding negative vibes. We talked calmly and constructively about the one-day series, and concentrated on tactics rather than personalities. It may sound a bit 'smart-arse' after the event, because it proved to be one of the decisive factors, but I was convinced that the batting power-play could work in our favour, and was determined to talk it through and devise strategies to ensure we made best use of it. We reached a consensus as a team that the power-play should be left, if all had gone well, until the 43rd or 44th over because we were preconditioned to belting it in the final five overs anyway, and with fielding restrictions we could be even more harmful. I believed that it was worth sacrificing a few runs in overs 38 to 44 in order to keep wickets in hand; whereas chasing 10 an over had been regarded as virtually impossible before the batting power-play was introduced, I believed it was far, far less intimidating with the new regulations.

Happily, that proved to be exactly the case in the first ODI, at the MCG on 16 January, when Albie walloped 40 off 18 balls to win the game just as everybody was writing us off. Nobody, they said, chased 270 at the MCG. The precursor to that, however, was a calm, mature fourth-wicket stand of 123 between JP and Neil Mac, which put us back on track from 90–3. Once again, Neil had answered the call and defied his detractors and critics – not that he ever allowed them to upset him. He was often unaware of how virulent certain people were in opposing his selection. That was an unfortunate part of my job. But Neil was aware of the undercurrents, and he showed his rare and priceless gift of being able to concentrate on what he was able to influence and ignore everything he couldn't. There are never many of his ilk around in world cricket at any given stage, let alone in one country. It is a great pity that they appear to be appreciated by their fellow professionals a lot more than by their bosses. Perhaps that says something about cricket in South Africa. I think it does.

The second game in Hobart, on 18 January, was ours to win. Australia won it, but as far as I was concerned we lost it – and it was partly my fault. Australia made 249, well below par for the conditions, mostly because they had an inexplicable reluctance to take on our spinners, Johan Botha and part-timer (although he was a lot better than that) JP Duminy. We had no information or inkling that the Aussie batsmen might be so hamstrung against our off-spinners, but they refused to sweep or hit the ball square on either side. It was peculiar, as it cut out 40 percent of their scoring options! JP bowled six overs for 23. It was an amusing reminder that, no matter how much research, planning and video analysis you do, you still have to think on your feet.

Sometimes a 'controlled' run-chase becomes stalled in third gear; as a coach, you need to make something happen to change that. We were calmly on course for much of the run-chase but lost by five runs, with Boucher and Morkel coming in at number seven and eight in the order. I had good reasons for not changing the order, for relying on those in place to get us home – for showing that I backed them and trusted them. But I got it wrong. It wasn't just because we lost; it was because I didn't read the conditions, the mood and the atmosphere correctly. I should have changed the order. I didn't. It was a bad mistake.

If chasing 270 at the MCG had been 'unlikely', it was regarded as 'impossible' at the SCG – largely because it had never been done before. Conditions change more markedly in Sydney over the course of 100 overs than anywhere else in Australia, and chasing runs in the second innings, under lights, was notoriously difficult. Chasing anything over 200 had, historically, proven to be extremely difficult.

Although the third ODI (23 January) was an all-round team effort, two innings really made the difference: one at the beginning and one at the end. Hersch was back to his absolute best, walking at bowlers and taking them on. When he hit Johnson over cover for six there could be no doubt that Herschelle still had all the qualities needed to be a match-winner – but with fewer of his old, less likeable off-field qualities. His 64 from 52 balls that night gave us breathing room in the middle of the innings, and meant that we still had wickets in hand when Albie once again teed off with spectacular results at the end. Another 40, this time from 22 deliveries, another batting power-play brilliantly used, another record run-chase and another victory.

Curiously, Australia seemed to have no idea of how they wanted to use the power-play. Even odder, their batsmen looked worse and worse against the spinners. Johan Botha took 3–32 that night, and JP was so effective that he bowled a full 10 overs. The Australians simply couldn't get them away, and they seemed strangely reluctant to try anything different. It was inexplicable.

Shaun Tait had been bowling seriously fast in the series up till then, but we had coped well in all three games, managing to score off him and deny him wickets. But he had a modicum of revenge in Sydney when a searing yorker crashed into Mark Boucher's foot and broke a bone. Not that Tait knew anything about it until the next day, when he saw Bouch on crutches. Call it brave or call it foolish, but Mark refused to acknowledge the pain or the potential seriousness of the injury while there was still a match to be won, and he batted on for over half an hour until the winning runs were scored. It was so typical of his attitude and approach to playing for South Africa, and further evidence, if any was needed, of why he was always one of the first names on my team list. (No doubt there was another administrative attack on his credentials waiting around the next corner. There always was. But I would be up for the fight. I always was.)

The Adelaide one-day international is always traditionally played on Australia Day (26 January). It is an occasion marked by jingoism of the highest order. All things Australian are cherished and celebrated almost to the point of extremism. If you aren't wearing a cork hat, blowing a didgeridoo or eating something off a barbie, then you just aren't entering into the spirit of Australia Day. Another tradition calls for the opposition at the Adelaide Oval to play along with things, put up a decent fight for the sake of providing entertainment, and then lose graciously. If they can't do that, then they should at least get thrashed quickly to provide some extra pub time at the end of the night.

I would be lying if I pretended that this felt just like any other game. The prospect of winning the series made sure it felt different, but so did Australia Day. I have yet to meet a cricketer who says he doesn't like touring Australia, but you have to understand that it can also be a very 'hard' experience – it's not for the faint-hearted cricketer. So this was an opportunity to hit back hard, to hit them where it really hurt. It was a chance to pull the school bully's pants down right in the middle of the playground, or to pull the wig off the fairy godmother right in the middle of the pantomime stage. And we were up for it.

Makhaya, whose place had been guaranteed in the squad by the president rather than the selectors, justified this intervention with the vital wickets of Warner and Ponting, and Dale was awesome yet again. They shared six wickets between them. Australia made yet another hash of the batting power-play, and we were left to chase an extremely modest 223 for victory. We were always overwhelming favourites for victory, but to win by eight wickets with 12 overs to spare really rubbed salt into Australian wounds. Hashim and AB both finished with unbeaten

80s. We had won the series – comprehensively, and with a game to spare.

Tactically, I was especially pleased with the solution we had found to counter Mitchell Johnson, who had been so effective (and occasionally devastating) during the Test series. The white ball swung less than the red one, which helped us of course, but we made a bold decision for the right-handers to bat on off stump against him, which meant that every delivery outside off stump was a 'free hit'. When he was forced to attack the stumps, we were able to work the ball away through the leg side.

When we arrived back at the team hotel and headed to the lobby bar for a celebratory drink, the players discovered that Australia had finally managed to gain some form of revenge. The bar was closed, despite it being Australia Day and only 10.45 pm! No matter. Our liaison guy organised a large kombi taxi and they all headed off into the night to find a 'recommended' nightclub. That wasn't really my scene, but I enjoyed an excellent glass of wine from the minibar in my room and went to sleep feeling very, very satisfied. Two series – two victories. It was extraordinary. I finally admitted to myself just how often I had thought about this tour over the last three years. Barely a day had gone by when I didn't think 'that will be useful in Australia' or something similar.

The one-day series concluded in Perth on 30 January, and my optimism about the future increased even further with the inclusion and subsequent performances of Wayne Parnell and Lonwabo Tsotsobe. With AB keeping wicket in place of Bouch, JP in the middle order and Vaughn van Jaarsveld also in the XI, it was a very different-looking team – a young and exciting team. And one that many expected to be bulldozed by the Australians, who were desperate to end with a consolation victory after the humiliation of Adelaide.

Instead, it was us who bulldozed them. Hashim was magnificent for his 97, while JP showed again that he was far more than just a skilful accumulator, with an aggressive, unbeaten 60 from 42 balls in our total of 288. Parnell and Tsotsobe both rose to the occasion in grand style. 'Parnie' just loves a stage; give him a crowd, give him a ball (or a bat, for that matter) and he will perform. He was still just 19 at that stage; he will need some help and good advice managing his personal life, but if he stays on track – and the right side of the tracks – he has a wonderful international career ahead of him. 'Lopsy' took 4–50 as we won the fifth game as comfortably as we had in Adelaide.

I couldn't have been more excited about the team – or about the squad, to be more accurate. With Graeme and Bouch set to come back, Dale resting and Roelof van der Merwe as a second spinning option back in South Africa, our depth in all areas was almost unprecedented. I was trying not to get too far ahead of myself, but it was very hard not to plan the path towards the 2011 ICC World Cup.

The victory took us to the number-one ranking in the world, and a short time afterwards we were number one in Test cricket as well. When I made my presentation to the board almost four years earlier, I made it clear that I believed we could achieve both goals, and set that as my target. We had done it. But I was still as driven to achieve more success as I had been on day one – more so, in fact. Reaching the top is addictive – you need it more and more. Before his departure, Graeme and I had spoken about that old truism in sport: becoming number one in the world is hard. Staying there is much harder.

After the game, a delighted Doc Nyoka came into the changing room. He gave a rousing speech in which he praised everybody for what they had achieved and for how proud they had made South Africans feel. It was all sweetness and light, all joy and happiness. There were no doubts, no references to what had happened before and no talk, even privately, about the future and how he and the executive board saw it. Doc Nyoka was impossible to 'read'. He would be polite, genial and even loving to your face, but so many people had told me how he could be when your back was turned. I found it difficult to trust him. His predecessor, Norman Arendse, had been brash, crude and tactless, but at least you knew where you stood and he spoke his mind. Doc Nyoka, on the other hand, seemed a bit of a Jekyll-and-Hyde character.

We arrived back to a packed reception at OR Tambo International Airport, and it was fantastic to have Graeme there, too, accepting the plaudits for the most successful tour South Africa had ever embarked on. 2008 had been South African cricket's greatest, and there was nothing wrong with enjoying and appreciating the happiness we had given people.

Unfortunately, none of that form or success would be repeated in 2009.

Chapter 12

Australia in South Africa

February to April 2009

Too much of a good thing can be dangerous and harmful. It's something every mother teaches her children. From the moment we set foot back on South African soil, the players experienced more demands on their time than ever before, and that applied across the board. The senior players, accustomed to requests from media and sponsors and happy to oblige, had them doubled. 'Juniors' like JP and Hashim, who had made such profound strides during the tour, were forced to live their lives one-handed for two weeks because the other one was constantly on their cellphone.

We saw and recognised the dangers. We could see the effect it was having on the squad and we knew it was a problem. A far bigger problem, however, was what to do about it. Not only did sponsors have a 'right' to ask for time from the players, but they deserved it too. As far as the media were concerned, the same applied, except that any refusal to cooperate with interview requests would almost inevitably result in negative reporting, bad relations and a tarnishing of what we'd achieved in Australia. It is difficult, if not impossible, to explain to a reporter who needs a story that you don't have time for the next six days. But that was the reality; it was the truth.

We had spoken so much as a squad about what we could achieve following the Australia tour, how we could build a legacy and create a period in cricket history that belonged to us, like the West Indies had done in the 1980s and the Australians had done in the early 2000s under Mark Taylor and Steve Waugh. We had everything going for us – talent, potential and now results. We shared a common goal, and we were passionate about achieving it. But none of us were prepared for the distractions that came with our newly achieved status.

Agents, managers and promoters were all over us – including me! Offers to speak at dinners, breakfasts and lunches came thick and fast, while endorsement deals with very attractive numbers were an appealing but nonetheless problematic distraction. If JP was blown away by the prospect of earning R250 000 doing a one-day television commercial for Lay's chips, his life was about to change forever when he was sold for $950 000 to the Mumbai Indians at the IPL auction. How could anybody keep their feet on the ground and stay level-headed in those circumstances? Three months earlier, JP wasn't even on the international radar; now he was the light flashing and bleeping the loudest. Let me say immediately that his character and personality did not change at all. Well brought-up in humble circumstances, he remained the same person. But I am intimidated to think about what might have been going on in his head.

In many ways it is unfair to single him out, but I do so simply because the change in his circumstances, both practical and financial, was the most extreme. Everybody else, though, was affected in some way or other. If you weren't doubling or tripling your salary, then you were wondering why not and looking at your teammates who were. Envy? Suspicion? There were several new emotions and feelings within the squad. Administrators, too, were wondering where their cut was. It was all very distracting.

'Arrogance' is a very harsh criticism in the world of professional sport, especially when it is used in the context of a team or individuals who consciously place themselves above their rivals in the context of physical or mental superiority. We never, ever did that. But I think we made the mistake of believing our own talk about 'dynasties' and creating our own chunk of history. Unbeaten for nine or ten Test series, number one in both (major) forms of the game, it is understandable (but entirely unforgivable) that many of the squad believed beating Australia on home soil would be 'easy', especially compared to winning on their turf.

Australia arrived in South Africa as a team reborn. A lot had changed: Matthew Hayden was gone, replaced by Philip Hughes; Marcus North was included, as were Ben Hilfenhaus, Andrew McDonald – a host of new faces, in fact. They went straight to Potchefstroom and began preparing with a single-minded determination and team spirit that was eerily similar to what we had done in Perth a couple of months earlier. On tour, things can be a lot easier to manage than they are at home. While we were battling to maintain our focus as a team, spending hours and days as individuals and responding to requests for our attention, Australia were working together as a unit and planning their response to the defeat at home. They were in combat mode, with no distractions. They were hungrier than us. They had a lot more to prove.

It showed, too, during the first Test, played at the Wanderers on 26 February – 2 March. We were soundly beaten, and deserved to be. At 296–7 in the first innings the game was in the balance, but the true test of great teams is how they react at crucial moments like that, and we could do nothing to stop North and Mitchell Johnson from adding 117 for the eighth wicket. North scored a century on debut and Johnson made 96 not out. Replying to 466 was always going to be hard.

AB made an unbeaten 104 in an otherwise feeble response, and we were left with an extremely unlikely victory target of 454 in the fourth innings. Graeme top-scored with 69, but, although it may sound harsh, the victory margin of 162 runs was more flattering to us than to Australia.

We had experience of being one-nil down in a three-Test series, and had come back from it, but everybody knew that this would be more difficult. We had all experienced the renewed vigour and determination of the Australian team and we knew how hard it was going to be.

There was barely time to regroup before the second Test, at Kingsmead in Durban on 6–10 March. Philip Hughes scored a hundred in both innings, and I must confess that rarely, if ever, did we get our strategy more wrong than we did against him. We felt he would be vulnerable if we could get him coming forward just outside the off stump, which was a reasonable approach. However, we were painfully slow to realise how proficient he was at the square cut and how painfully small the margin for error was in terms of length. Like many short batsmen with a low centre of gravity, he could cut deliveries that many fast bowlers would have regarded as a 'good' length when they let them go.

He also hit a lot of his cut shots in the air close to gully and backward point, which gave us the impression that he was not in control and could be dismissed at any time. The bowlers initially didn't mind conceding a few boundaries to third man because they felt he was vulnerable in that area. Unfortunately for us, the opposite was true. He was so proficient at cutting the ball that he was placing it beyond the fieldsmen with the accuracy of a marksman!

What we should have been doing was attacking him at the body and chest, tucking him up and cramping him from room.

The mistake was made even worse by the fact that we had evidence to suggest he wasn't comfortable against the short ball. At the Wanderers, he had twice gloved a couple of rib-high deliveries down the leg side but been given 'not out'. Everybody was still finding their feet with the new Umpire Decision Review System, and we'd already got a couple of early referrals wrong so we didn't ask the third umpire to have another look in case the deflection wasn't clear. It's the kind of good fortune most batsmen need.

Kingsmead is unique in world cricket for the inexplicable way in which conditions can change. There are the obvious things like cloud cover and humidity, but these exist to a greater or lesser degree around the world. Heat and wind direction always play a part, too. But none of these factors can explain sufficiently how conditions can be near perfect on one day and virtually impossible the next – and back to featherbed again after that. Locals have many theories, the most popular being that it all depends on the tide. Personally, I really do think there is something in that. Days one, two and three of the Kingsmead Test were the perfect example of this changeability. There was absolutely nothing to encourage the bowlers on a stinking hot first day, and the openers, Hughes and Simon Katich, both cashed in with centuries. By the close of play, the visitors were 303–4 and we were in trouble.

On the second morning, the ball could hardly stop singing and dancing. There was bounce, seam movement and plenty of swing through the air. The batsmen were suddenly struggling, and we took the last six wickets for just 49 runs. The bowlers were delighted, and convinced that we were back in the game. The batsmen weren't quite so sure, while the pitch was having one of its infamous, menopausal hot flushes.

Over the years, many bowlers have made the mistake of believing that the pitch, in one of its 'moods', will do the hard work for you. Wrong. You still have to work hard, hit the deck hard and land the ball in the right place. Mitchell Johnson did everything right. He was so focused that you could feel the energy from 100 metres away. His rhythm was superb, his pace was up there with anybody in the world, his aggression was channelled towards a couple of very specific points and he blew the top order away. It rates amongst the top three spells of fast bowling I have ever seen. And he broke Graeme's hand while he was at it. Again. For good measure, he also hit Jacques Kallis on the head, necessitating a few stitches. In cricketing terms, it was like heckling a sermon by Archbishop Desmond Tutu.

We made 370 in the fourth innings, which was a very good effort – but not when we were chasing 546. We had been well and truly hammered for the second Test in a row, and that was the series gone. It hadn't even been close. We were devastated. It remains one of my biggest disappointments.

At least we had resolved our difficulties as a team about how to approach 'dead' Test matches, and nobody had any doubt that we would give a better account of ourselves in Cape Town during the third Test (19–22 March). However, I was extremely disappointed when the selection panel chose to make two changes to the team. I felt strongly that Neil McKenzie and Morné Morkel deserved to have the same chance to make amends as all the other players, and I hated the idea that they were being made scapegoats. But when you lose two in a row – three if you include Sydney – then the selectors are made to feel that they are not doing their job if they don't make 'hard decisions'.

Selectors sit in the President's Suite during Test matches, and they are exposed to many opinions, some of which I often found quite frightening in their naivety. But there is no escape for the selectors, and sooner or later, I believe, they lose the strength or desire to stick up for what is right. Consistency in selection had been one of the cornerstones of our success during the preceding eighteen months and ten unbeaten series. Neil and

Morné had played massive roles in that success.

But if you are going to drop a couple of regulars, then there is a time and a way to do it that shows respect and an appreciation for what they have done. Appallingly, both men were told that they would not be going to Cape Town before they had even left the field at Kingsmead. Such treatment showed an utter disregard for the effort they had put in, and singled them out for blame in what had been a very under-par team performance. Morné burst into tears in the changing room; he was made to feel responsible for the result, and, in the immediate aftermath of the contest, with emotions swirling, he began to have doubts about his international career. I put an arm around his shoulders and assured him that he would play many, many more Test matches, and I reminded him once again of the special talent that he had been blessed with. I believe South Africa may well have the number one and two fast bowlers in the world for many years to come if Dale and Morné can stay fit and healthy.

Neil was old and wise enough to realise that it was probably the end of the road for him. Instead of the congratulation and thanks he deserved for contributing as much as he did to the greatest year of South African cricket's history, he was tossed aside like an empty fast-food container. They had taken what they wanted from him, and now didn't care. Typically, Neil accepted his fate like a gentleman. He was the only one who did. The rest of us were either furious or deeply saddened. Or both.

Graeme and I took some consolation from the fact that we had helped to revive his international career and given him the chance to prove to everybody, perhaps most importantly himself, what an exceptional cricketer he was. The difference between his 'first' career and his second could hardly have been more pronounced. As a young man still learning his game, he played 41 Tests and averaged 33.24. As a mature cricketer with a developed understanding of the mental side of the game and a sound knowledge of his technique, he played another 17 Tests and averaged 47.11 with three centuries, three 50s, a world record and many other milestones. But that's only the stuff you can measure.

Neil's presence and influence in the changing room was immeasurable. The advice he gave the captain not only helped win games, but also was paramount to maintaining a happy working environment in which everyone knew where they stood on every issue. Neil was a classic example of why captains and coaches clash with selectors who pick teams based exclusively on statistics and numbers rather than a more rounded package of information about what a cricketer contributes. Jonty Rhodes might not have played as much as he did had he been selected purely on averages – but without him the team would have won a hell of a lot less than they did.

Perhaps there is scope to develop a system that would quantify a player's worth off the field. The captain and coach could rate a player in five categories: willingness to help teammates prepare physically; willingness to share knowledge; ability to lift players when down; tactical value to captain; and effect on team discipline. Then, when the selectors are wavering between two players or considering whether to drop a player after a couple of indifferent games, at least they might take into account the value he adds to the team if he has a captain/coach rating of 45 out of 50.

Like so many young South African players, Neil he was probably selected prematurely, given no back-up, support or advice and left to find his own way in international cricket. Two people are more qualified than any others to work with Cricket South Africa in the future to make sure the same thing doesn't happen again: they are Neil McKenzie and Boeta Dippenaar. I wonder whether the national administrators will keep them involved in the system and make use of their expertise. They would be extremely foolish not to.

The forty-eight hours before the Test were marred by the disagreement between Ash and the management team. He was clearly very disappointed – angry, even – not to have been brought straight back into the team for the first Test when his finger was healed, but JP had made himself 'undroppable' in Australia. It was an unprecedented situation. South African teams had always operated on a policy of injury replacements making way when the first-choice player was fit again, but on this occasion an exception was made for the first two Tests. Perhaps Ash had reason to feel aggrieved, but sport is about rising to challenges, not being angry about them.

For the record, I did vote for Ashwell's return at the beginning of the series and JP's return to the bench. It was one of the hardest selection decisions I'd ever faced, but there was no point in me being so stringent about maintaining consistent policies that players could rely on and then changing my mind. Ultimately I was outvoted by the other selectors, and I really didn't feel strongly enough about it to have another war of words – with anyone.

Ash's return to the team as captain, replacing Graeme, was announced before it was made clear to him that he was also replacing Graeme as an opener! When that did become clear, Ash said that captains were not told what role they had to play, and, therefore, if he was going to be asked to open the batting under protest, then he would rather not be captain. So Jacques was given twenty-four hours' notice to take charge on a temporary basis for the umpteenth time. It was hardly ideal preparation. There was right and wrong on both sides, but there was no point in complaining about Ashwell being obstinate and stubborn because these were exactly the qualities which made him such a fine Test cricketer!

Possibly my best bit of coaching during the whole week in Cape Town was to arrange a team trip up Table Mountain, a couple of days before the match, to have an early meal. As team-building exercises go, it was a tremendous success, although a few of the Gautengers were caught seriously unprepared for the ten-degree drop in temperature the moment the sun disappeared. There was a mad scramble for spare clothes. I think the souvenir shop at the upper cable station sold at least half a dozen sweatshirts.

At Newlands, we went a very long way towards winning the Test on the first day by bowling Australia out for just 209, Dale leading the way once again. Ashwell made light of the embarrassing controversy surrounding his return to the team by scoring 150 as we piled up a mountain of runs in reply. Jacques also scored a hundred, and AB was absolutely sublime during an innings of 163. Albie, who had been selected for a Test debut in place of his brother Morné, belted a quick 50 at the end as we piled up 651. Harris bowled a monumental spell to take 6–127, and Mitchell Johnson made it exciting at the end with a maiden century, but we still won by an innings – South Africa's biggest win against Australia. It was the only Test in either country not to reach the fifth day – and did we appreciate the extra rest!

The ODI series

After taking the two T20 matches on 27 and 29 March, we cemented our place as the number-one team in the world with a seriously convincing 3–2 win in the ODI series, which wasn't as close as the score line might suggest. We lost the fifth match, at the Wanderers on 17 April, when the minds of the majority of the players were emphatically distracted by all things Indian, with the second season of the IPL about to start in South Africa.

You could probably have got long odds against us winning so handsomely, or winning at all, after the first game at Kingsmead (3 April), where we lost by 141 runs. It was hard to explain – we were just really, really bad that day. One of the many funny things about cricket is that good and bad form is contagious. The same is true of many sports, I suppose – think of how often you play well or badly at golf depending on how your partners are playing. But we started badly and got worse on that day. Mike Hussey made an unbeaten 83 in their 286, and we replied with 145, thanks to 52 from Graeme.

There was one performance from our side that stood out – for the wrong reasons. Makhaya went for 67 in nine overs, and seemed helpless to stop the flood of runs. In my mind, it was the end of the road in ODI cricket for him, no matter what the politicians and board members would say. We felt that all Makkie could still offer was an occasionally probing spell with the new ball. But he had very little variation in the middle overs, and whereas he'd always been a risk bowling at the death, now he had become a straight liability. I knew it would leave me politically vulnerable once again, but Makkie wasn't doing himself or the team justice. In his reaction, I believe Makhaya let himself down once again. Despite overwhelming cricket evidence – run rates of seven an over and very few wickets – over a significant time frame, he reacted with considerable petulance, preferring the conspiracy theory to the facts.

The nature of defeat in the second game, at Centurion on 5 April, was equally emphatic, but this time it was Australia on the receiving end. Ponting elected to bat on the basis that 'there might be something in it for the first hour but it should be a good track to bat on after that'. In many ways he was absolutely right, except that, instead of 'a bit' in the first hour, there were six wickets. Wayne Parnell took Makhaya's place and formed a devastating new ball pairing with Steyn, sharing eight wickets on the day. At 40–6 in the 13th over, they did reasonably well to get to 131, but the game was over soon after lunch – victory by seven wickets. Incidentally, Ponting was also right about the pitch becoming good to bat on later in the match. So his reading of the pitch had been perfect – sort of.

In Cape Town on 9 April, the Australians added some late

runs to reduce the margin of defeat to just 25 runs, but they were never, ever in the game once we'd made a mighty 289 and reduced them to 114–5. Roelof van der Merwe once again looked the part with 3–37, but it was a genuine team effort.

We clinched the series in Port Elizabeth (13 April) on the back of a highly charged and emotional century by Herschelle, which led us to a total of 317. He cried twice that day, once as soon as he reached three figures and once again in the changing room after the match, when he stood up and publicly thanked me and Doc Moosajee personally for the decision we had taken earlier in the season. By being tough, we had been kind. By making him face some painful realities, we had given him the chance to get things right and put them behind him. Coaching 'the person', as opposed to simply coaching 'the cricketer', was central to my philosophy, and it was deeply rewarding to see Hersch emerge as a better man. He was always an outstanding cricketer.

The only negative on an otherwise outstanding day, celebrating yet another series win, was the news that Johan Botha had been reported by the umpires for having a suspect action. It was disappointing and a little unfair, not so much because his action was completely pure and innocent, but because there were so many other bowlers in the world with similar idiosyncrasies who were never reported. We felt, perhaps, that Botha was a soft target, although I confess he was having some difficulties with his 'doosra' at that stage of his career.

You never, ever regard any international fixture as unimportant let alone irrelevant, but it was very hard to give the fifth game the attention it deserved, with several players having to fly to Cape Town immediately after the game to play in the IPL double-header at Newlands the following day. The IPL franchises had been making demands on their players' time in the build-up to the game, and, as we had just seen before the Test series, sponsors' commitments and photo shoots weren't the best way to prepare for international cricket.

At the Wanderers that day, Australia made 300 and won by 50-odd runs. But their victory did not leave a sour taste or detract from the series win. Parnell and Van der Merwe had added yet another couple of dimensions to the squad, and although there were still questions to be answered and a couple of areas where we could improve, I felt we had 15 players undoubtedly capable of winning at least one of the next three ICC events. The Twenty20 World Cup, postponed from Pakistan a year earlier, was just a couple of months away, and the Champions Trophy on home soil barely four months after that, to be followed by the World Cup in Asia in 2011. I couldn't have been more optimistic.

Chapter 13

ICC World Twenty20

June 2009

T he ICC World Twenty20 tournament, the second of its kind, was held in England in June 2009. I was convinced that we were good enough to win the tournament. Like many coaches and players, I had been pretty sure that good cricketers would be successful in any form of the game, but over the course of the previous couple of years, during which more 'science' had been applied to the 20-over format, I became far less sceptical about the use of specialists in that form of the game.

So while T20 games afforded us the opportunity to give more exposure to younger players, I was completely happy that a player like Yusuf Abdulla, for example, deserved his place in the squad. He had already been given a chance in the second T20 against Australia, played at Centurion on 29 March, and had looked the part. It was just a case of me, and a few others, getting over our old-fashioned perceptions that all cricketers should be conditioned to play first-class cricket and be able to bat for six hours or bowl 25 overs.

The composition of the squad was an extremely important

concern for everybody. Whereas I had always believed that the Test squad could not be 'compromised', even if it fell short of 'targets', everybody was in agreement that the T20 squad was a golden opportunity to show the nation – and the rest of the world – how much progress we were making with transformation.

Nonetheless, having transformation so paramount in our priorities also made it uncomfortable at the time, and it's uncomfortable repeating it now. The objective was always honourable, but the reality – especially for the players involved – was often unpleasant. Whereas we tried to select the Test squad on the basis of who deserved to be there, we found ourselves 'counting numbers' ahead of the T20 tournament. So guys like Robin Peterson and Justin Ontong had their places unfairly questioned. Robbie P was a whole-hearted, passionate and committed cricketer whom I'd respected for many years. If anything, he was a victim of being a jack of all trades rather than a specialist. He could cover three or four positions, from opening batsman to middle order, all-rounder and specialist spinner. Justin was in a similar position and had enjoyed a very successful domestic season.

We played warm-up games against Pakistan and Sri Lanka, which we won comfortably using what I believed was our best starting XI. It was always a conundrum: do you give all of the fringe players an opportunity to get some game time, or do you try to build momentum with the first-choice players? I believed in the latter approach. However, I had enough respect for the contrary point of view to go out of my way, with the colossal assistance of Goolam Rajah, to organise a third, unscheduled, warm-up game against Ireland in which all of the 'reserves' played. And played very well – we won that game comfortably, too.

We played our opening game against Scotland at The Oval on 6 June, winning by 130 runs. There wasn't just a mountain between the teams; there was a mountain range. But, at the risk of sounding patronising, and perhaps unconvincing, I believe that Scotland, because of the way they presented themselves and competed, deserved their place on the international stage. Not many teams will lose by 130 runs in a T20 international, but they competed and did not look out of their depth. AB de Villiers scored 79 off 34 balls, and to be honest he could have done it against anybody, such is his talent. I support the inclusion, on merit, of minor teams in major ICC events. What's the point of them having dreams if there is no prospect of fulfilling them?

The second match, against New Zealand at Lord's (9 June), was a triumph in reading conditions. Our total of 128 looked extremely modest, but was only about 10 or 15 runs short of par, in extremely awkward conditions. Nonetheless, we had batted badly and needed to make amends with the ball and in the field, which we did. Much of the conversation within the squad before the tournament had been about how, on a bad day, the bowlers would help the batsmen, and vice versa. There was none of the old batsman/bowler antagonism. It was one for all and all for one. We won that game by one run. There is no closer margin, but strangely we never looked, or felt, like losing. Winning had become a habit, I guess, and I expected it to continue at every stage.

We moved safely and securely into the Super Eight phase, where we were scheduled to meet England (11 June), West Indies (13 June) and India (16 June), each of whom we beat with something to spare. Wayne Parnell took 3–14 against England at Trent Bridge in Nottingham as they were bowled out for 111. Kallis, Smith and Gibbs all scored heavily and quickly against the West Indies at The Oval to take us to 183, which was 20 too many for the West Indies. Then our spinners, Botha and Van der Merwe, bowled eight overs for only 29 runs as we restricted India to just 118 chasing our score of 130 on a really tricky surface at Trent Bridge. By winning the West Indies game, we were already pretty much assured of top spot in the group and a semifinal against the team finishing second in the other group, to be played also at Trent Bridge. (Lord's or The Oval would probably have suited us better, but given the way we had been playing we were absolutely confident that we had a team for all conditions and all opposition.)

Before the India game, we had some big decisions to make once again. It was a familiar dilemma, but it didn't get any easier. Should we play all the 'reserves', or stick with the winning formula and try to keep the momentum going? Every time the situation arose I tried to consider it with a fresh perspective, but I always came to the same conclusion – although not necessarily for the same reasons. I always believed strongly in the basic tenet of keeping a winning team together, and not disrupting successful partnerships and combinations, but on this occasion I was also thinking ahead to the semifinal on 18 June, which we knew would probably be against Pakistan. The Trent Bridge square was getting drier by the day, and it was obvious that spinners would play a big role in that match. There was no better preparation for the semifinal than playing against India at the same venue. The decision to field an unchanged XI would later be used as 'evidence' against me.

The India game was our seventh successive T20 victory, and an international record. We were comfortably the most consistent team in the tournament, and, tactically, we always seemed to be one step ahead. We looked better prepared than anybody else, and we were certainly the best fielding side. No matter what some cynics might say, fitness and fielding are two aspects of cricket that are very much measurable – and our guys all measured up pretty well (although I think Yusuf would be the first to admit that he wasn't in the most aerodynamic shape possible).

I was supremely confident before that semifinal, principally because we had already beaten Pakistan comprehensively, and I felt we were a better-organised team with more bases covered and more options. We'd won consistently, and had no negative thoughts. That's not to say we were overconfident, or that we were taking our opponents lightly. Our preparation was as thorough and meticulous as it had been before every other game, and there was no lack of respect for how dangerous Pakistan could be on their day.

Shahid Afridi smashed 51 from 34 balls to set up a total of 149–4, which was about a dozen or so above par. Conditions at Trent Bridge were even trickier than they had been during our game against India. We did not bowl well, and for the first time in the tournament our fielding was also a little tentative and below the standards we had set ourselves. Nonetheless, we still knew that we could, and would, win the game if we played well, and played to our potential.

Kallis anchored the innings from the top of the order with 64 from 54 deliveries, but Afridi bowled Gibbs and De Villiers cheaply in the seventh and ninth overs, and the pressure was really on. Umar Gul bowled superbly at the death of the innings, and JP was simply unable to score, finishing 44 not out from 39 deliveries. We lost the game by seven runs. That was the story of the match in purely cricketing terms, but once again we had to ask the hard questions. Were we affected by the fact that it was an ICC semifinal? Were we affected by the pressure? Did we choke? These questions will continue to be asked of every South African team until they can get the monkey off their backs.

I tended to think we were simply outplayed on the day. It was a pity that so much attention was focused on our performance, rather than on the brilliance of Afridi and Gul, but that was inevitable given our record.

There may have been times during the early part of my career when I turned a blind eye to signs of discord, unhappiness or nervousness; more often than not these pass as quickly as they arrive. I knew the team was nervous before the Lord's Test match, for example, but thought it wiser to adopt an attitude of 'it will be all right on the night' rather than risk making a mountain out of a molehill. This time, however, I was determined to get as close to every player as possible, and to really probe for any doubts or potential weaknesses – and equally determined to help them resolve their issues. I had one-on-one chats with almost all of them to make sure they were clear about their roles and were keeping everything in perspective.

But I encountered nothing but positive intent, positive thoughts and a calm, authoritative confidence. They sounded, looked and felt ready for any situation. Nothing fazed them, which is why I still tend to give them the benefit of the doubt regarding that match and believe that they were simply outplayed on the day by a very good Pakistan team. That can happen in any form of the game, but particularly in 20-over cricket. But we had shown before the semifinal that it was still possible to take much of the element of chance out of the game and utilise high-percentage strategies.

Doc Nyoka came into the changing room after the game and gave us another affectionate speech about how we could still be proud of ourselves and how we had played up until that day. He said the right things, although the level of disappointment among the players was so high that it was difficult for them to accept his attempts to console them. I found his words slightly curious, almost as though he didn't really mind what had happened, or at least not nearly as much as we did.

Then, on his way out, I saw him look at our media manager, Michael Owen-Smith, and overheard his aside: 'Well, at least *your* job is safe.' It took several minutes for his comment to sink in. I was completely stunned. After all that we had achieved, and after his apparent satisfaction with our efforts, he was sharpening a knife. Alarm bells started ringing when I had least expected them to.

* * *

We had been back at home for two days after the tournament when I received a phone call from Gerald Majola, asking me to go to Johannesburg for a dinner meeting with Doc Nyoka, Ray Mali and himself. I suspected what might be on the agenda and asked whether they could invite Doc Moosajee as well. As team manager, it seemed only appropriate that he be there. Besides, he is a man of enormous integrity and real moral fortitude; I felt extremely comfortable and confident that, even if Doc did not agree with me, his presence would facilitate an atmosphere in which we could all listen to each other and be heard.

The occasion turned out to be very cordial and constructive, with plenty of open and honest discussion, which I enjoyed. There was no innuendo or talking in circles, which can be so frustrating. At the end of it, thankfully, I felt that the 'big picture' was a lot clearer and I knew where I stood. Makhaya had not been in the T20 squad in England, which was a problem, but not nearly as much of a problem as the fact that we did not have a single black African on the tour. The fact that I had chosen only three players of colour in our starting XIs had also presented a significant problem. Once or twice, for solid cricketing reasons, might have been acceptable, they said, but not throughout the tournament. And certainly not for the game against India, when we had already qualified for the semifinal.

Doc Nyoka made it perfectly clear that he and his executive were coming under extreme pressure from the government and the Ministry of Sport and Recreation, and that something had to be done about it. At one point during the evening, when the 'nitty-gritty' subjects were first being raised, there was a surreal moment of silence after Doc Nyoka accused me of having selected only *two* players of colour throughout the tournament. He obviously wasn't joking, but I felt he couldn't be serious either. Then, when we talked through the starting XI, it transpired that he knew that Herschelle and JP were players of colour, but not Wayne Parnell. It was extraordinary.

I flew back to East London the following morning with a lot
going on in my head. But I was determined to enjoy a couple of
weeks' leave before refocusing on the ICC Champions Trophy,
to be held on home soil in September.

Chapter 14

Falling stars

September to October 2009

After a year of what felt like constant work, a record-breaking, fantastic 2008, we had all enjoyed a proper break. The players had two months to recover from the niggling injuries which had been 'managed' for so long rather than properly treated; for myself and the rest of the management, there was an opportunity to reflect on what we had done well, what we could improve upon and what our goals would be for the next few months and years.

In the run-up to the ICC Champions Trophy – the sixth tournament, and the first to be played on home soil – I was concerned that it might be difficult, and take some time, to get everybody back into work mode after such a long break, so I organised for our pre-tournament camp to take place in Potchefstroom two weeks before the opening game.

My concerns proved well founded. There was a peculiar lethargy and 'flatness' that I had never encountered before. It was difficult to get anybody really 'up' for their work, to rekindle the passion, energy and enthusiasm that had been such a crucial part of our squad. When you speak of 'motivation' within a sports team, and suggest that it might be lacking, it is perceived – and taken – as a deep personal insult. Sometimes it shouldn't be. Occasionally, there are practical reasons why players feel flat. But they were certainly lacking a bit of inspiration.

I was unable to put my finger on the problem. One of my strengths, as I'm sure my coaching staff and colleagues would agree, lies in identifying problems or 'issues' which might be affecting the energy of a squad. So it was unusual that I couldn't see what the problem was. It occurred to me, quite seriously, that it might have been the fact that we were preparing for another ICC event. Perhaps there was mental 'scar tissue' remaining from the T20 experience? It wasn't something easily confronted as a coach. Once again, I ran the risk of creating a problem rather than solving one, but if there was something to be tackled then I was completely committed to doing it – no matter what the fallout.

Perhaps it had something to do with selection. This was supposed to be a private and confidential process, but, as every player, fan and journalist knows, most selection meetings are leakier than a sieve. (I also know from experience that, most of the time, these are not 'deliberate' leaks, but more a result of human nature.) I had flown to Johannesburg to discuss the composition of the squad for the tournament, and, after a typically robust meeting ended in a satisfied, mutual agreement, returned to East London with my mind at rest. The following day the squad was announced to the media. In place of Morné Morkel, whom I had felt was critical to the attack, was the name of Makhaya Ntini.

If I had been told during the selection meeting that we were obliged to select Makhaya, then we could have made a plan. But to agree on a squad and then change it the moment the coach walks out of the door seemed unnecessarily underhanded and unlikely to foster a relationship of trust and understanding. I was disappointed and angry.

One of the outcomes of my dinner meeting with Ray Mali and Doc Nyoka a couple of months earlier was that there would, at all times, be a minimum of one black African in every squad thereafter. And I was completely comfortable with that decision. I understood that political demands were a reality and that we had to make every effort to make cricket look and feel acceptable to the majority of the nation. I always maintained my belief that kids, of all colours and creeds, would be more likely to be attracted to a winning sport rather than a multicoloured one, but I still fully understood and endorsed the requirements. And let me say here that Lonwabo Tsotsobe was an exciting prospect and certainly no 'quota selection'. A tall, left-arm swing bowler with the ability to get a bit of extra bounce, he was exactly the sort of player we needed to have in the squad, to train with the team and to learn. I had no doubt in my mind that he would make huge progress and very soon be a regular member of the team.

But the decision to remove Morné from the squad and replace him with Makhaya was one I found very difficult to understand, or accept. Morné was a world-beater in the making; Makhaya was a South African icon whose best days were left in the Test arena. He was struggling in ODI cricket, and was even less likely to make an impact in T20.

When I was told by selection convenor Mike Procter that Makhaya had been included because he had a history of bowling well at SuperSport Park in Centurion – venue for our three group games – I found it almost laughable. Conditions have far less influence in the selection of bowlers in T20 than in ODI or Test cricket. They only have to bowl four overs in T20! Getting each ball in the right place and executing a simple plan is far more important than conditions. I always got on well with Proccie, but his explanation for the last-minute change in the squad was wafer thin. As one of the greatest players of all time, with a wonderful knowledge of, and 'feel' for, the game, his cricketing pedigree was second to none. But he could be easily swayed by people who knew far less than him, and he often took the easy route instead of fighting for what he believed in.

It was now abundantly clear to me that the mysterious 'agendas' that had been simmering under the surface throughout my tenure, mysterious demands that were implied rather than stated, were now coming to a boil. I had been made to understand, willingly, that every squad should have at least one black African. But was that the issue? Or was it that every squad should contain one Makhaya Ntini? That seemed more likely. I went back a long way with Makhaya; I loved him as a person and a cricketer and had supported him on many, many occasions. This *was* personal. I would have loved him to be in the side on merit, but he wasn't producing his best cricket at that stage. And when we gathered in Potchefstroom, Morné's absence made it feel a bit like a family bereavement. Everybody knew he was one of the best cricketers in the country, if not the world, and it felt very odd to the players not to have him with us.

If I sat in front of a panel of social scientists and experts in 'nation-building' and was presented with evidence to suggest that the nation needed to have Makhaya Ntini in every team, and that his presence was more important than picking the best team, I wouldn't doubt them for a second. I don't have the expertise to know that. But I *was* qualified to pick the best team available within the stipulated criteria.

The tournament was a disaster for us. I don't know whether somebody else would have been able to lift the physical or mental level of the squad, but I wasn't. I experienced a slow, numbing realisation that my fate might be out of my hands. I was still largely oblivious to the situation during the tournament, hoping for the best. In some ways it felt sudden, but on reflection the signs had been there all along. The meetings, the comments, the handshakes – all meaningless platitudes. When the administrative sharks circle, they don't swim away without a kill. And they don't mind if it takes a while to get their prey.

The pressure from the board was hard to quantify; it came in the form of comments, remarks and sarcastic wit from friends of board members. None of these were significant on their own but were powerful when added together. I was clearly at loggerheads with the board, and it was starting to worry me. Up until then, I had always been able to put such concerns to one side for days, even weeks, at a time. Now, however, it was impossible not to feel that I was the object of a conspiracy, and it did not make for an easy or pleasant working environment.

The first game, against Sri Lanka on 22 September, was a car crash. We were nervous and tense, and it showed, Wayne Parnell went for 79 in his 10 overs, and Albie went for 10 an over in his 4. Tillekeratne Dilshan scored a century in a total of 319, and rain turned an extremely stiff target into a Duckworth/Lewis mountain. We lost by 55 runs, and were never in the game.

Parnell made up for the first game with a five-wicket haul against New Zealand (although he still conceded over seven an over) on 24 September, and we knocked off the 215 for victory with almost 10 overs to spare. But it was a false dawn, and the shoddiness of the bowling and fielding returned in the third match, against England, who scored 323–8. All our front-line bowlers went for six runs an over, or more. There was an outside chance of qualifying through the back door by scoring 312 and lifting our net run rate above that of Sri Lanka, but even that was beyond us. It was an especially bitter pill for Graeme to swallow, having scored a career-best 141 from just 134 balls.

Our performances had been completely unacceptable for any South African team at any time, let alone the number-one-ranked team in the world playing on home soil. I could think of reasons for our underperformance but absolutely no excuses.

Not for a second had I ever considered that we might not reach the semifinals, at the very least. We hadn't trained well enough, and although the coach can't do the training for the players I still take responsibility for it. I wasn't able to get the atmosphere right or address the problem areas.

At the board meeting shortly after the tournament ended, I encountered barely contained, let alone concealed, hostility. I had always tried to be very open with the board about my plans for the future, the players I hoped to use and how they could be best utilised, in my opinion. The hostility started with questions about why neither Makhaya nor Lonwabo had played any of the three games. I defended myself, my pride and my integrity on cricketing grounds and with cricket reasons and logic. There were sound and solid reasons for every selection made. Yet again, I also found myself defending the places of Kallis and Boucher in the team.

The board members all deferred to Doc Nyoka and Ray Mali. Their way of showing support was simply to join in the 'free for all', launch their own attacks on me and question every selection made. Some of their questions revealed a spectacular lack of cricket knowledge but a deeply entrenched bias towards their own region – and, of course, to racial composition. They did not know enough about balancing the cricketing components of a team. They knew only what the balance of white players to players of colour was and that it was not a 'fair' split. Which it wasn't. Gerald tried to back me up during that meeting, but the air had turned cold in the room and I knew that I was travelling a different road to the board. Whereas I had always been mindful of the need to transform the demographics of the team without compromising quality, they just wanted transformation – at any cost. I could see that by the way they reacted when we lost. For them, it was simply another opportunity to usher in change – and to get rid of me.

I was under attack for a sustained period of time, and

eventually I snapped and hit back. Doc Nyoka said he didn't believe I was the right man to take the Proteas forward and to win an ICC event; he said he was of the opinion that a change needed to be made. We left it at that. But I had lost respect for the board, and they probably had lost respect for me, too. It wasn't a healthy or a happy situation to be in. I didn't know how it would resolve itself, but I resolved to myself to get back to the team and help them start winning again. The worst thing about playing so poorly, and losing, in the Champions Trophy was that it gave the board the ammunition they needed to take cheap, uninformed pot-shots at us.

In November, we had an ODI series against Zimbabwe coming up before England arrived for the summer's main attraction. The selectors gathered to select a squad for that series, and, yet again, we stalled over Makhaya's inclusion. Mike Procter said we needed to include him, but I said that would negatively affect the team in the medium to long term: Makhaya wasn't going to get any better, and we could instead be giving valuable exposure and experience to a younger player. Mike concluded the meeting by agreeing that it was time to look ahead and move forward without Makhaya, and that we should waste no more time in finding his replacement. It made a bit of a mockery of his Champions Trophy decision to include him because we had played no cricket at all since then.

Proccie then facilitated a meeting between him, me, Doc Moosajee and Makhaya in East London, at which I told Makhaya exactly where he stood in the big picture, exactly what he needed to do and exactly where I saw his career heading. I was completely honest and open with him – as I have always been with every player I ever coached. I have no hidden agendas; if I upset certain players by telling them the truth, then that is something we both have to live with. It is not something I am going to apologise for. Similarly, in the context of the East London meeting, I wasn't going to apologise for backing players who had performed consistently and won games over and over again. Proccie was the consummate professional and an outstanding gentleman during that meeting. He made certain that everybody knew exactly what the others were thinking.

I cannot claim to have been correct all of the time – no coach can – but I can claim to have been honest all of the time, including when I felt players were nearing the end of their careers and needed to consider an exit strategy. I sat in that meeting and offered Makhaya an exit strategy. Because he no longer featured in our long-term ODI plans, I suggested that he might consider retiring from one-day cricket before the Zimbabwe series, but that he play in all three games in order to give the nation an opportunity to say goodbye in a manner that was proper and fitting for an icon of the game. Sure, it wasn't Australia, but we can't control the fixture list.

I also made it abundantly clear that he remained, for the time being, our number-one bowler in Test cricket, and that he would still be taking the new ball for the foreseeable future. In fact, I guaranteed him the new ball in the opening couple of Tests against England: the first at Centurion (his 100th) and the second, the Boxing Day Test, at Kingsmead. After that, we could review where he stood with regard to Test cricket. I didn't believe that it would be right or fair to give him just one Test match; it had to be two. Anybody could have a bad game, especially with the likelihood of so many distractions and celebrations of the landmark game at SuperSport Park.

Makkie wasn't in the slightest bit interested. He was completely defiant and said that he wasn't going to retire, and that if we wanted to drop him then we should do it. I guess he'd been rescued by politicians before so was banking on being rescued by them again. So we did drop him. We had no choice. And, predictably, Makhaya went to Gerald, Ray and Doc Nyoka and claimed that he was being victimised because Graeme and I didn't want black men in the team. It was as horrible as it was hurtful. It feels inappropriate, even now, to dignify such an accusation with a response. But for those who require it, here it is: nothing could be further from the truth.

The England Tour (November 2009–January 2010)

The first two games on the itinerary were T20s, so we selected Loots Bosman because he was a specialist in that format and I believed he could play a role for us in the ICC T20 World Cup in the West Indies in April-May 2010, which was the next ICC event on the calendar. I went back a long way with Loots; I had coached him in Galeshewe township, outside Kimberley, when I began my career, and had mentored him during the start of his professional career with Griquas. I knew only too well how effective he could be, especially on flattish wickets, and he remained amongst the three cleanest hitters of a cricket ball in the country. I had no doubts at all that he could add considerable value.

Fortunately, we had put behind us an unpleasant bust-up that occurred in 2007 during a tour of Zimbabwe – a warm-up to the inaugural ICC T20 tournament. Having been selected for the squad, Loots had crashed badly into an advertising hoarding while fielding during one of the games and hurt his back a little more seriously than he was keen to admit. He was desperate to play in the tournament, and, I believe, refused to admit how much pain he was in. There was no way I was going to leave it to a decision between me and him, so I asked for medical advice – not only from Shane Jabaar, but from a third party. The advice was that he was not, and would not be, fit for the tournament.

When I withdrew him in 2007, Loots responded by going public with a burst of emotional vitriol, claiming that we were making a convenient excuse to leave him out of the squad. It was very clearly implied that it was a colour issue. I was stunned at first, and then furious. For Loots to say that about me, or to imply that about me, after all we had done together and shared, was hard to believe. He involved anybody and everybody he could, eventually even going to the premier of the Northern Cape to get her to intervene. It was malicious, even vicious, behaviour, and I told him so. In South Africa, with its brutal history of apartheid and racism, the merest insinuation of bias – let alone a full-on accusation – can stain somebody forever. Yet Loots burst out with a series of statements with scant regard for the consequences – and he was extremely economical with the truth.

But we spoke about it later, and cleared the air. He admitted that he had been out of line and he apologised to me, without reservation. Apart from his own emotions affecting his judgment on that occasion, there had been comments made to him by influential people who should have known better – but who had more interest in causing trouble and spreading bad blood.

So I had absolutely no doubts about his credentials as a T20 player, and he proved them in emphatic fashion by scoring an amazing 94 from 45 balls in the second of the two games against England – at Centurion on 15 November – during a record opening stand of 170 with Graeme, who made 88. We would have won the first game, too, had rain and Duckworth/Lewis not denied us. Loots and I had a beer together after the game and a great chat – I was so enthused about what he had done and the prospects for him in the T20 format. He had booked his place in the squad for the ICC T20, and I sincerely hoped that it would be the making of him as an international player. However, he had just recently returned from knee surgery, and I had been told in very clear terms by the medical team that his progress needed to be gradual and carefully monitored.

When I turned my phone on after the game, I was dismayed. There was a message from Proccie, who had spent his evening in the President's Suite, saying that it had been decided that a

sixteenth name would be added to the squad for the ODI series
due to start on 20 November. Not only was it a complete knee-
jerk reaction to Loots's wonderful display of clean-hitting, but it
showed a complete disregard for the processes which we had in
place for selection and which the rest of the squad had come to
trust and believe in.

I had been working with Hashim Amla for a long time,
preparing him as the 'next batsman' in line for the ODI team,
and specifically as the next opener. The move to promote Loots
so suddenly, and without any input from me, was destructive
in the extreme. So much work and preparation had gone into
Hashim's elevation to the ODI team; it all felt meaningless if the
team was going to be selected from the President's Suite. Hash
was far better technically, and had the ability to score freely and
quickly in the first 15 overs of an ODI without taking risks.

I stood my ground, and argued long into the night to keep
things as they were. We had selected our 15 players for the
England ODI series, all the players knew where they stood, and
I believed it was vital that we maintain the status quo for the
confidence and security of the players. They needed to know
how the process worked and that it could be relied upon, not
that it could be usurped at any point by administrators with
no knowledge of the workings of the team and the squad.
Eventually I called my great ally, Gerald Majola, who concurred
that a squad, once selected, should be left intact barring sudden
changes in health, fitness or form (or for disciplinary reasons).

This episode left my relationship with Proccie even further
strained, although, bizarrely, I still enjoyed his company as a
person and appreciated his knowledge. We could still have great
conversations, and debate general things well into the evening,
but talking 'specifics' was becoming more and more difficult,
even impossible. I was left with the impression that he was a
little too happy to acquiesce to the nudges of the many people
with agendas beyond the field of play.

To me, the principle was so simple. I had made a promise to Hashim, just as I had done to JP Duminy and André Nel and several others before them, that he was the 'next in line'. Players responded positively to knowing the succession order and where they were on it. I was aware at the time of how I might be fuelling the board's argument that I was stunting the involvement of black Africans in the national team; that concerned me, but not as much as the thought that I might compromise my principles in order to try and keep my job. If I had cared only about my salary, I could so easily have thrown my arms open and selected teams to satisfy political demands first and playing requirements second. If I had, I might have kept my job. But I don't think so. Winning games is what keeps coaches in jobs, and they have to pick the best team – not the best individuals – in order to win. Perhaps I was unduly concerned about the impact on players of being selected with a bias to skin tone. But I had personal experience of seeing how negative the reaction could be, and was always keen to avoid that.

I had been doing the job for five years, and the 'issues' around the team and its infrastructure were beginning to wear me down. I was still passionate about making the Proteas the best in the world – or rather keeping them there – but the politics that came with the job were beginning to make life miserable. The inferences that I was anti-black African appalled me. No other criticism could have been more hurtful – or more incorrect.

On a more practical level, I began to wonder whether I had said and done all I could for the players in the squad. Perhaps they needed a new voice, new ideas and a new approach. Five years is a long time for a national coach. Despite the passion I still had for the national team, I began to accept that, perhaps, my time was done. There are only so many times you can say the same thing. I had begun to feel that it might be time to move on. It was a very hard thing to accept, and I knew the players would never say it, but there comes a time for most relationships to end.

I can honestly say that I never carried on with any part of my job in a half-hearted manner. Even though I knew the writing was on the wall, I gave it my all. We endured an insipid ODI series against England in which nothing went our way – mostly the weather – losing it two-one. We never gained any momentum, and it seemed impossible to change things. There is an interesting passage in Michael Vaughan's autobiography, *Time to Declare*, in which he states that, when it is time for your star to fall, everything will conspire to go wrong at the same time, and there is nothing you can do about it. His demise was very similar to mine!

Chapter 15

The England Test series

November 2009 to January 2010

Whenever I think about the role that Lady Luck played in my career, particularly on her bad days, I will reflect on the Test series against England, which would turn out to be my last as national coach. In my opinion we were, by some considerable distance, the better team and I believe we proved it on the field. We were two balls away from winning the series 3–1, and yet somehow we walked away to salvage a drawn series, having won the final game.

The first Test, at Centurion on 16–20 December, will always be remembered for Makhaya's century of caps. The fuss and fanfare around the occasion was everything we expected it to be, and although it was a distraction it was a very happy distraction, and we were prepared for it. Jacques and Hashim both scored centuries, allowing us to declare and leaving ourselves about 95 overs to bowl England out. At 27–3 we were well on our way, but Jonathan Trott and Kevin Pietersen built a long partnership together, and Paul Collingwood batted for the last two-and-a-half hours to steer England to a draw – with last man Graham

Onions surviving 12 balls and celebrating afterwards as though he'd won the Ashes. I know that sounds harsh and uncharitable; it was fair enough to be pleased, but a bit less of the fist-pumping would have been appropriate! Still, it was great drama and wonderful entertainment, set up by an excellent spell of fast bowling with the second new ball late on the final afternoon from debutant Friedel de Wet.

Jacques had been unable to bowl in the match, having only just returned from a serious side-strain. I doubt England would even have come close to escaping if we'd had our regular, five-man attack. Like so many other things, I used to wonder what direction my career would have taken if Jacques had been fit to play as an all-rounder.

I was very confident as we headed towards Durban for the Boxing Day Test, principally because Jacques would be able to bowl, but also because, on the evidence of what we'd seen, my belief that we were a far better team than England had been confirmed.

We were thrashed. By an innings and 98 runs.

Batting first, on 160–2 with Kallis and Smith in the 70s, I was just beginning to relax on the first day, and was looking forward to posting a very big total. Graeme Swann had Jacques caught at slip, and moments later Graeme was run out in a horrendous mix-up with AB de Villiers. JP Duminy was quickly trapped LBW by Onions, and we were 170–5. At 285–9 I thought we were in serious trouble, but Dale Steyn smashed 47 and added 58 for the last wicket with Makhaya. I felt happier with a total of 343, but in truth it was probably 100 short of par. England emphatically proved that by racking up 574, with hundreds from Cook and Bell and another 90 from the ever-reliable Collingwood.

But it was events off the field that were concerning me as much as what was happening on it. The board had discussed the need to have a meeting to address the problem of the team's 'inconsistent performances'. We weren't even halfway through the series, and already there was a 'crisis meeting' being planned. Alarm bells were ringing louder than ever in my head, especially when Swann bowled brilliantly once again, adding five more wickets to his four in the first innings to dismiss us for just 133. I could barely remember a time when the team had so underperformed.

With just three days before the New Year's Test at Newlands (3–7 January), I needed to make some hard decisions. I was happy with the squad chosen by the selectors for both Tests. I had the say on the composition of the final XI, but once again I found myself with a ticking bomb. The politically prudent thing to do was to select an unchanged team. The sensible thing to do from a cricket point of view was to make a change in the bowling attack. Steyn and Morkel had taken five wickets between them, and looked dangerous at times. Makhaya had taken 0–114 and looked flat, never threatening. So I took a very deep breath, literally as well as metaphorically, and prepared myself for the consequences of leaving him out of the third Test.

Straight after the Kingsmead Test, I asked Gerald Majola to meet me in a small office at the back of the changing rooms. I asked him what my options were and whether we were still dealing with a 'straight' pack of cards; was there still an authentic cricket context for decision-making, or was it now political only? It was a no-win situation for me: play the best team to try and square the series, or keep the politicians and Makhaya happy. A lot of people asked me later why I didn't take the 'easy' option and avoid all the resultant aggro, but that would not have been fair to the team, and, whether you believe it or not, it would not have been fair to Makhaya either.

I explained to Gerald how it felt to me: fail to win the series and my job was on the line. Leaving Makhaya out of the team meant I would disrupt the hornet's nest of politicians and board members, who would do all they could to put my job on the line. He sympathised, but gave me his blessing to do what I believed was in the best interests of the team. Whatever decision I took would be right and wrong in so many people's opinions.

I took the decision to leave him out, and the rumblings started immediately. Doc Moosajee was summoned to the President's Suite, on the first morning of the Newlands Test, to be told that the board was very unhappy with Makhaya's omission. The board members then, I believe, again talked about the need for a 'crisis meeting' to discuss the inconsistent performance of the team, and did so, significantly, without Gerald being present. It was very obvious that I was both the subject and the 'target' of their discussions. It emerged that they believed I had too much power, and that I had failed to transform the team sufficiently. All this was taking place with a very important Test match in progress. I wondered whether they had watched any of it. I knew, deep down, that we had to win it for me to keep my job.

I had changed over the preceding couple of months. The uncertainty and backstabbing had undoubtedly got to me; I was a little less fun to be around for my family, which upset me greatly. Yvette has always been extremely perceptive, and in Durban she had mentioned the change in atmosphere among those who effectively employed me. Now, at the start of the New Year festivities in Cape Town, she did her best, as always, to put a brave face on the situation, and to stay positive. My mother and father had come for the match; with my brother and sister both living in Cape Town, it was a great opportunity to be together as an extended family and share some quality time. But none of them could ignore my state of mind; one by one, they told me that, for the first time in five years, it looked as if the pressure was getting to me and I was showing signs of strain. In fact, they went so far as to say that I had become a completely different person. They were probably too kind to say it, but I wasn't too much fun to be around.

Players respond best when they know they are backed and supported by the coaches and management team, and aren't constantly on trial. The same principle applies to coaches, who need to know that they are not being judged from result to result and being made to feel that any mistake, or a single bad match, could result in being fired.

I still felt that I had the support of the team, although I must admit that relationships had become a little more strained. There were never any bust-ups or meltdowns, but we'd been together for more than five years – a lifetime in coaching these days – and the combination of over-familiarity and the pressure I was under meant that dialogue between us had started to become more fractious. But that had nothing to do with the termination of my contract.

On the field, meanwhile, the Test match had swung decisively our way after an even first two innings. Graeme led the way with a brilliant 183 in our second innings score of 447–7, and England were set a target of 466. More importantly for us, however, was the fact that we had almost five sessions to bowl them out. Surely there could be no escape this time, as there had been at Centurion. Surely not?

England's top three – Strauss, Cook and Trott – all batted more than two-and-a-half hours, and then the obdurate Collingwood hung around for over four-and-a-half hours to make 40, and Bell lasted almost five hours for his 78. For hour after hour I sat and watched, wondering whether time was running out more quickly for the team ... or for me. I was convinced that my job depended on victory. Eventually the wickets began to fall again, and we were left with three overs to claim the last one. But Swann and Onions hung on once again to deny us. I was emotionally spent. I know the newspaper headline writers enjoyed having some fun with the surname of the England number 11 on that tour, but I must say I may have been a step ahead of them when the last ball of the match was defended. 'Onions make Arthur cry,' I thought to myself. Only 17 Test matches in 130 years had previously been saved by the last-wicket pair. And now it had happened twice in the space of three matches. Perhaps it was a message to me.

They say your life flashes before your eyes moments before you die. At that moment, my career in charge of the Proteas, all the relationships I had built and all the experiences I had had, flashed before my eyes. I thought about what I would miss: working with Graeme, and all the time we spent strategising; the companionship of Jacques Kallis; the never-say-die contributions of Mark Boucher; Hashim Amla, whose career was now in full flight after a difficult start; Paul Harris, pulled from impending obscurity and given an extended run in international cricket; Wayne Parnell, a youngster but so talented; Ashwell Prince, a man whose life and career had been intertwined with mine; Dale Steyn and Morné Morkel, in whom I'd invested so much time and commitment, now set to dominate the fast bowling world for years to come. And then there was AB de Villiers, a young man whose international career started almost at the same time as mine, and whom I had backed and supported almost like no other. I told him from the early days that he could be number one in the world, and would be if he was prepared to do the work. I was hard on him, I pushed him, but I was also there to listen when he needed me. And of course I thought of Vinnie Barnes, quite simply my closest friend in cricket. I trusted and respected him more than any other. There is no need to say any more here.

They had all been part of my family, and I'd been part of theirs. There was true and genuine respect, admiration and love. It wasn't over officially yet, of course, but I knew the end was near. It was hard: I could feel our time coming to an end, and yet time was standing still. Everybody starting changing a bit. They could sense me, a senior, being ousted from the 'pack', and they didn't know how to react. I'm not sure I did.

If I was going out, which I suspected I was, then I wanted to go out with a 'bang' at the Wanderers during the fourth Test

(1–7 January). No more caginess, no more reticence – we would show England how we could play in our own conditions. I spoke to Chris Scott, the Wanderers curator, and enquired about the possibility of him leaving a bit of extra grass on the pitch and ensuring we had a 'result wicket'. He knows his trade better than anyone in South Africa, and was only too willing to assist. Funnily enough, I never, ever thought at any stage that it was a gamble, that it might backfire and lose us the series. I just wanted to hit England as hard as possible and win with a day to spare. I wasn't just confident we would do that; I *knew* we would.

And we did. Not in four days, but in three. I still didn't know for sure that it would be my last match, but at least we'd hammered England in emphatic style. We'd shown what we were capable of.

I walked out onto the Wanderers outfield to savour the atmosphere of victory. Doc Nyoka was there, parading among the players and offering his congratulations. He ignored me for as long as he could, and then deigned to say 'well done'. I later heard that, in the President's Suite, he had expressed his 'disappointment' that there was no black African in the squad.

A short time after the Test, I heard that Doc Moosajee had been told, again, that he was being 'bullied' by me, with the consequence that CSA transformation policy was not being implemented. As far as I was concerned, I'd done everything I could to balance the requirements of winning games and selecting players of colour. The specific requirement for black Africans in the team had been a recent development, and I had tried to adhere to it. Resources were not abundant, and it felt wrong to me to promote players who were not ready. There were ten black Africans registered as professionals between the six professional franchises. The presidents of those franchises were the ones who were about to sack me. I had been told often enough by the players themselves how unpleasant it was to be selected because of a quota.

I tried to stay as positive as possible during the post-match celebrations, but it was difficult. Even close friends and acquaintances were avoiding my gaze; I felt like a 'dead man walking'. I tried to celebrate, and I think I did good job of that. When it came to singing our team song that afternoon in the changing room, I gave it everything my lungs could produce. I sang until there were tears in my eyes and I could hardly breathe. Moments before we gathered in our huddle, I finally accepted the truth which had been staring me in the face for months beforehand. This was it. The last time I would ever do it. There were tears then, for sure, but they were probably lost on everybody else. They didn't notice. Or if they did, they would have been disregarded as 'beer and victory' tears. But they were tears of genuine, deep sadness.

I flew home to East London that night on the last available flight. It didn't seem right that I stay in Jo'burg, and I had no inclination to do so. My family is what had sustained me, and I wanted to be with them – with Yvette. The meeting with the board was still scheduled for the morning after the scheduled finish of the Test match, so I would have one full day at home. At OR Tambo, I was approached by a BBC journalist, microphone in hand, who asked me whether it was true that I was about to resign in two days' time. The thought of resignation had never, ever crossed my mind. Sacking, yes, but not resignation. I was flummoxed. But obviously my fate had already been leaked.

Two days later, the entire management team – Doc Moosajee, Graeme, me, Vinnie Barnes, Jeremy Snape and Mike Procter – were called to a meeting with the board, at which their reservations were expressed. They weren't just 'reservations', however; that much was clear. It was obvious that I was gone – in their minds. Somehow, I'm not sure how, I was still clinging to the possibility that I could fight my way back – that I could persuade everybody to understand the sense of my approach. How ridiculous.

Chapter 16

The end

After the meeting with the board, I flew home as soon as I could to be with my family. Once again, Yvette was extremely perceptive, and knew instantly how bad the situation was. The girls, too, knew that Dad wasn't happy – at all – but they all gave me their love, which helped to put life and work into perspective.

The truth is, I had lost faith in the people who ultimately sat in judgment of me, and we were never going to see eye to eye. I wanted to win cricket matches, first and foremost, and, to a great degree, I thought that was the best way of ensuring long-term, sustainable transformation. They wanted the team transformed, first and foremost, and were prepared to sacrifice results along the way if that was necessary.

In many ways, I did still want the job – the camaraderie, the sense of adventure, the shared goals. We had become the best team in the world, and, although we'd slipped since then, once you've tasted success like that, it's very, very hard not to want more. And I did want more. We had a short tour of India coming up, which was being billed as a 'Test Championship' because they had taken over the number-one ranking and we were number two.

But I also knew that I couldn't work with the board anymore, and that was an insurmountable obstacle. It was over. I'd known it for a while, but it was taking time to sink in. I couldn't help reflecting on how far I had come with the team and how much further we could still have gone together. I had been planning for six months on how to win in India, and the World Cup had been at the heart of my one-day plans for over two years. They were objectives I would have loved to achieve.

On the other hand, perhaps I should walk away and be happy with how far I had come and all I had achieved. Four years earlier, I had sat in a cold hotel room in Hobart, feeling more miserable and insecure than I can describe. I wanted to sleep under the floorboards, but it was a concrete floor. We had lost the Test series and just been knocked out of the triangular in humiliating fashion. I was able to enjoy the subsequent victories all the more because I never forgot that day. When we won in Australia three years later, the memory of that Hobart hotel room accompanied virtually every sip of Champagne. But for all the highs, there were many lows which I had to keep to myself. I am naturally an emotional person, with a tendency to wear my heart on my sleeve, but for five years I had kept my emotions to myself and internalised many of my stronger feelings. Only Yvette ever knew what I was really feeling at any given stage.

When I walked into the room for that final management meeting with the board, the atmosphere changed immediately, conversations stopped and nobody greeted me; most couldn't even make eye contact.

Each member of the management team had been asked to make a presentation to the board, assessing how we thought our role and contribution to the team was going, how we could improve and how we saw the future. These presentations needed to be done individually and not as a management group, as had sometimes been the case in the past. Before we made our presentations, Doc Nyoka announced to everybody that no fingers were being pointed at any individual, that there was no witch-hunt; it was simply an effort by the board to get to the bottom of why the team had been performing so inconsistently. As he was saying it, I looked at the board members on either side of him and not one of them could look me in the eye. Nyoka was absolutely right: there was no witch-hunt. There was no need for one. They already had their man.

My presentation was interrupted by a couple of messy verbal fights with Nyoka, who chipped in with comments and questions while I was speaking. I took offence to some of the things he said, and told him so. I told him that he did not have sufficient experience of being at the coalface of international cricket, and that he had very little idea of how a team actually functioned or of the consequences of forcing 'artificial' selections. At least these exchanges appeared to wake up the other board members, because they, too, began to quiz me about various issues. Many of the questions betrayed their deep lack of cricketing knowledge or even empathy for team dynamics. I had no wish to cause offence for the sake of it, but sometimes that was unavoidable with an honest answer.

I was asked repeatedly to clarify my stance on transformation. For the thousandth time, I repeated that I was a man who believed wholeheartedly in transformation, not just that it was 'necessary', but that it was a good thing. But I also said that it could be a bad and destructive thing if pushed too hard or too quickly. I also said that I didn't believe transformation should be allowed to adversely affect a team's chances of victory.

Doc Nyoka said that he, and the board, wanted to bring in an outside team of management consultants to work with me and oversee my decision-making. I said that would not be acceptable to me. In my view, the head coach of a cricket team was in charge of cricket issues and policies. Having 'outsiders' involved in key decision-making processes may be a successful strategy in the world of corporate business, but in my view it was a recipe for disaster in a cricket team.

The board cleverly adopted a 'divide and rule' strategy around the presentations. Other members of the management team went before me, so by the time it was my turn they were able to say things like 'we have been told that ...' and 'it has come to our attention that ...' They made some statements about my management style which were fundamentally incorrect and extremely upsetting. I didn't know whether someone before me had fed the board this misinformation, or why. But the point was to breed suspicion and mistrust among us.

'Silence is golden' and 'No news is good news' are two phrases we hear a lot in everyday life – but I think they pertain mostly to children! I didn't hear a word from anybody for five days after that meeting; none of us did. It was a very long time to be lying on your back looking up at the guillotine blade. I spoke to Graeme and Doc Moosajee at least once a day to check whether they had heard anything, and the answer was no. Five days after the meeting, it was a Sunday and I was determined to try and relax. So I switched my phone off, invited some friends over and had a braai. When we had finished and said our goodbyes at the end of the day, I switched it back on to check my messages. And there was Gerald, sounding a little terse, telling me to catch a flight to Jo'burg as soon as possible on Monday morning. I knew instantly that my future would be decided inside the next twenty-four hours. There would be no more waiting or uncertainty. That, at least, was a positive.

When I thought about it logically, there was no way around the impasse with the board; there was no solution. They would never back down on anything, and I would not have been capable of doing the job if I had backed down on any of my key principles. And yet, as bizarre as it may sound, I boarded the plane on Monday morning still hoping for a miraculous intervention. But it wasn't desperate hope. I had already come to terms with life without the Proteas.

I met with Gerald first of all, and it became very clear, very quickly that there was going to be no miracle. We chatted for at least half an hour, and he presented me with what he believed to be the best 'exit strategy'. How ironic. He was keen for me to keep my dignity and pride intact, and he gave me the choice, of course. We had worked closely together for five years and become very fond of each other – our relationship was forged out of mutual respect. He wanted my reputation to remain intact, and for me to be remembered for all the successes we had achieved during my tenure rather than for a bout of unnecessary and pointless mudslinging in the final weeks. I was, and remain, grateful to him for that.

Once we had agreed that I would announce my resignation at a press conference in my hometown of East London on Wednesday, two days later, we both shed a tear or two as we reminisced further about the good times, and bad, that we had shared.

It was hard to walk out of Gerald's office for the last time as national coach and try to keep a straight face and behave as though it was 'situation normal' for the benefit of the CSA staff. Gerald escorted me to the door, and I did my best to say a cheerful goodbye to everybody. It was a very strange feeling.

I dialled Yvette as soon as I walked out of the door and said: 'It's over.' She didn't need to say a word. I could feel both her relief and support as surely as if she was standing by my side with her arms around me. For so many years, she had been both mother and father to our girls: she had run the household, attended school meetings and fetched and carried to school and all the extracurricular activities. She had done everything for the majority of the time while I was away fulfilling my life's ambition and taking the Proteas to number one in the world.

Added to all of that, in the last year she had to cope with the stress and unhappiness of my deteriorating relationship with my employers. I don't know how she coped. I was determined to do all I could to make up for the lost time with Ashton, Brooke and Kristin. Never again would I be away for months at a time. Wherever I went, and whatever I did, they would be with me from now on. Yvette finished with the words: 'Now our lives can begin again.'

I started the car, and began to drive away from the Wanderers offices for the last time when I saw Doc Nyoka sitting in his car in the car park. He had been there the whole time. As I drove out, he got out of his car and walked towards the front door. Maybe I was wrong – perhaps he'd been on the phone – but the overriding impression I was left with was of a man who didn't have the balls to say goodbye to me, let alone thank-you. He had left the dirty work to the chief executive, something thankfully I never did when it came to dropping players from the team. I would have respected him so much more if he had shaken my hand for a final time and said: 'Thank you for what you did, I'm sorry it didn't work out in the end.' But he sat in his car instead.

On the drive to the airport, I called my father, Yvette's father and my great friend Wayne Schonegevel. The three of them, along with Yvette, had been my greatest allies and closest confidants. The rest of the world could wait until Wednesday, but those four needed to know immediately what had happened.

Any bitterness or resentment that may have accumulated over the last few months disappeared on the drive to OR Tambo. I was relieved, and began to enjoy a sense of freedom I hadn't felt for a long time. But most overwhelming was the feeling of gratitude I had for five fantastic years. Most people might go through their entire lives without the opportunity to experience even a fraction of the intensity of competition and emotion that I had enjoyed. I felt extremely lucky – and grateful. The feelings I had endured towards Norman Arendse, Doc Nyoka and the board members were gone, consigned to history. All I felt was the satisfaction of a job done as well as I could possibly have done it. When I sat in my interview five years earlier, I said I would take the team to the number one ranking in the world in both forms of the game. And we did it.

The turmoil I woke up to on Tuesday morning was completely unprecedented in my life. It was the one and only time in my professional life when I did not take, or at least return, all the phone calls from the media. (I apologise to those who were disappointed with me – but it was the only time I let you down!) I had always been open and honest with the media – too open, some would say – but it meant they all had my telephone number. And, boy, did they use it! I couldn't take all their calls, but I did my best.

There was much wild speculation about a 'rift' between me and Graeme, which was absolute nonsense. Right up until the press conference on that Wednesday (27 January), and right up until now as I sit writing in Perth, Western Australia, I regard Graeme as a true friend, and a man I can trust. We had our disagreements along the way, and exchanged a few hot words during the England series – when everybody's nerves were frayed – but never, ever did our relationship break down. It was a sign of the strength of our working bond, and the depth of our mutual respect, that we could debate things at full throttle. If it wasn't for that relationship I doubt we could have achieved what we did with the team. He continued to SMS me during the India tour and thereafter. We remained in regular contact, even when I'd moved to Perth.

I felt very sorry for Graeme throughout the Tuesday and Wednesday morning, when 90 percent of the speculation about my impending resignation focused on a 'rift' between us. We spoke three or four times during the day to reassure each other. He was blamed for my demise, which was rubbish. He is a very strong character, and he is the first to admit that he made some decisions early in his career that were a little too 'strong' for his own good, or the good of others, but that period of his life was over well before the time came for me to depart.

When I finally announced my resignation, I sat with immense pride and joy behind that table in East London. I had Gerald, Graeme, Doc Moosajee and incoming coach Corrie van Zyl alongside me – all men I trusted implicitly and respected. I never did get the chance to chat to Corrie about the board, and what he might expect, but he is his own man and no doubt he will sort something out.

Among all the shirts, stumps and silverware, the 'trophies' I will cherish most are the messages I received from the players on that Tuesday. There were voice messages and e-mails thanking me for everything I had done to resurrect, to keep on track and, in some cases, to kick-start their careers.

My life was suddenly a bundle of opportunity. I feared it might be a void, but it was quite the opposite. Rather than a vacuum, which every freelancer fears, there were phone calls and offers from far and wide. I was deeply flattered and humbled, but most of all I was relieved. I knew I had done a good job – a very good job – with the Proteas, but it was still reassuring to hear it from elsewhere. Cricket Australia even enquired about my availability to work with their team as a consultant. I had a phone call from Australia coach Tim Nielsen, whom I always got on well with, and from Michael Brown, their director of cricket operations. It proves the old adage: never burn your bridges. I was interested and tempted. But too much of my heart and loyalty still belonged to Cricket South Africa and the Proteas. It was far too soon. It would have felt wrong. But if the opportunity ever presents itself again in the future ...

The level of excitement I feel about the challenge of driving the Western Australia Warriors back to the top of Australian cricket is as great as it was when I took on the challenge of getting the Proteas to the top of the world rankings – maybe even a little more, because I have so much more belief and confidence, having been successful at international level.

As I write this, we are in the final phases of moving the entire Arthur family to Perth and making the city our home. There will be ample braai opportunities with fellow South Africans, but our objective is to integrate as completely as possible. There is absolutely no point in settling if you regard it as a temporary measure. I love Perth, and the family loves it even more. I am South African, for now and forever. And I will follow the Proteas' progress and results almost as closely as I did when I was coach. But I am also committed enough to my new life to say there is no limit to the time I will spend here. If I am successful and stay for the rest of my working career, there will be no regrets.

But who knows, maybe one day in the future somebody may employ me as a part-time CSA consultant ...

Chapter 17

Yvette's story

Imet Mickey in Kimberley's Halfway House Inn, the oldest drive-through pub in South Africa. It was November 1988, a year after I matriculated from Kimberley Girls High School. I was studying in Port Elizabeth, and I had returned home just a week earlier. I never drank in those days, although like many young people I spent my first (and only, in my case) year at varsity catching up.

I had popped in to have a glass of water (honestly!) with this poor bloke who was off to the border the following morning to do his national service. As I was leaving, I literally bumped into this guy in dirty cricket whites. I kept on walking, climbed into my car, put the key into the ignition and started the car. Then I thought, 'Hell, that oke looks like Tom Cruise.' (You have to imagine Mickey slimmer and with more hair.) It wasn't like me at all, but for some reason I went back in and told him. A couple of days later (he took his sweet time!), he traced me to the law firm where I was working and invited me to see the movie 'Cocktail' – starring Tom Cruise! I know it sounds cheesy, but it's true.

We hit it off immediately, and were inseparable from day one – well, probably day three. He never had a car – or even a licence! – so we got around in my yellow 1974 model Citi Golf. I soon realised that he played cricket, and what the implications were going to be for me. I'd never been to a match, and knew nothing about the game – except that it was obviously a test of endurance for players and spectators alike.

The next 750 weekends of my life were to be taken up with cricket, in one way or another – at least, that's how it felt. In the beginning he was either playing club cricket or for Griquas, home or away. The weekdays were our own, and were spent between his poky little flat, across the road from the railway station, and my parents' home, where I still lived. Weekends were spent around the cricket club fields of Kimberley, or alone at home when he was travelling.

Five months into the relationship we faced a huge decision. He was committed to playing for Coventry in the Birmingham League in England for six months. He invited me to go with him. Some might say he begged! I couldn't believe it when my very strict, conservative parents said 'yes, no problem, go.' I think they were worried that if Mickey went and left me behind I might return to my 'wild varsity' days.

We knew the trip would either make or break our relationship. There was a heck of a lot of cricket, a lot of socialising, meeting new people – mainly cricket folk. We didn't have our own accommodation at any stage. We moved three times, sharing each time with either fellow club players or committee members. It wasn't ideal, and sometimes I longed for the privacy of his little flat – no matter how full of old cricket socks.

The highlight of the six months was a week-long holiday to St Ives in Cornwall. At last I had Mickey to myself. We swam in the chilly sea and tried to sunbathe, but I never got any browner. English summers aren't really very hot. At least, that one wasn't.

We went out to sea on a fishing boat trip, and borrowed a couple of bikes for a day. It was innocent bliss.

Our big 'test' came three days into the holiday, when Mickey admitted that we had virtually no money, and that our budget was £5 per day – for everything. The way he was behaving, I wondered if it was actually less than that! The holiday was right at the end of the season, and we were due to fly home two days after returning to Birmingham. I was devastated. I really wanted a nice holiday, not fish and chips in newspaper every night! I threw my toys, and told Mickey I was going to call my dad and ask him to wire some money. He refused to let me. I didn't eat a single scrap of the fish and chips he bought me that night, and when he bought me the smallest ice cream he could find, to try and cheer me up, I threw it over the railing of the pier into the sea. I was the ultimate, ungrateful spoilt brat. But Mickey was completely unfazed by my behaviour. He put his arms around me and said: 'We'll be OK, we'll survive.'

And we did survive. We returned to South Africa a very happy couple, closer than ever.

I realised Mickey was a cricket tragedy pretty much from that first day. Who comes into a pub wearing whites? And really dirty ones, too. Who walks through a shopping mall with an imaginary bat playing air shots and making that noise with your tongue that means you've hit it well? (Especially when you're supposed to be impressing a potential girlfriend.) Who still smiles after fielding for eight hours in the Kimberley sun? And then goes back out to do the same the following day? Who really thinks their girlfriend will still be there, an hour and a half after play has finished, because it's 'important to have a few beers with the boys' despite the girlfriend having been there, waiting, all day? Who walks out of the changing room after four or five beers, with a huge, innocent grin on his face, and thinks everything is just great because they're only 20 behind with six wickets left?

Mickey's playing years were nerve-wracking. I didn't enjoy them. I was always very nervous, and would want to kill if anyone had anything negative to say when he failed. I could hardly bear to watch. He took it very seriously, and was the most dedicated member of any team he was in. When he played for Free State, we made many good friends in Bloemfontein. Tina Donald and I became best buddies. Wherever the guys were playing, we would follow. Flying was too expensive, so we went on many road trips in my battered old Golf.

There was one unforgettable trip to Durban. Tina and I stayed with Mickey's folks. We weren't married yet. The guys had to stay in the hotel. Those were the rules back then – no wives or girlfriends in the team hotels. Free State were playing Natal in Pietermaritzburg in a day-night game. Tina and I had lunch with Liz Symcox, Pat's wife (she was my maid of honour at our wedding). We had arranged to meet up with my future in-laws at the start of the match, after we'd had lunch.

We opted for a civilised pub lunch, but we got very clever after that. Given that we had a couple of hours to kill before the game, Liz decided she wanted to teach us a game she had just perfected. We bought a bottle of Sambuca, and went to her house to learn how to set your finger alight and then put it out in your mouth. Well, we never did make it to the cricket. We finished the whole bottle. Nobody knew where we were – it was pre-cellphone days. I had forgotten to let my in-laws know that we were meeting Liz. Poor Tina ended up in hospital for a short while! And my poor, dear in-laws had to drive us back to Durban after finally tracking us down to the Symcox residence. I think we got back as the sun was coming up.

I was also bosom buddies with Rudi Steyn's wife, Ilze. We lived around the corner from one another in Langenhoven Park, Bloemfontein. In fact, the whole Free State team lived in Langenhoven Park. The Steyns and the Arthurs braaied together every second day, and in between the wives cooked – sometimes for both families. We lived in each other's pockets, and heard a lot about cricket! Sometimes we even chipped in if we thought the boys were talking rubbish. When we found out we were both expecting our first babies within a week of each other it made for big conversation. Free State's opening batsmen were obviously developing quite a partnership.

To make it even funnier, I phoned Ilze on 10 August 1992, a very cold, wet winter evening, to tell her I thought I was in labour. She replied: 'Me too!' Mickey and Rudi were at practice. On their return, we all rushed off to the Universitas Hospital maternity wing. We walked the corridors together, with our separate gynaecologists, for 29 hours! Brooke was eventually born, by Caesarian section, at 11 pm on 11 August, and Sune, their daughter, at 3 am the next day, also by Caesarian. We both went on to have two more children. We had Kristin two years later, on 13 August 1994, and Ashton three years after that, on 17 August 1997.

It's a good job we never discussed the practicalities of Mickey being away for so long before we started a family. It probably would have been too intimidating. For instance, there was a time when Dad took the children for bike-riding lessons, and then quickly removed the stabiliser wheels before leaving again on tour. I put it straight out of my mind. Luckily we all got on with life, and the girls learned everything quickly. I used to get very short-tempered and aggressive when I was doing 'Dad' things as well as 'Mum' things, so the girls knew they were better off learning for themselves.

It's a blessing that Mickey never had any sons. He doesn't know which end to hold a screwdriver, the difference between a lawnmower and an edge-cutter and, worst of all, whether a switch is on or off! Over the years, I've had to get friends' dads to stand in for the yearly 'muffin morning' and 'Fathers' Day' functions. The annual 'Dads and Daughters Camp Out' also had to be with an adopted dad. Maybe it was just as well; with

Mickey's DIY and practical skills, they might not ever have had a roof over their heads. Later, towards the end of his time with the Proteas, I was the one who gave potential boyfriends the fatherly 'once-over'. I tried to remember what my dad had said about some of my boyfriends! Luckily, Brooke was the only one interested, and she chose well. Mickey can take care of the other two!

I don't mind admitting that I was devastated when Mickey decided to pursue a career in coaching. After being a player's 'widow' for so long, I wanted a normal life. I even suggested we go our separate ways. I'd had enough, in a big way. And I really hated the 'limelight' aspect of our lives. I really wanted my husband to go to work in the morning, come back for a home-cooked lunch, have a couple of afternoon strolls, help with a quick dinner and then settle down for a game of cards or dominoes after putting the children to sleep. I did manage to get him to move from Bloemfontein to Kimberley in the hope of him taking over my dad's business in Barkly West, half an hour outside Kimberley.

In the end, it was me who ended up driving to Barkly West every morning and returning at lunchtime. I had even convinced my dad I could take over the business. But after a year of leaving Brooke and Kris in the care of our domestic worker, I threw in the towel: my kids were not going to have two absent parents. I also realised that Mickey would never be able to work there. It wasn't in his make-up to run a supermarket or a second-hand car sales business. I suppose that year made me realise that Mickey actually couldn't do anything else but cricket. That was what he was good at, pure and simple. If I wanted food on the table, it was best I just accept what life had dished up. We never discussed coaching or his career again. At least, we never discussed alternatives.

When Mickey became national coach, everyone believed that our lifestyle, with all the travel to wonderful destinations, would be a dream come true. And in some ways it was – but only a very, very small percentage. Don't get me wrong; we all loved parts of it. I mean, four girls soaking up the sun in the Caribbean? How is that not a dream come true? In London, we saw fantastic shows, walked in Hyde Park, shopped in the King's Road, saw Madame Tussauds and went on the London Eye. We explored the English countryside, saw every castle we could and experienced the Glastonbury festival (I've never seen so many stoned people in my life!). We even ate rock candy on the cobbled streets of St Ives to show the girls where our family began.

We have toured the whole of Australia twice, seen every zoo and been to every beach – including Bondi, and it is as good as they say. We've ridden on every bus, water-taxi, ferry, train and monorail in that country. It is truly a fantastic place. We all fell in love with Perth on our very first tour five years ago, and are so excited and happy that this is going to be our new home. But all of this came at a price.

After every day of all these wonderful experiences, we always came back to ... a hotel room. I ended up despising them. The girls always had their own interlinking room to ours, which did help with some privacy for all of us, but in a hotel room you can't open your own fridge and cut a piece of cheese, or grab an avocado and Tabasco sauce; you can't cook your own dinner. After six weeks of eating hotel breakfasts and going to restaurants for lunch and dinner, all you crave is some normality. Then there was the dirty laundry ... the first thing I always did on arrival at a hotel was to ask the concierge to direct me to the nearest laundromat. As all mothers know, you *must* be in control of washing and clothes.

All the wonderful, touristy experiences I've mentioned were done alone with the girls. No Mickey. Ever. He was either practising or playing. Or planning. Or in meetings. So yes, what a wonderful opportunity we had, but it was lonely. We did include the other wives at times, but I really preferred sharing these memorable times with my girls. I would have preferred to share them as a family, of course – even occasionally – but that wasn't possible. But we usually had an hour together in the evening, and we tried to be grateful for that.

Over the years, I tried to limit the amount of school the girls missed. We would leave for a long tour a week before school broke up and return a week after opening day. If the Proteas were playing a Test match in South Africa, we would fly on the Thursday afternoon and return on the first flight Monday morning and go straight to school. The Clarendon Prep, Primary and High Schools in East London have been very understanding and sympathetic to our situation. They did query some trips, but the girls would be given any missed work on their return and we made sure they caught up.

There is an old and suspicious saying among cricketers that 'what happens on tour stays on tour'. It's probably wise, but seeing as I'll never be on tour again, let me break the rule (a little bit). At one match, the 'Wags' (wives and girlfriends) were in our hospitality suite, right at the top of the stand, at a very special venue (I won't say where in case I jeopardise future invitations to SA wives!). We were always treated well on tour; I don't know if it was the same for every team's Wags, or whether the South African wives have a reputation for enjoying good wine, but we were always provided with a well-stocked bar. Anyway, it was late in the afternoon, and the tiniest Wag of all heard a rather derogatory comment that was obviously about her boyfriend. 'What did you say, Bruce?' she screamed. Well, next thing she was shouting to her boyfriend who was at least 500m away and trying his damndest to concentrate amid all the jeers and noise around him. 'Kill him! Take his head off! Decapitate him ...!' she screamed.

We soon found out that we were, in fact, sitting behind the Members' Stand, and that such comments were not appreciated.

It was a little embarrassing, but I can't help chuckling when I think back to that day. It was emotion, not malice. Anyway, we were all summoned to see the manager at the end of the day. It was our first disciplinary hearing! We were all contrite and apologetic, although there were a few small giggles. We promised to behave better in future.

Another memorable occasion was in December 2008 when we beat Australia at the WACA for the first time in ... how long was it? I don't recall. The first time in a thousand years, judging by how the players were reacting. We were invited into the boys' changing room, for the first time ... ever! It was not exactly first thing in the morning; in fact, it was well after the Boeing had flown over, and the fridge in our suite had been stocked with some of Western Australia's finest Chardonnays and Sauvignon Blancs.

So, as good Wags do, we made our way obediently across the ground to the changing room side. We bumped into the Aussie players on our little journey, and offered them our sincere condolences and commiserations. 'Better luck next time, fellas.' 'How does it feel to lose?' 'Don't be too upset, Rick!'

We were eventually marshalled into the 'correct' changing room, and had a good celebration with our men. When we were told that our company was no longer 'required', as they had a fines meeting to get through, we decided 'why not have our own fines meeting?' We went via the 'Arthur suite' back at the hotel, raided the minibar, and shoved everything that we could into nappy bags and my daughters' handbags. We found the perfect celebratory venue in the pool area upstairs. Our team meeting ended in the early hours of the next morning. The men had to do the babysitting, as our meeting outlasted theirs by a couple of hours!

Whenever he came home between tours, Mickey would try so, so hard to switch into husband and father mode, and I will always be grateful for that. It was not always with great success, though. I suppose when you are living in your teammates' pockets for three months at a time, you do become automatically 'connected'. Even on days when his cellphone was off and he wasn't taking calls on the land line, I could see that his mind was thinking about the next tour or wondering what Bouch or Vinnie's golf round was like. He would very sweetly decline golf outings with his mates in order to spend the mornings with me. That made me determined to take up golf so I could spend time with him doing something he obviously loves. I started taking lessons in April 2010; ever since, he has patiently spent almost all of his golf time with me. We have had many a laugh on the course. Weekends away now mean that a trailer has to be hitched to the car, as we have two golf bags to squeeze in as well as all the stuff required by three teenage girls.

We love taking the girls into the Katberg Mountains, in the Eastern Cape. They love it, and it's almost the only place in this country where I'm not checking on them 24/7; they only have to report at meal times. Many a great family memory has been captured there. At least once a year, we also plan trips to our parents' homes – his in Durban and mine in Kimberley. These visits give us an opportunity to catch up with all of our school friends.

But Mickey's biggest thrill when home is taking the girls to and from school, as well as doing the afternoon taxiing to and from sport. He will also never, ever miss a hockey, tennis or water polo match when in town, and even watches their practice sessions – much to the girls' embarrassment. He has also very diligently sat through many a ballet lesson, showing much interest and always having a few words with the teacher afterwards.

Finally, the hardest and most time-consuming task he has when he's home is putting out all the fires that erupt with four Leos under one roof. He is the peacemaker, so I decided long ago not to get into screaming sessions with the girls. Brooke has dislocated her knee three times by stamping the floor too hard. Our *au pair* once took her to the emergency room and returned with crutches. Now I won't scream back, not when Mickey can just sit them down and explain the lie of the land. And they lap it up and walk out friends. It's much less stressful.

My view is that Mickey handled himself impeccably, and with great restraint, when all the political crap starting crowding into his job. Of course I'm biased, but I think he deserves a medal. Sorry Mr Arendse, and Dr Nyoka, but he deserved a little better – a lot better, actually. He was forced into a corner, slowly but surely, and eventually there was no way out. Nobody will ever know better than me how much pain and anxiety it caused him. The suggestion that he didn't care about transformation is laughable. He would get so, so angry, but never despondent. He loved the game and the boys on a far bigger scale than any politically driven selector, board member or one-eyed politician could ever have dreamt to imagine. And that is what drove him to argue and try his best to get his point acknowledged. Ultimately politics did win, though, and Mickey was asked to stand down. Sadly for them, South African cricket lost my husband. But it's been my gain. He is the old, relaxed, stress-free person that I met many a year ago.

How hard was it for us? On a scale of one to ten, I'd say nine. I should say five, or six, given the reality of the world, but that is our truth. There were more tears of anguish and anger than tears of joy.

By the time you read this chapter, we will all be settled in our new city, Perth. Brooke hasn't quite decided what she wants to do when she finishes school; being the wicked witch that I am, she won't be having a gap year in my lifetime. Mickey has organised for her to do some promotional work. Krissy will be going into Grade 11 at Perth Ladies College from October, and I will be accompanying her over. She and Mickey are very excited to be living together until the end of the year. Ash will be attending the same school and goes into Grade 8 from January next year.

I see our future in Australia as a new beginning. I won't know anyone in the supermarkets, and I'll have to find a new hairdresser, GP, dentist, gym and, most importantly, golf course. I look forward to a structured and law-abiding society. I think I might even take up surfing with the girls. The beaches in Perth are magnificent, clean and safe. We are hoping to find a piece of land and build a home according to our needs – and dreams. I realise that there will be obstacles, and many a tear will be shed, especially in saying goodbye to family and friends. We feel we are doing the right thing. Mickey needed a new challenge, and we are very grateful for the opportunity. All of us. Perhaps we all needed a change of scenery.

Goodbye South Africa. A new dawn breaks. No regrets.

Appendix

Mickey Arthur

A statistical profile compiled by Andrew Samson

Playing career

First-class

Season	For	M	Inns	NO	Runs	HS	Avg	100	50	Ct
1986/87	Griqualand West	6	10	0	99	39	9.90	0	0	2
1987/88	Griqualand West	6	12	1	400	123	36.36	1	2	6
1988/89	Griqualand West	7	13	1	311	80	25.91	0	3	2
1989/90	Griqualand West/ Bowl XI	5	10	1	522	131	58.00	2	1	5
1990/91	Orange Free State	10	19	0	548	94	28.84	0	4	8
1991/92	Orange Free State	7	13	1	566	120	47.16	1	5	3
1992/93	Orange Free State	7	13	0	318	81	24.46	0	3	3
1993/94	Orange Free State/ South Africa A	9	17	1	600	106	37.50	2	3	4
1994/95	South Africa A in Zimbabwe	2	3	0	87	53	29.00	0	1	1
1994/95	Orange Free State/ South Africa A	9	17	0	523	85	30.76	0	3	5
1995/96	Griqualand West/ SA Invitation XI	6	10	1	267	109	29.66	1	1	7
1996/97	Griqualand West	8	16	1	539	86	35.93	0	3	7

258

1997/98	Griqualand West	8	16	0	309	58	19.31	0	1	7
1998/99	Griqualand West	9	17	0	690	148	40.58	2	2	4
1999/00	Griqualand West	7	14	1	606	128	46.61	3	2	3
2000/01	Griqualand West	4	7	0	272	165	38.85	1	0	7

Totals

Competition	M	Inns	NO	Runs	HS	Avg	100	50	Ct
SuperSport Series ('A Section')	68	130	4	4177	165	33.15	7	21	44
UCB Bowl ('B Section')	27	49	4	1444	131	32.08	4	6	20
Other First-class	15	28	0	1036	106	37.00	2	7	10
Grand Totals	**110**	**207**	**8**	**6657**	**165**	**33.45**	**13**	**34**	**74**

For each team

Competition	M	Inns	NO	Runs	HS	Avg	100	50	Ct
Free State	41	77	2	2511	120	33.48	3	18	23
Griqualand West	64	121	6	3934	165	34.20	10	15	48
South Africa A	3	5	0	131	53	26.20	0	1	1
South African Invitation XI	1	2	0	13	12	6.50	0	0	0
Combined Bowl XI	1	2	0	68	38	34.00	0	0	2

Bowling: He bowled one over in first-class cricket. It was a maiden.

Centuries

Score	For	Against	Venue	Season
123	Griqualand West	Natal B	Kimberley	1987/88
131	Griqualand West	Orange Free State B	Virginia	1989/90
112*	Griqualand West	Orange Free State B	Kimberley	1989/90
120	Orange Free State	Transvaal	Johannesburg	1991/92
105*	Orange Free State	Eastern Province	Port Elizabeth	1993/94
106	Orange Free State	England A	Bloemfontein	1993/94
109	Griqualand West	Transvaal B	Kimberley	1995/96
137	Griqualand West	KwaZulu-Natal	Durban	1998/99
148	Griqualand West	Boland	Paarl	1998/99
128	Griqualand West	Gauteng	Kimberley	1999/00
113*	Griqualand West	Easterns	Benoni	1999/00
105	Griqualand West	UCB Invitation XI	Kimberley	1999/00
165	Griqualand West	Gauteng	Johannesburg	2000/01

Leading run-scorers in first-class for Griqualand West

Name	Years	M	Inns	NO	Runs	HS	Avg	100	50
W Bossenger	1996-2010	108	190	30	5893	168	36.83	8	37
MI Gidley	1994-2004	76	144	10	5345	215*	39.88	12	26
MJD Doherty	1965-1985	85	160	10	5238	130*	34.92	12	23
JM Arthur	1986-2000	64	121	6	3934	165	34.20	10	15
AP McLaren	1999-2010	52	93	8	3823	164	44.97	14	17
DJ Schonegevel	1966-1977	49	88	6	2863	138*	34.91	6	14
EJ Draper	1954-1968	57	106	7	2725	118	27.52	4	13
PH Barnard	1995-1999	37	70	6	2719	250	42.48	7	1
AP Beukes	1971-1987	64	117	5	2686	91	23.98	0	16
CD Helfrich	1945-1958	46	84	4	2599	165	32.48	6	13

As at the end of the 2009/10 season

On retirement, he was the second-highest run-scorer for Griqualand West, behind Mike Doherty. He was also the leading limited overs run-scorer for the team at the time, with 1864 (avg 31.06).

Arthur and Martyn Gidley are the most prolific opening pair for Griqualand West in first-class cricket and he also had a successful opening partnership for the team with another future international coach, Andy Moles.

The following opening pairs have aggregates of more than 1000 runs for Griqualand West:

Batsmen	Inns	Unb	Runs	Best	Avg	100	50
JM Arthur & MI Gidley	75	1	3072	254	41.51	6	13
MJD Doherty & NL Heale	57	0	1727	146	30.29	4	9
JM Arthur & AJ Moles	31	1	1166	112	38.86	4	6
MI Gidley & BH Tucker	30	1	1081	129	37.27	3	5

His 254 with Gidley against Gauteng at Johannesburg in 2000/01 remains the record opening partnership for Griqualand West in first-class cricket as at the end of the 2009/10 season.

List A Limited Overs

Season	For	M	Inns	NO	Runs	HS	Avg	100	50	Ct
1987/88	Griqualand West/ Impalas	9	9	0	187	38	20.77	0	0	2
1988/89	Griqualand West/ Impalas	11	9	0	124	43	13.77	0	0	0
1989/90	Griqualand West/ Impalas	10	10	1	246	111*	27.33	1	0	2
1990/91	Orange Free State	12	12	0	325	73	27.08	0	2	2
1991/92	Orange Free State	13	13	1	419	126*	34.91	1	1	4
1992/93	Orange Free State/ SA Pres XI	13	13	0	320	56	24.61	0	2	2
1993/94	Orange Free State	12	11	1	208	44	20.80	0	0	2
1994/95	South Africa A in Zimbabwe	2	2	0	38	29	19.00	0	0	1

1994/95	Orange Free State	12	12	1	288	91*	26.18	0	1	6
1995/96	Griqualand West	10	9	0	155	52	17.22	0	1	4
1996/97	Griqualand West	13	13	1	444	84	37.00	0	4	1
1997/98	Griqualand West	10	10	0	279	63	27.90	0	2	5
1998/99	Griqualand West	13	13	0	371	83	28.53	0	2	6
1999/00	Griqualand West	10	10	0	370	75	37.00	0	4	4

Totals

Competition	M	Inns	NO	Runs	HS	Avg	100	50	Ct
Benson & Hedges Series/ Std Bank Cup	118	115	4	2966	126*	26.72	1	17	35
Nissan Shield/ Total Power Series	24	24	1	692	111*	30.08	1	2	4
Other Limited Overs	8	7	0	116	34	16.57	0	0	2
Grand Totals	**150**	**146**	**5**	**3774**	**126***	**26.76**	**2**	**19**	**41**

For each team

Competition	M	Inns	NO	Runs	HS	Avg	100	50	Ct
Free State	61	60	3	1548	126*	27.15	1	6	16
Griqualand West	63	62	2	1864	111*	31.06	1	13	21
Impalas	23	21	0	312	44	14.85	0	0	3
South Africa A	2	2	0	38	29	19.00	0	0	1
South Africa Pres XI	1	1	0	12	12	12.00	0	0	0

Bowling: He bowled one over in List A Limited Overs for 2 runs.

Centuries

Score	For	Against	Venue	Season
111*	Griqualand West	Western Transvaal	Potchefstroom	1989/90
126*	Orange Free State	Western Province	Bloemfontein	1991/92

Coaching Career

Griqualand West

First-class

Season	Played	Won	Lost	Tied	Drawn	%Won
2000/01	10	2	3	0	5	20.00
2001/02	8	3	4	0	1	37.50
2002/03	5	1	3	0	1	20.00
2003/04	8	2	5	0	1	25.00
Totals	**31**	**8**	**15**	**0**	**8**	**25.80**

Limited Overs

Season	Played	Won	Lost	Tied	NR	%Won
2000/01	10	4	6	0	0	40.00
2001/02	9	3	5	0	1	37.50
2002/03	7	4	3	0	0	57.14
2003/04	10	5	5	0	0	50.00
Totals	**36**	**16**	**19**	**0**	**1**	**45.71**

NB: %Won calculation excludes 'No results'

Warriors

First-class

Season	Played	Won	Lost	Tied	Drawn	%Won
2004/05	10	1	6	0	3	10.00

Limited Overs

Season	Played	Won	Lost	Tied	NR	%Won
2004/05	10	4	5	0	1	44.44

NB: %Won calculation excludes 'No results'

Standard Bank Pro20

Season	Played	Won	Lost	Tied	NR	%Won
2004/05	7	4	2	0	1	66.66

NB: %Won calculation excludes 'No results'

South Africa

Tests

Series	Venue	Season	Played	Won	Lost	Tied	Drawn
v Australia	Australia	2005/06	3	0	2	0	1
v Australia	South Africa	2005/06	3	0	3	0	0
v New Zealand	South Africa	2005/06	3	2	0	0	1
v Sri Lanka	Sri Lanka	2006	2	0	2	0	0
v India	South Africa	2006/07	3	2	1	0	0
v Pakistan	South Africa	2006/07	3	2	1	0	0
v Pakistan	Pakistan	2007/08	2	1	0	0	1
v New Zealand	South Africa	2007/08	2	2	0	0	0
v West Indies	South Africa	2007/08	3	2	1	0	0
v Bangladesh	Bangladesh	2007/08	2	2	0	0	0
v India	India	2007/08	3	1	1	0	1
v England	England	2008	4	2	1	0	1
v Bangladesh	South Africa	2008/09	2	2	0	0	0

v Australia	Australia	2008/09	3	2	1	0	0
v Australia	South Africa	2008/09	3	1	2	0	0
v England	South Africa	2009/10	4	1	1	0	2
Totals			**45**	**22**	**16**	**0**	**7**
v Australia			12	3	8	0	1
v Others			33	19	8	0	6

Winning Percentage: 48.88

Limited Overs Internationals for South Africa

Series	Venue	Season	Played	Won	Lost	Tied	NR
v New Zealand	South Africa	2005/06	5	4	0	0	1
v India	India	2005/06	4	2	2	0	0
VB Series	Australia	2005/06	8	3	5	0	0
v Australia	South Africa	2005/06	5	3	2	0	0
v Zimbabwe	South Africa	2006/07	3	3	0	0	0
Champions Trophy	India	2006/07	4	2	2	0	0
v India	South Africa	2006/07	4	4	0	0	0
v Pakistan	South Africa	2006/07	5	3	1	0	1
World Cup	West Indies	2006/07	10	6	4	0	0
v Ireland	Ireland	2007	1	1	0	0	0
v India	Ireland	2007	3	1	2	0	0
v Zimbabwe	Zimbabwe	2007	3	3	0	0	0
v Pakistan	Pakistan	2007/08	5	3	2	0	0
v New Zealand	South Africa	2007/08	3	2	1	0	0
v West Indies	South Africa	2007/08	5	5	0	0	0
v Bangladesh	Bangladesh	2007/08	3	3	0	0	0
v England	England	2008	5	0	4	0	1
v Kenya	South Africa	2008/09	2	2	0	0	0
v Bangladesh	South Africa	2008/09	2	2	0	0	0
v Australia	Australia	2008/09	5	4	1	0	0
v Australia	South Africa	2008/09	5	3	2	0	0
Champions Trophy	South Africa	2009/10	3	1	2	0	0
v Zimbabwe	South Africa	2009/10	2	2	0	0	0
v England	South Africa	2009/10	3	1	2	0	0
Totals			**98**	**63**	**32**	**0**	**3**

Winning Percentage: 66.31 (calculation excludes 'No results')

Limited Overs Internationals for Africa

Series	Venue	Season	Played	Won	Lost	Tied	NR
v Asia	South Africa	2005/06	3	1	1	0	1

T20 Internationals

Series	Venue	Season	Played	Won	Lost	Tied	NR
v New Zealand	South Africa	2005/06	1	0	1	0	0
v Australia	Australia	2005/06	1	0	1	0	0
v Australia	South Africa	2005/06	1	1	0	0	0
v India	South Africa	2006/07	1	0	1	0	0
v Pakistan	South Africa	2006/07	1	1	0	0	0
World T20	South Africa	2007/08	5	4	1	0	0
v New Zealand	South Africa	2007/08	1	1	0	0	0
v West Indies	South Africa	2007/08	2	1	1	0	0
v Bangladesh	South Africa	2008/09	1	1	0	0	0
v Australia	Australia	2008/09	2	0	2	0	0
v Australia	South Africa	2008/09	2	2	0	0	0
World T20	England	2009	6	5	1	0	0
v England	South Africa	2009/10	2	1	1	0	0
Totals			**26**	**17**	**9**	**0**	**0**

Winning Percentage: 65.38 (calculation excludes 'No results')

Arthur's reign as South Africa's coach was from 21 October 2005 to 17 January 2010 (from the start of his first game to the end of his last game in charge).

The following are the results of the coaches of the ICC Full Member countries in that period:

Tests

Coach	Played	Won	Lost	Tied	Drawn	%Won
TL Penney (SL)	3	3	0	0	0	100.00
JM Buchanan (Aus)	16	15	0	0	1	93.75
TJ Nielsen (Aus)	32	17	8	0	7	53.12
RJ Shastri (Ind)	2	1	0	0	1	50.00
JM Arthur (SA)	45	22	16	0	7	48.88
G Kirsten (Ind)	19	9	3	0	7	47.36
TH Bayliss (SL)	22	10	6	0	6	45.45
TM Moody (SL)	14	6	5	0	3	42.85
RA Woolmer (Pak)	18	7	5	0	6	38.88
P Moores (Eng)	22	8	6	0	8	36.36
CG Borde (Ind)	3	1	0	0	2	33.33
JG Bracewell (NZ)	22	7	11	0	4	31.81

GS Chappell (Ind)	16	5	4	0	7	31.25
A Flower (Eng)	16	5	3	0	8	31.25
LS Rajput (Ind)	7	2	2	0	3	28.57
DAG Fletcher (Eng)	18	5	9	0	4	27.77
J Dyson (WI)	19	3	9	0	7	15.78
Intikhab Alam (Pak)	11	1	6	0	4	9.09
D Williams (WI)	3	0	2	0	1	0.00
DJA Moore (WI)	4	0	3	0	1	0.00
GF Lawson (Pak)	5	0	2	0	3	0.00
AJ Moles (NZ)	7	0	3	0	4	0.00
BA King (WI)	13	0	8	0	5	0.00
JD Siddons (Ban)	13	2	10	0	1	15.38
S Williams (Ban)	3	0	3	0	0	0.00
DF Whatmore (Ban)	6	0	5	0	1	0.00

Limited Overs Internationals

Coach	Played	Won	Lost	Tied	NR	%Won
Mushtaq Ahmed (Pak)	1	1	0	0	0	100.00
RJ Shastri (Ind)	2	2	0	0	0	100.00
TL Penney (SL)	3	3	0	0	0	100.00
DJA Moore (WI)	6	4	1	0	1	80.00
HWD Springer (WI)	4	3	1	0	0	75.00
JM Buchanan (Aus)	56	40	15	0	1	72.72
GF Lawson (Pak)	28	19	9	0	0	67.85
TJ Nielsen (Aus)	67	42	20	0	5	67.74
Talat Ali (Pak)	3	2	1	0	0	66.66
G Kirsten (Ind)	55	34	17	0	4	66.66
JM Arthur (SA)	98	63	32	0	3	66.31
CG Borde (Ind)	12	7	5	0	0	58.33
DF Whatmore (Ban)	45	26	19	0	0	57.77
JG Bracewell (NZ)	71	38	28	1	4	56.71
GS Chappell (Ind)	52	27	22	0	3	55.10
LS Rajput (Ind)	22	10	9	0	3	52.63
TH Bayliss (SL)	64	32	29	0	3	52.45
BA King (WI)	46	23	22	0	1	51.11
TM Moody (SL)	65	31	30	0	4	50.81
A Flower (Eng)	22	11	11	0	0	50.00
Intikhab Alam (Pak)	23	11	12	0	0	47.82
RA Woolmer (Pak)	35	15	17	0	3	46.87
AJ Moles (NZ)	22	8	10	0	4	44.44
P Moores (Eng)	36	14	18	1	3	42.42

WR Chawaguta (Zim)	34	14	20	0	0	41.17
DAG Fletcher (Eng)	44	17	26	0	1	39.53
JD Siddons (Ban)	52	19	33	0	0	36.53
J Dyson (WI)	38	9	25	0	4	26.47
KM Curran (Zim)	39	9	28	1	1	23.68
RD Brown (Zim)	9	1	8	0	0	11.11
D Williams (WI)	3	0	3	0	0	0.00
S Williams (Ban)	3	0	3	0	0	0.00

NB: %Won calculation excludes 'No results'

T20 Internationals

Coach	Played	Won	Lost	Tied	NR	%Won
GS Chappell (Ind)	1	1	0	0	0	100.00
DF Whatmore (Ban)	1	1	0	0	0	100.00
Intikhab Alam (Pak)	11	9	2	0	0	81.81
GF Lawson (Pak)	14	11	2	1	0	78.57
JM Buchanan (Aus)	3	2	1	0	0	66.66
TM Moody (SL)	3	2	1	0	0	66.66
JM Arthur (SA)	26	17	9	0	0	65.38
LS Rajput (Ind)	9	5	2	1	1	62.50
TH Bayliss (SL)	22	13	9	0	0	59.09
AJ Moles (NZ)	12	7	4	1	0	58.33
J Dyson (WI)	13	7	5	1	0	53.84
RD Brown (Zim)	2	1	1	0	0	50.00
RA Woolmer (Pak)	2	1	1	0	0	50.00
P Moores (Eng)	10	5	5	0	0	50.00
TJ Nielsen (Aus)	19	8	10	0	1	44.44
G Kirsten (Ind)	10	4	6	0	0	40.00
A Flower (Eng)	9	3	5	0	1	37.50
JG Bracewell (NZ)	15	5	9	1	0	33.33
S Williams (Ban)	7	2	5	0	0	28.57
WR Chawaguta (Zim)	4	1	2	1	0	25.00
DJA Moore (WI)	4	1	3	0	0	25.00
KM Curran (Zim)	1	0	1	0	0	0.00
BA King (WI)	1	0	0	1	0	0.00
DAG Fletcher (Eng)	3	0	3	0	0	0.00
JD Siddons (Ban)	5	0	5	0	0	0.00

NB: %Won calculation excludes 'No results'

South Africa: Individual playing records with Arthur as coach
Tests
Batting & Fielding

Name	M	Inns	NO	Runs	HS	Avg	100	50	Ct	St
HM Amla	38	66	4	2709	176*	43.69	7	16	34	0
N Boje	8	15	2	289	48	22.23	0	0	6	0
J Botha	2	2	1	45	25	45.00	0	0	1	0
MV Boucher	45	70	7	2005	117	31.82	1	14	158	8
AB de Villiers	45	77	7	2867	217*	40.95	6	16	64	0
F de Wet	2	2	0	20	20	10.00	0	0	1	0
HH Dippenaar	5	9	0	207	52	23.00	0	1	4	0
JP Duminy	10	17	2	503	166	33.53	1	3	11	0
HH Gibbs	20	37	1	940	94	26.11	0	8	37	0
AJ Hall	6	10	1	201	64	22.33	0	1	4	0
PL Harris	27	38	5	401	46	12.15	0	0	12	0
JH Kallis	41	71	6	3220	186	49.53	11	15	59	0
JM Kemp	1	2	0	62	55	31.00	0	1	0	0
I Khan	1	1	0	20	20	20.00	0	0	1	0
CK Langeveldt	2	2	1	1	1*	1.00	0	0	1	0
ND McKenzie	17	29	3	1225	226	47.11	3	3	17	0
R McLaren	1	1	1	33	33*	–	0	0	0	0
JA Morkel	1	1	0	58	58	58.00	0	1	0	0
M Morkel	21	27	2	336	40	13.44	0	0	6	0
A Nel	21	30	4	305	34	11.73	0	0	13	0
M Ntini	42	55	28	244	28*	9.03	0	0	9	0
WD Parnell	1	0	0	0	0	–	0	0	1	0
RJ Peterson	1	1	0	4	4	4.00	0	0	1	0
SM Pollock	14	24	7	648	67*	38.11	0	3	7	0
AG Prince	40	69	11	2648	162*	45.65	9	8	26	0
JA Rudolph	8	16	1	441	102*	29.40	1	1	6	0
GC Smith	41	73	4	3316	232	48.05	9	14	60	0
DW Steyn	33	41	7	446	76	13.11	0	1	9	0
M Zondeki	1	1	0	0	0	0.00	0	0	0	0

Bowling

Name	M	Balls	Runs	Wkts	Avg	RPO	BB	5I	10M
HM Amla	38	42	28	0	–	4.00	–	0	0
N Boje	8	1725	966	12	80.50	3.36	4-111	0	0
J Botha	2	225	178	4	44.50	4.74	2-57	0	0
AB de Villiers	45	30	34	0	–	6.80	–	0	0
F de Wet	2	426	186	6	31.00	2.61	4-55	0	0
JP Duminy	10	533	294	10	29.40	3.30	3-89	0	0

AJ Hall	6	810	464	14	33.14	3.43	3-75	0	0
PL Harris	27	5980	2759	. 82	33.64	2.76	6-127	3	0
JH Kallis	41	4753	2343	76	30.82	2.95	5-30	1	0
JM Kemp	1	84	71	1	71.00	5.07	1-58	0	0
CK Langeveldt	2	516	377	7	53.85	4.38	3-117	0	0
ND McKenzie	17	18	5	0	–	1.66	–	0	0
R McLaren	1	78	43	1	43.00	3.30	1-30	0	0
JA Morkel	1	192	132	1	132.00	4.12	1-44	0	0
M Morkel	21	3983	2328	74	31.45	3.50	5-50	2	0
A Nel	21	4357	2341	61	38.37	3.22	4-81	0	0
M Ntini	42	8485	4785	169	28.31	3.38	6-59	9	2
WD Parnell	1	66	35	2	17.50	3.18	2-17	0	0
RJ Peterson	1	174	94	6	15.66	3.24	5-33	1	0
SM Pollock	14	3039	1404	44	31.90	2.77	4-35	0	0
AG Prince	40	42	25	1	25.00	3.57	1-2	0	0
JA Rudolph	8	148	123	0	–	4.98	–	0	0
GC Smith	41	234	190	1	190.00	4.87	1-41	0	0
DW Steyn	33	6787	3970	177 .	22.42	3.50	6-49	12	3
M Zondeki	1	88	42	3	14.00	2.86	2-10	0	0

Note: Boucher and De Villiers are the only players to appear in all 45 of Arthur's Tests as coach.

Limited Overs Internationals

Batting & Fielding

Name	M	Inns	NO	Runs	HS	Avg	SR	100	50	St	Ct
HM Amla	22	21	3	848	140	47.11	82.65	1	6	10	0
GH Bodi	2	2	0	83	51	41.50	62.87	0	1	1	0
N Boje	3	1	1	3	3*	–	100.00	0	0	0	0
LL Bosman	11	9	0	202	88	22.44	90.17	0	1	3	0
J Botha	48	25	9	266	46	16.62	78.46	0	0	21	0
MV Boucher	90	73	21	1909	147*	36.71	91.69	1	10	120	6
AB de Villiers	81	77	11	2841	146	43.04	87.36	4	19	49	0
HH Dippenaar	19	19	2	661	125*	38.88	67.03	2	3	7	0
JP Duminy	49	42	11	1264	111*	40.77	82.66	1	6	20	0
HH Gibbs	76	70	3	2553	175	38.10	87.22	6	15	35	0
AJ Hall	38	21	6	286	56*	19.06	72.04	0	1	10	0
PL Harris	3	0	0	0	0	–	–	0	0	2	0
JH Kallis	75	70	14	2706	128*	48.32	75.73	3	21	18	0
JM Kemp	50	41	14	871	100*	32.25	75.93	1	4	18	0
GJ-P Kruger	3	2	1	0	0*	0.00	0.00	0	0	1	0
CK Langeveldt	47	14	7	42	12	6.00	43.29	0	0	9	0
J Louw	3	1	0	23	23	23.00	328.57	0	0	0	0
ND McKenzie	5	4	0	108	63	27.00	65.45	0	1	2	0
R McLaren	5	4	1	11	6*	3.66	45.83	0	0	2	0

JA Morkel	38	26	7	539	97	28.36	107.58	0	2	10	0
M Morkel	20	7	2	59	23*	11.80	95.16	0	0	4	0
A Nel	45	16	8	119	30*	14.87	85.61	0	0	10	0
M Ntini	57	20	9	55	9*	5.00	61.11	0	0	6	0
JL Ontong	7	4	0	80	27	20.00	72.72	0	0	3	0
WD Parnell	9	2	1	11	10*	11.00	45.83	0	0	1	0
AN Petersen	10	8	1	342	80	48.85	89.52	0	4	0	0
RJ Peterson	14	7	3	56	22	14.00	103.70	0	0	4	0
VD Philander	7	5	2	73	23	24.33	87.95	0	0	2	0
SM Pollock	61	44	15	857	90	29.55	91.75	0	4	12	0
AG Prince	32	23	3	490	47*	24.50	62.82	0	0	17	0
AG Puttick	1	1	0	0	0	0.00	0.00	0	0	1	0
JA Rudolph	6	6	1	156	53	31.20	58.20	0	1	2	0
GC Smith	80	79	6	3004	141	41.15	90.40	4	25	49	0
DW Steyn	33	8	4	45	17*	11.25	91.83	0	0	5	0
R Telemachus	4	3	0	41	29	13.66	204.10	0	0	2	0
T Tshabalala	4	1	1	2	2*	–	66.66	0	0	0	0
LL Tsotsobe	3	0	0	0	0	–	–	0	0	2	0
RE van der Merwe	10	5	2	17	6*	5.66	73.91	0	0	3	0
JJ van der Wath	10	8	2	89	37*	14.83	127.14	0	0	3	0
VB van Jaarsveld	2	2	0	9	5	4.50	60.00	0	0	1	0
MN van Wyk	5	5	0	178	82	35.60	64.96	0	2	1	0
M Zondeki	5	0	0	0	0	–	–	0	0	1	0

Bowling

Name	M	Balls	Runs	Wkts	Avg	RPO	BB	4I
GH Bodi	2	6	8	0	–	8.00	–	0
N Boje	3	84	58	2	29.00	4.14	2-26	0
J Botha	48	2280	1691	46	36.76	4.45	4-19	1
JP Duminy	49	565	462	15	30.80	4.90	3-31	0
AJ Hall	38	1812	1387	56	24.76	4.59	5-18	4
PL Harris	3	180	83	3	27.66	2.76	2-30	0
JH Kallis	75	2012	1662	50	33.24	4.95	3-3	0
JM Kemp	50	410	329	11	29.90	4.81	3-21	0
GJ-P Kruger	3	138	139	2	69.50	6.04	1-43	0
CK Langeveldt	47	2265	1929	61	31.62	5.10	5-39	1
J Louw	3	156	148	2	74.00	5.69	1-45	0
R McLaren	5	204	163	4	40.75	4.79	3-51	0
JA Morkel	38	1420	1258	37	34.00	5.31	4-29	2
M Morkel	20	1024	827	26	31.80	4.84	4-36	1
A Nel	45	2157	1624	63	25.77	4.51	5-45	3
M Ntini	57	2867	2318	82	28.26	4.85	6-22	4
JL Ontong	7	16	28	1	28.00	10.50	1-28	0
WD Parnell	9	477	462	22	21.00	5.81	5-48	3
AN Petersen	10	6	7	0	–	7.00	–	0

RJ Peterson	14	472	366	8	45.75	4.65	2-27	0
VD Philander	7	275	209	6	34.83	4.56	4-12	1
SM Pollock	61	3258	1754	70	25.05	3.23	5-23	2
AG Prince	32	12	3	0	–	1.50	–	0
GC Smith	80	712	617	14	44.07	5.19	3-30	0
DW Steyn	33	1633	1449	49	29.57	5.32	4-16	3
R Telemachus	4	216	213	7	30.42	5.91	3-34	0
T Tshabalala	4	150	151	3	50.33	6.04	1-30	0
LL Tsotsobe	3	144	114	6	19.00	4.75	4-50	1
RE van der Merwe	10	525	425	13	32.69	4.85	3-27	0
JJ van der Wath	10	526	551	13	42.38	6.28	2-21	0
M Zondeki	5	240	245	5	49.00	6.12	2-40	0

T20 Internationals

Batting & Fielding

Name	M	Inns	NO	Runs	HS	Avg	SR	100	50	Ct	St
YA Abdulla	2	0	0	0	0	–	–	0	0	0	0
HM Amla	2	2	0	52	26	26.00	104.00	0	0	0	0
GH Bodi	1	1	0	8	8	8.00	32.00	0	0	0	0
N Boje	1	0	0	0	0	–	–	0	0	0	0
LL Bosman	6	6	1	257	94	51.40	170.19	0	3	0	0
J Botha	16	9	7	59	28*	29.50	122.91	0	0	9	0
MV Boucher	20	16	4	239	36*	19.91	99.17	0	0	13	1
AB de Villiers	23	22	5	396	79*	23.29	128.57	0	3	23	2
HH Dippenaar	1	1	0	1	1	1.00	20.00	0	0	0	0
JP Duminy	18	18	4	372	78	26.57	124.00	0	2	11	0
HH Gibbs	20	20	1	359	90*	18.89	130.07	0	3	3	0
AJ Hall	2	1	0	11	11	11.00	110.00	0	0	0	0
T Henderson	1	1	0	0	0	0.00	0.00	0	0	0	0
JH Kallis	10	10	1	288	64	32.00	122.55	0	2	4	0
JM Kemp	8	7	3	203	89*	50.75	126.87	0	1	3	0
RK Kleinveldt	1	1	1	3	3*	–	100.00	0	0	0	0
GJ-P Kruger	1	1	0	3	3	3.00	60.00	0	0	0	0
HG Kuhn	1	1	1	5	5*	–	125.00	0	0	1	0
CK Langeveldt	4	2	1	2	2	2.00	40.00	0	0	1	0
J Louw	2	1	1	1	1*	–	100.00	0	0	0	0
ND McKenzie	2	1	1	7	7*	–	87.50	0	0	0	0
R McLaren	2	1	1	1	1*	–	100.00	0	0	0	0
JA Morkel	24	20	5	361	43	24.06	139.38	0	0	11	0
M Morkel	9	1	1	1	1*	–	33.33	0	0	1	0
A Nel	2	1	1	0	0*	–	0.00	0	0	1	0

Name										
M Ntini	9	3	1	9	5	4.50	100.00	0	0	1	0
JL Ontong	3	2	0	20	14	10.00	71.42	0	0	0	0
WD Parnell	8	0	0	0	0	–	–	0	0	0	0
RJ Peterson	5	2	0	42	34	21.00	107.69	0	0	2	0
VD Philander	7	4	0	14	6	3.50	50.00	0	0	1	0
SM Pollock	12	9	2	86	36*	12.28	122.85	0	0	2	0
AG Prince	1	1	0	5	5	5.00	83.33	0	0	0	0
JA Rudolph	1	1	1	6	6*	–	85.71	0	0	0	0
GC Smith	20	20	2	642	89*	35.66	131.02	0	4	10	0
DW Steyn	14	2	1	2	1*	2.00	66.66	0	0	3	0
R Telemachus	3	1	1	5	5*	–	166.66	0	0	0	0
AC Thomas	1	0	0	0	0	–	–	0	0	0	0
LL Tsotsobe	1	1	0	1	1	1.00	14.28	0	0	0	0
RE van der Merwe	9	3	0	49	48	16.33	125.64	0	0	5	0
JJ van der Wath	8	4	1	46	21	15.33	117.94	0	0	0	0
VB van Jaarsveld	3	3	0	15	12	5.00	65.21	0	0	0	0
MN van Wyk	2	1	0	1	1	1.00	25.00	0	0	1	0
M Zondeki	1	1	0	0	0	0.00	0.00	0	0	0	0

Bowling

Name	M	Balls	Runs	Wkts	Avg	RPO	BB	4I
YA Abdulla	2	42	44	2	22.00	6.28	1-16	0
N Boje	1	24	27	1	27.00	6.75	1-27	0
J Botha	16	318	330	13	25.38	6.22	3-16	0
JP Duminy	18	36	41	3	13.66	6.83	1-3	0
AJ Hall	2	48	60	3	20.00	7.50	3-22	0
T Henderson	1	24	31	0	–	7.75	–	0
JH Kallis	10	84	120	3	40.00	8.57	2-20	0
JM Kemp	8	6	5	0	–	5.00	–	0
RK Kleinveldt	1	6	20	1	20.00	20.00	1-20	0
GJ-P Kruger	1	24	29	0	–	7.25	–	0
CK Langeveldt	4	84	106	5	21.20	7.57	2-14	0
J Louw	2	42	54	2	27.00	7.71	2-36	0
R McLaren	2	48	59	4	14.75	7.37	3-33	0
JA Morkel	24	346	449	15	29.93	7.78	2-12	0
M Morkel	9	203	212	13	16.30	6.26	4-17	1
A Nel	2	48	42	2	21.00	5.25	2-19	0
M Ntini	9	168	252	6	42.00	9.00	2-22	0
JL Ontong	3	12	25	1	25.00	12.50	1-25	0
WD Parnell	8	173	192	11	17.45	6.65	4-13	1
RJ Peterson	5	65	86	6	14.33	7.93	3-30	0
VD Philander	7	83	114	4	28.50	8.24	2-23	0

SM Pollock	12	243	309	15	20.60	7.62	3-28	0
GC Smith	20	24	57	0	–	14.25	–	0
DW Steyn	14	306	359	23	15.60	7.03	4-9	1
R Telemachus	3	72	90	2	45.00	7.50	1-22	0
AC Thomas	1	24	25	3	8.33	6.25	3-25	0
LL Tsotsobe	1	12	16	1	16.00	8.00	1-16	0
RE van der Merwe	9	204	221	12	18.41	6.50	2-14	0
JJ van der Wath	8	186	231	8	28.87	7.45	2-31	0
M Zondeki	1	18	41	1	41.00	13.66	1-41	0

Test batting under Arthur and previous coaches

| | Arthur | | | Before Arthur | | | |
Name	M	Runs	Avg	M	Runs	Avg	Diff
MV Boucher	45	2005	31.82	84	3007	30.68	+1.14
AB de Villiers	45	2867	40.95	11	967	53.72	-12.77
HH Gibbs	20	940	26.11	70	5227	47.09	-20.98
JH Kallis	41	3220	49.53	93	7337	56.87	-7.34
ND McKenzie	17	1225	47.11	41	2028	33.24	+13.87
A Nel	21	305	11.73	15	32	4.00	+7.73
M Ntini	42	244	9.03	59	455	10.34	-1.31
SM Pollock	14	648	38.11	94	3133	31.33	+6.78
AG Prince	40	2648	45.65	12	523	37.35	+8.30
GC Smith	41	3316	48.05	39	3441	55.50	-7.45

Minimum of 10 Tests before Arthur and 10 under Arthur

Test bowling under Arthur and previous coaches

| | Arthur | | | Before Arthur | | | |
Name	M	Runs	Avg	M	Runs	Avg	Diff
JH Kallis	41	76	30.82	93	183	31.60	-0.78
A Nel	21	61	38.37	15	62	25.45	+12.92
M Ntini	42	169	28.31	59	221	29.21	-0.90
SM Pollock	14	44	31.90	93	377	22.09	+9.81

Minimum of 10 Tests before Arthur and 10 under Arthur

Limited Overs International batting under Arthur and previous coaches

Name	Arthur			Before Arthur			
	M	Runs	Avg	M	Runs	Avg	Diff
MV Boucher	90	1909	36.71	193	2567	25.16	+11.55
HH Gibbs	76	2553	38.10	169	5507	35.52	+2.58
AJ Hall	38	286	19.06	50	619	22.10	-3.04
JH Kallis	75	2706	48.32	215	7674	45.40	+2.92
JM Kemp	50	871	32.25	29	500	33.33	-1.08
CK Langeveldt	47	42	6.00	16	5	2.50	+3.50
A Nel	45	119	14.87	34	8	4.00	+10.87
M Ntini	57	55	5.00	115	144	12.00	-7.00
RJ Peterson	14	56	14.00	21	91	13.00	+1.00
SM Pollock	61	857	29.55	233	2336	24.08	+5.47
AG Prince	32	490	24.50	17	450	64.28	-39.78
GC Smith	80	3004	41.15	68	2609	40.76	+0.39

Minimum of 20 Limited Overs Internationals before Arthur and 20 under Arthur

Limited Overs International bowling under Arthur and previous coaches

Name	Arthur			Before Arthur			
	M	Runs	Avg	M	Runs	Avg	Diff
AJ Hall	38	56	24.76	50	39	28.92	-4.16
JH Kallis	75	50	33.24	215	194	31.89	1.35
JM Kemp	50	11	29.90	29	18	32.55	-2.65
A Nel	45	63	25.77	34	43	30.48	-4.71
M Ntini	57	82	28.26	115	183	22.85	5.41
SM Pollock	61	70	25.05	233	317	24.14	0.91
GC Smith	80	14	44.07	68	4	83.50	-39.43

Minimum of 20 Limited Overs Internationals before Arthur and 20 under Arthur